JOAN CRAWFORD
THE LAST WORD

*   *   *   *   *   *   *   *   *   *   *

ALSO BY FRED LAWRENCE GUILES

Norma Jean: The Life and Death of Marilyn Monroe
Marion Davies
Stan: The Life of Stan Laurel
Jane Fonda: The Actress in her Time
Tyrone Power
Hanging On in Paradise
Andy Warhol: Loner at the Ball

*   *   *   *   *   *   *   *   *   *   *

★ ★ ★ ★ ★ ★ ★ ★ ★ ★ ★

JOAN CRAWFORD
—
THE LAST WORD

Fred Lawrence Guiles

A BIRCH LANE PRESS BOOK
Published by Carol Publishing Group

★ ★ ★ ★ ★ ★ ★ ★ ★ ★ ★

★ ★ ★ ★ ★ ★ ★ ★ ★ ★ ★

A Birch Lane Press Book
Published by Carol Publishing Group
Birch Lane Press is a registered trademark of Carol Communications, Inc.
Editorial Offices: 600 Madison Avenue, New York, N.Y. 10022
Sales & Distribution Offices: 120 Enterprise Avenue, Secaucus, N.J. 07094
In Canada: Canadian Manda Group, One Atlantic Avenue, Suite 105,
Toronto, Ontario M6K 3E7
Queries regarding rights and permissions should be addressed to
Carol Publishing Group, 600 Madison Avenue, New York, N.Y. 10022

Carol Publishing Group books are available at special discounts for
bulk purchases, sales promotions, fund-raising, or educational
purposes. Special editions can be created to specifications. For
details contact: Special Sales Department, Carol Publishing
Group, 120 Enterprise Avenue, Secaucus, N.J. 07094

Manufactured in the United States of America
10 9 8 7 6 5 4 3 2 1

Library of Congress Cataloging-in-Publication Data

Guiles, Fred Lawrence.
Joan Crawford : the last word / by Fred Lawrence Guiles.
p. cm.
"A Birch Lane Press book."
ISBN 1–55972–269–X
1. Crawford, Joan, 1908–1977.   2. Motion picture actors and
actresses—United States—Biography.   I. Title.
PN2287.C67G85 1995
791.43'028'092—dc20
[B]   94–42058
CIP

★ ★ ★ ★ ★ ★ ★ ★ ★ ★ ★

★ ★ ★ ★ ★ ★ ★ ★ ★ ★ ★

Dedicated to
MAX GARTENBERG, SUZANNE HOLETON,
JEFFREY SIMMONS and HIRAM WILLIAMS

★ ★ ★ ★ ★ ★ ★ ★ ★ ★ ★

CONTENTS

ILLUSTRATIONS

★ ★ ★ ★ ★ ★ ★ ★ ★ ★ ★

ACKNOWLEDGEMENTS

I am especially grateful to Joan Crawford's private secretary, Betty Barker, to Douglas Fairbanks, Jr, and to Cindy Crawford Jordan, for sharing their memories of her with me.

Over the years of my research, I have become indebted to the following persons, who were friends or colleagues of Miss Crawford, for their time and memories:

Beatrice Ames*
Eleanor Boardman d'Arrast*
Joseph J. Cohn (Vice Pres., Metro, '20s and '30s)
Matthew Curran
Milton Feitelson
Francis Goodrich and Albert Hackett
William Haines*
Anne Power Hardenbergh
Helen Hayes (MacArthur)*
Joan Feldman Porter Hollander
Leo Jaffe
Bethel Leslie
Anita Loos*
George Oppenheimer*
Henry C. Rogers
Cesar Romero*
John Springer
J. Watson Webb, Jr
Ken Young
* Deceased

This book has been much enriched by the photographs, many never published before, from the collections of J. Watson Webb, Jr, Joseph Yranski, and Douglas Fairbanks, Jr, and I thank them most sincerely.

I am also in the debt of the following persons whose support and hospitality allowed me to continue with my research on Miss Crawford in New York and Los Angeles:

Bob Board
Gordon Herigstad
James B. Lahey

Others whose encouragement and backing allowed this project to continue were Harold Haskins, Leonard Kesl, Carlos MacMaster, Jeffrey Simmons, Avonell Williams, and Hiram Williams.

I wish to thank, too, the librarians at the Lawton Constitution, the director of Documents Section (FOIA), the Federal Bureau of Investigation, the Margaret Herrick Library at the Academy of Motion Picture Arts and Sciences, the Charles Feldman Collection at the American Film Institute, the Billy Rose Collection at the Lincoln Center Library of the Performing Arts, and the Alachua County Library in Gainesville, Florida. Lastly, I would like to thank Douglas Fairbanks, Jr for taking the time to correct those sections of the book in which he was involved.

FRED LAWRENCE GUILES, 1995

★ ★ ★ ★ ★ ★ ★ ★ ★ ★ ★

★ ★ ★ ★ ★ ★ ★ ★ ★ ★ ★

CHRISTOPHER CRAWFORD:
'As usual, she has the last word.'

CHRISTINA CRAWFORD:
'Does she?'

Closing lines from the film *Mommie Dearest*, based on the book
by Christina Crawford.

PREFACE

A s I write this in the winter of 1993, Joan Crawford's memory lies in tatters – her 'punishment' for being a bad mother. Her posthumous reputation is similar to that of the celebrated torch singer, Libby Holman, who introduced the song 'Moanin' Low' and a dozen other popular songs which have become standards in our time. Holman was a critic's darling and her male admirers were legion, but it was the scion of the Reynolds Tobacco Company who won her and persuaded her to retire to a magnificent estate in North Carolina. Once there, however, boredom set in and the Reynolds manse became a prison to Libby.

There were drunken brawls and jealousy was rife on both sides, and then one morning young Reynolds was found shot to death. As she had been on the premises, Libby was accused of murder, and her rambling account (as any alcoholic's would be) of the night before did nothing to give her an alibi. She was booked, freed on bail and then tried for the murder of Reynolds.

The jury was moved by Libby's tearful courtroom appearance in her widow's weeds, and she was acquitted. She picked up her career again, yet she could never quite live down the notoriety. When she died, Libby Holman was remembered mainly for the crime which she claimed she did not commit, and, in a similar way, Joan Crawford is remembered chiefly not for having had the longest career on the screen of anyone who ever worked before the camera but for being a monstrous mother. [Mary Astor made her screen début in September 1921 and retired from the screen in March 1965 (ironically with *Hush, Hush, Sweet Charlotte*, the film in which Joan was to have starred with Bette Davis, but, because of their disagreements on the set, Joan left the production on the pretext of illness). She was replaced by Olivia de Havilland. Astor was therefore technically on the screen longer than Joan Crawford, but in roles of diminished importance.]

Film stars are traditionally thought of as poor mothers. Many have indulged in unmotherly behaviour – Judy Garland, Ingrid Bergman, Bette Davis, Gloria Swanson, Marlene Dietrich and Lana Turner, to name but half a dozen – and few have evaded the relentless eye either of the gossip columns of the past, or the tabloids of today. The extraordinary lives which these women led, and the unique stresses placed upon them, makes it foolish to expect any of them to have behaved like normal human beings, yet many would argue that this remains a very poor excuse – or no excuse at all – for their treatment of their children.

Joan Crawford's posthumous reputation is the worst of any of them. Unfortunately for Joan, her transgressions as a mother were paraded before the world in a best-selling memoir called *Mommie Dearest* (subsequently made into a film) by an articulate adopted daughter, Christina. Fiercely disciplined and highly organized, Joan sought to impose that same discipline on her role as a mother. It worked with her youngest two children, her twins, because they never questioned her, fought back or rebelled in any way. It failed dramatically with the two oldest children, Christina and Christopher.

In the pages ahead we will see why it failed. If undue emphasis has been placed on putting her role as a mother in proper perspective, it was forced upon her biographer. *Mommie Dearest* has left in its wake a lot of tales which must be re-examined, some inventions and exaggerations and a great deal of truth, because film stars are by their very nature self-absorbed, vulnerable to criticism, and trying to cope – not always sensibly – in a pressure-cooker environment.

There is no earthly reason why Joan Crawford's life should be so tarnished by her daughter's writings that we should view her story only through the latter's eyes. Joan Crawford was simply the most successful American screen actress in the history of film. She was not the *greatest* actress, nor was she the most beautiful of the superstars, but she survived longer in the cinema than any other female star.

★   ★   ★

It may be true that Joan Crawford's memory lies in ruins, yet there are clues abounding that this ignominy is neither universal nor permanent. Much to the dismay of the Academy of Motion Picture Arts and Sciences, her Oscar went on auction after her death and sold for $68,000 when the auction house had predicted a top bid of $15,000. Rather like the curse of King Tutankhamun, the career of Faye Dunaway, who played the monster mother in the film version of *Mommie Dearest*, went into a steep decline following the release of the film. In a recent interview, Miss Dunaway offered a disclaimer, saying that she had made a mistake in doing the film. Anne Bancroft, who was originally cast, worked for six weeks on the picture and then decamped, leaving her agent to work out a settlement with Paramount Pictures.

Christina Crawford claims to have written her book as a classic study of child abuse, but, incidentally, has earned slightly more from it than the sum total of her mother's estate at the time of her death. Perhaps it is time that the scales were balanced, and that the voices of the many who saw Joan Crawford from a different perspective, as their lives touched, were finally heard. No other film star of Crawford's magnitude has suffered so greatly in terms of their reputation. Fatty Arbuckle, Charlie Chaplin, Mabel Normand, Lana Turner, Judy Garland and Elizabeth Taylor were all superstars who were seared by tabloid journalism every bit as damaging as the charges brought against Joan, yet only Fatty Arbuckle went into total eclipse. Of the rest, only Joan and Lana Turner (whose Mafioso lover was stabbed to death by her daughter) were branded as 'not very nice people' by the public.

Even Joan's dearest friends concede that she was not the best of mothers. There will be no attempt here to challenge most of Christina's allegations, but there will be a conscientious effort made to show that, for every instance when Joan lost control (or imposed her own fierce control) over those around her, there was an instance of generosity or simple humanity which had little to do with the 'bitch-goddess' syndrome all too often used to describe her behaviour.

The legend which took Joan Crawford half a lifetime to create may have been unmade by her daughter for some people, but, for fair-minded readers, here is the whole story, including her good deeds and fundamental decency. It would be grossly unfair if we allowed a prejudiced account of this great film star's life to obscure the human being within. So here is the unbiased and unvarnished truth of the incredible passage of Lucille LeSueur from Kansas City to a near half-century as the legendary Joan Crawford.

INTRODUCTION

I f she had been anyone but Joan Crawford, nearly everyone would have said that she was at the end of the road. She had just completed her seventy-eighth movie after nearly forty years on the screen. *Strait Jacket* was a cheap programmer, but Joan was given a large percentage of the profits as an inducement, and now she was making a personal appearance tour to promote the film.

In early 1963, her producer, William Castle, a veteran in the genre, knew that he was exploiting her success of the previous year, *What Ever Happened to Baby Jane?*, in making this blatant screamer. He and Joan must have known that both fans and film critics would wonder why the most durable star in American films was making a career of horror films. To Joan, it did not seem a matter of taste or discrimination. She wanted to work and Castle had sent the script of a film which she believed she could do. And she wasn't doing it just for the money either – her ten per cent of *Baby Jane* was going to make her a millionaire all over again, and she was then also being paid $40,000 a year as a board member of the Pepsi-Cola Company.

Strait Jacket was not a very good script, and perhaps Joan knew that, even though it was by Robert Bloch (the writer of *Psycho*). Still, this tale of an axe murderess released from custody after twenty years might have succeeded if Joan had been supported by at least one or two heavyweight peers – a Laughton or a March, perhaps, or even a James Mason. As it was, it succeeded only as a second-class thriller and a late-night TV programmer. As a lark, one of Pepsi-Cola's vice presidents, Mitchell Cox, played the role of the doctor from the mental institution who follows her post-release progress with growing dismay. It was not a production which Joan took very seriously.

She toured all the key theatres in the Loew's chain, going from her home town of Manhattan as far north as New Rochelle. She would go on stage with newspaper columnist and TV celebrity Dorothy Kilgallen to be 'interviewed', a ploy which seemed to work as a way of getting her out there before her fans. Of course, the applause was always deafening when she appeared. As one of the four most-written-about women of all time (the others being Cleopatra, Elizabeth Taylor and Marilyn Monroe), she was familiar to everyone in the audience from the veteran fans of the 1920s to the hippies of the '60s: Joan Crawford, the lady with the big eyes and big mouth who always played all those tense emotional scenes in an operatic bravura style, even though she looked as if a Mack truck could not truly impinge upon her will.

Her 'in-person' tour was drawing huge crowds and turning the film into a hit wherever she went. From New York, she flew in the Pepsi-Cola executive plane to Philadelphia, where she encountered a February blizzard and could not fly on to Pittsburgh, where she was to appear that evening. She scrubbed Pittsburgh, boarded the Boston Express at the 30th Street Station, and settled back in Drawing-Room A, where the lights went out soon after they left the city. She was informed that the heat had gone off as well, and that the diner had run out of food. Joan asked 'Mamacita' Brinke, her personal maid and companion, to get down two of the hampers she had brought along, lit some candles and began a picnic with chicken, hard-boiled eggs, pickles and plenty of vodka.

As well as Mamacita, Joan also travelled with two Pepsi-Cola pilots, a press agent, a photographer, twenty-eight pieces of luggage and one prominent prop – an axe said to have been used in the film, which Joan always hefted for the attendant newspaper photographers and TV cameras.

On the road Joan changed as often as ten times a day – hence the need for the trunks of clothes carried from city to city. A security guard from Pinkerton's was always employed to guard her hotel suite, and Joan rarely left her rooms during a visit except for the theatre appearances. Pepsi bottlers were brought to the suite for an audience with the great lady. It was marvellously effective, and their impressions of her visit to their city would be vivid and lasting ones.

★   ★   ★

Although Joan made some money from *Strait Jacket*, encouraging her to go right into another horror film for William Castle, her life was far from serene at that moment. Her brother, Hal LeSueur, had died during the winter of a ruptured appendix. Joan paid the funeral expenses, but did not attend the services and did not send flowers. [Hal LeSueur was buried in Forest Lawn, and not in the local Potters Field, as was alleged by some reporters.] She had effectively kept her mother and brother away from her life for nearly forty years. She considered them to have been losers in life, and she kept an antiseptic distance from that contamination.

Bette Davis, Joan's co-star in *What Ever Happened to Baby Jane?*, had been nominated for an Academy Award for the film the previous year, which had infuriated Joan. Rumours circulated that she had campaigned *against* Davis, asking friends around New York who were voting members of the Academy not to vote for Davis. Joan clearly was bitter and resentful. She knew that it was she who had courted Davis so that she would be receptive to the notion of appearing in a film as Joan's co-star. Joan had done this with some trepidation – she considered Davis a great actress and herself a great star, and she knew the difference.

Joan knew in advance that the film was going to be a huge success, just as she knew that her performance as Blanche Hudson was one of the best performances of her career, but now Davis was getting all the praise in the showier part of Baby Jane. Joan waited in vain for Davis to do the gracious thing and say, 'We mustn't overlook Joan Crawford,' but Davis never once mentioned Joan's name in connection with the film, always speaking of it as a star vehicle. Of course, Joan's campaign against Davis's Oscar was successful (although in truth a waste of time because Anne Bancroft was always the favourite for her role as Helen Keller's teacher, Annie Sullivan, in *The Miracle Worker*).

Joan, still fuelled by bitterness, and in Bancroft's absence from the Award ceremony, actually collected the Oscar on her behalf. She even gave a party for the younger actress, at the theatre in New York where Bancroft was playing the title role in *Mother Courage*. It was in character for Joan occasionally to do self-destructive things. As a tenth owner of the film, she knew that she was only hurting herself by sabotaging Bette Davis's Oscar chances for their film. Fall-out over her displeasure and her campaigning for Bancroft continued throughout 1963, and in the early summer of that year, when the Cannes Film Festival invited Joan to be an honoured guest, her director in *Baby Jane*, Robert Aldrich, had her disinvited.

And then there were the children. Christopher, now nearly twenty and totally estranged from Joan, would marry and have children whom she would never see. Christina had written a long article for *Redbook* magazine in 1960, in which she said that she had at last realized that her mother had done her a good turn by being so strict a disciplinarian during her childhood. At one stroke, Christina had edged away from Joan's control of 'the legend' and had broken the long silence about her childhood. She did not yet say that she had been abused, but now Joan was going to be mentioned along with Barbara Stanwyck as stars who were not very good mothers.

Joan was no fool. Having been in the spotlight all those years, she knew that she had enemies. She had written off her son Christopher because he had told her to her face that he hated her. There were also members of the Pepsi-Cola board who were beginning to gripe about her 'huge' salary of $40,000 a year. This news had sent Joan into a frenzy, although Herbert Barnet, the company's President, had come to her aid with a newspaper quote that her salary was 'peanuts' compared with her worth to the company. He was probably right, because for nearly ten years the public had begun to couple Joan Crawford with Pepsi-Cola in their minds.

★　　★　　★

In June 1963 production began on Joan's second co-starring film with Bette Davis (a kind of 'sequel' to *What Ever Happened to Baby Jane?*) entitled *Hush, Hush, Sweet Charlotte*. Robert Aldrich was directing once again, and nothing of his earlier hostility to Joan, when he had had her disinvited from the Cannes Film Festival, was mentioned. After all, he must have reasoned, *Baby Jane* had made a fortune for everyone concerned with it, including himself and both of his stars. On the official production starting date, Los Angeles Mayor Sam Yorty proclaimed it 'Joan Crawford–Bette Davis Day' and handed a scroll to Davis, who was alone for the ceremony as Joan was in the hospital with viral pneumonia.

Aldrich shot around Joan for nearly a week, and then Joan and her doctor announced that she would be well enough to resume her film work the following Monday. There was some feeling coming from the Davis trailer that Joan's problem was one of temperament and not in her lungs. The truth was that Bette Davis was scathingly sarcastic around Joan. While Joan tried to ignore it, she began to sicken and then her temperature, which never failed her in an emergency, began to rise and her doctor forced her to enter Cedars of Lebanon Hospital.

In actual fact, Joan believed that the script of *Hush, Hush, Sweet Charlotte* was inferior to that of *What Ever Happened to Baby Jane* and she did not appreciate having to spend long weeks working with an actress whom she had come to detest, only to emerge with a losing proposition. However, if she allowed her health to shut down a big-budget film production, she might become uninsurable. That, of course, was unthinkable, and so back she came from the hospital. She did this twice, until finally, on 13 July, Aldrich threatened to shut down the film production after incurring losses due to Joan's illness of half-a-million dollars.

Joan pleaded with Aldrich not to do this, insisting that she would be all right by the following week. She and Davis had yet to do a single scene together, and it now seemed to be that confrontation which Joan was fearing more than anything. She appeared on the set, shot shorter scenes which took no more than two hours of the day, and then 'collapsed' again as Aldrich announced that he was ready for Joan's first scenes with Davis. Once more, Aldrich shut down the production and Joan, no longer in the hospital, rested in her Bristol Avenue home.

In August, Joan was told by her doctor that she could not resume work for a month, and at that juncture, Aldrich announced that she might be replaced. When Joan tried to reach him to discuss this possibility, she was told that he was out of town. In fact, Aldrich was in Switzerland conferring with Olivia de Havilland. Then, on 25 August, Joan was informed by a newspaper reporter of a *fait accompli* – de Havilland had been signed to replace her.

'Wouldn't it have been nice if they had told me?' Joan said to the press. 'I still believe in this business and there should be some gentleness. I think it takes a lot of guts to make pictures, and I'm going to make a lot more of them. But I'm going to make them with decent, gentle people.'

Afterwards, as she told friends, she cried for nine straight hours, and said, 'I've never been replaced before. I'm used to having people look me right in the eye . . . and not this indirect treatment.' That was what Joan said, and the reporters believed her. They had no reason not to. The lady was by then a legend – 'a living legend' as they often called her – despite her aversion to clichés. *Hush, Hush, Sweet Charlotte* was made without her and was only a modest success.

There were to be no more big-budget films starring Joan Crawford. Perhaps producers were afraid that she might break down again mid-production. Who knows? She made horror programmers and TV movies during her last years, yet some of the sting was taken out of even that development, because she knew that Bette Davis was now doing the same.

New York City, May 1977

The role was one which she had played half-a-dozen times during the forty-five years she was in motion pictures. She sat alone in her apartment, seeing no one except her housekeeper. As her health rapidly declined, she called in a Christian Science practitioner, Mrs Markham, whom she had known for forty years and who began coming every day. A devoted fan hovered, running necessary errands, handling vital correspondence and standing in as a private nurse.

Joan Crawford had learned to live with fear, for death threats had become a regular occurrence, but what she had not learned was to live with threats from total strangers. There had been many of these over the years of her fame, despite the ease with which she had slipped into the role of victim, from the silent films of Lon Chaney up to that of the wheelchair-bound sister of a demented Bette Davis in *What Ever Happened to Baby Jane?*. On 21 October 1976, an FBI special agent, following up on an extortion letter received by the actress, had telephoned to ask whether she had ever heard of the author of the letter, a woman requesting no less than $50 million dollars, and Joan swore that she had not. Some faceless woman wanted her dead, or at least wanted her to pay for the privilege of life which this tormentor was willing to grant her for an absurd price. After the death threats, security became a major concern as Joan secluded herself within her East Side apartment in Manhattan's Imperial House.

She rarely went out, and she complained to her close friend, Leo Jaffe, then President of Columbia Pictures, that someone had tried to break into her apartment, located in one of the most secure buildings on the upper East Side with two doormen guarding the two entrances on East 68th Street and East 69th Street. The head doorman, Matthew Curran, was especially vigilant to possible intruders and strangers, and said he looked upon all of the owner-tenants of the co-op building as 'my own family'.

Still, Jaffe went over to reassure Joan and to check out the premises. He saw no evidence of a break-in, but the police were called and guards were stationed in the corridor for several days and nights. 'Extra locks were installed, but she seemed to be living in mortal terror,' Jaffe recalled. He was, however, relieved to see that Joan's sobriety seemed to have become permanent, as about eighteen months earlier, during a vodka binge, she had fallen and seriously hurt her head. Always hopeful, Jaffe would call her and make dates to have lunch at a nearby restaurant, but invariably she would telephone ten minutes before she was due to leave the building and cancel. 'She would make dinner dates and cancel. She did this to everybody.'

The crisis ended ironically when Joan's cancer-ridden body silently informed her that she would soon be leaving this life on her terms, not on those of some extortionist. On 8 May 1977 she gave away her closest companion, her shi-tzu, Princess Lotus Blossom, knowing that she could no longer look after the dependent little creature herself. She was rapidly wasting away, down now to eighty-five pounds. She had pain pills for her back, which she took as needed. She discharged her beloved Mamacita, telling her that she could no longer afford her services, which was simply not true.

Then, on 10 May, she took the last of her pills and quietly slipped into a sleep from which she would never awaken. Her maid found her mid-morning. Joan would have denied it, but she was seventy-two.

★　　★　　★

But how had it all begun, this longest-running film-star saga? Joan Crawford had come up from nothing – from a status far below the background of Marilyn Monroe, who had at least lived in a series of bungalows and had never worked as a child to help support a family. Yet in their iron determination to succeed as film actresses, they were much very much alike. The difference between Monroe and Crawford was that, whereas Monroe invented herself, and promoted that invention to success in the film marketplace, Crawford was the creation of her studio, Metro-Goldwyn-Mayer. We will be privy to that studio processing — taking on an overweight chorus girl with cultural deficiencies, and turning her into their most dependable star, and eventually a legend and a power in Hollywood.

ONE

BILLIE THE TOILER

T he south- and middle-west of America are very different from the unending cities, towns and suburbs and the Europeanized culture of the east. There is more space in Texas, Oklahoma and Missouri for the individual spirit. Somewhere on the horizon, children think they see the smoke of Indian camp fires. Indian culture forms the link between the south- and mid-western child and the past. Tepees. Arrowheads. Tomahawks.

Some notorious killers — Baby Face Nelson, Dillinger, the Barker Gang, Bonnie and Clyde — came out of the south- and mid-west, and before these were others with a licence to kill — Sitting Bull and Wyatt Earp. Just south of Kansas City, where Joan Crawford was raised to adulthood, is St Joe, home of the Pony Express and Jesse James.

Growing up with that kind of cultural inheritance, as Joan did, girls who were not closely watched by their parents sometimes suddenly appeared in scarves and sandals as 'Greek' dancers (Ruth St Denis), with some ties to the old Indian mythology, or as exotics (Josephine Baker) finding audiences abroad and international reputations.

In Joan Crawford's youth, there was no great ignominy in being poor in Kansas City when the local newspaper, *The Kansas City Star*, could be bought for two cents and connect Billie and her family to the world. The Sunday rotogravure section was her finishing school. The fashions of the day and the dances were illustrated, often with charts — the Black Bottom, the Foxtrot, and the Charleston. Valentino made the roto section regularly, as did Mary Pickford and her husband Douglas Fairbanks. Through those pages, Billie toured the rooms of Pickfair (Pickford and Fairbank's California home) years before she actually trod them as the Fairbanks's daughter-in-law.

★ ★ ★

Joan Crawford was born Lucille Fay LeSueur to Anna Belle (Johnson) and Thomas LeSueur, a French-Canadian, on 23 March 1905 in San Antonio, Texas. It is said that Thomas abandoned the family shortly before her birth. There were two other children born to the couple – Daisy, who died in infancy, and Hal Hayes, who was nearly two years older than Lucille.

Five years later, Anna LeSueuer had a sudden and unexpected relationship with Henry Cassin, a small, agreeable man known as 'Billy' to his friends. Cassin was a back-country impresario who travelled about the south-west in search of talent for his theatre in Lawton, Oklahoma – talent that he could afford, as most of his performers were either just starting out or close to retirement. Henry wanted Anna to accompany him back to Lawton, but she insisted on bringing her two children, even though her parents offered them a temporary home in Arizona. Henry therefore arranged for the mother and children to travel to Lawton by train. (There was a rail line near the town, as it was close to Fort Sill, a major army installation vital in the last half of the nineteenth century in waging war against the Indians, who were largely decimated by that time.)

In Lawton in 1911, the year of Anna's arrival with the children, Henry ('Billy') Cassin operated Cassin's Air-Dome Theatre, a five-hundred-seat alfresco affair open during the summer at which touring companies appeared. Cassin also managed the Ramsey Opera House, a permanent theatre with a balcony, which offered more cultured fare, such as the 'American Pavlova', a ballerina who had appropriated the famous Russian dancer's name, with her small troupe. To ensure a steady income, Cassin also kept an office open for five days a week, where he recorded deeds and acted as a notary public and bail bondsman.

Lucille quickly attached herself to her new father and even took on his nickname, changing the spelling to 'Billie'. [Joan's private secretary, Betty Barker, informed me that she believed 'Billie' to be a common nickname for Lucille.] The affection was mutual and Cassin indulged his stepdaughter, allowing her to linger around the theatre during performances and play in a barn behind their house in which scenery was stored − much of it left behind and never claimed by touring companies or acts which had folded.

Before she was seven years old, some of Cassin's dancers passing through had taught Billie the time step (tap) and buck-and-wing. 'Pavlova' gave the girl a pair of worn-out ballet slippers, several sizes too large. Another dancer helped her into greasepaint and discarded costumes. Joan later wrote:

'It was entrancing to watch the dancers backstage at the theatre. Once a ballerina in flaming-red tarlatan let me kneel before the lighted mirror on her dressing-table while she put purple eye shadow and pink rouge on my face. I inhaled the smell of greasepaint, the musty scent of scenery, the dancers flying about, light dazzling in their spangled skirts. And I literally danced through the days, a butterfly, a bird . . .'

Mother Anna did not approve. In fact, she did not approve of anything Billie did, saving her affection instead for her son Hal. Once, when her brother trampled her mother's nasturium bed, Billie was the one who 'got' it, and was caned on the legs − an often-administered punishment.

Billie was something of a tomboy and preferred the company of boys to that of girls, but Hal was not interested in playing with his younger sister. He and a friend were 'exploring' the sewer tunnels then being dug all over town, but Billie would be chased if she tried to join them. Her peers among the town girls were even more inclined to shun her. She was much too eccentric, once climbing the town water-tower, throwing aside her skirt and climbing up to the very top in her muslin petticoat and knee-length underwear. Christina Swanson, a local girl of just Billie's age, said that she was forbidden by her mother to play with her.

The Swansons, as well as the Blanding family (Don Blanding, a contemporary of Billie's, was later to become a noted and much-published poet) lived near the Cassins on D Avenue in the 800 block. Their homes were identical bungalows with wide verandahs where porch swings or sofas, all bought from Sears or 'Monkey' (Montgomery) Ward catalogues, hung from chains to the porch ceilings, with eight identical steps leading to the decks from the sidewalk.

In good weather, which was all that Billie lived for (she later said that, in winter, which was severe, she simply endured like a hibernating creature), she invariably went barefoot. When she was eight years old, she leaped off the front porch, landing in some bushes on a broken milk bottle and severing an artery in her foot. Don Blanding picked her up and carried her into her home. The doctor, who came at once, told her parents that she would never walk without a limp, but Billie found that unacceptable and, after two operations, with her stepfather's encouragement she not only walked normally but thought of little else but her plans to become a professional dancer. During her convalescence, her tiny mother (who weighed just over seven stone) carried her around the house – from living-room to porch to dining-room – and the child came to learn that Anna really did love her in her own way.

It has been written that Joan Crawford came from riff-raff, from 'the wrong side of the tracks', but, in fact, the Cassins were a respected family until an unforeseen scandal drove them out of town. The Cassin theatres staged literate theatrical productions, often on low budgets but always with high pretensions, and represented culture to Lawton residents. The exception to this was during the summer, when the huge Chautauqua tent was erected and the locals saw 'in person' such exalted creatures as future President Woodrow Wilson, John Philip Sousa and His Band, opera star Mme Ernestine Schumann-Heink, pianist Ignace Paderewski, fire-brand orator William Jennings Bryan, humourists and Russian folk dancers. When the Chautauqua was in full swing, Henry Cassin shut down his theatres.

Despite the Chautauqua and Cassin's efforts, in that period before America entered the First World War the south- and mid-west still retained vestiges of the pioneer days. Conestoga wagons with their canvas covers were a common sight in barns, and the spirit of those hardy folk still prevailed in Oklahoma, Texas and other south-western states. Ambition in even the poorest child was often limitless.

Billie hated school and often played truant. When she entered a classroom, she felt a knot in her stomach that never left her until she was away from the school grounds. She learned very little, and her parents did not insist that she try – Anna through apparent indifference, Henry through an indulgence of the child that was as harmful to her later development as it was balm to her spirit. To Billie, formal schooling was unimportant; what she felt she had to do was to work very hard at learning to dance, and to keep improving every day until she emerged as one of America's greatest dancers. Maurice was the biggest name in ballroom dancing at that time, and was often featured in the local *Lawton Constitution*. Billie's ambition was simply to become Maurice's partner.

One Lawton resident, John March, recalls that Billie's brother Hal had rigged up a trapeze from beams in the barn, in order to work at his ambition of becoming a circus acrobat. Billie decided to put together a little 'revue', consisting of a solo dance by herself and a turn on the trapeze by Hal with another boy as his partner. Their stepfather abetted them, allowing them to use a backdrop from a *Robin Hood* performance by a wandering troupe long gone from the scene. Cassin also suggested that they improvise footlights from tin cans split down the middle with candles inside.

When the huge barn doors slid open, as theatre curtains might part, Billie was revealed in her gypsy costume of red and turquoise, which she had made herself from scraps and discarded costumes. She wore her over-sized 'toe slippers' and danced to *'Wait till the sun shines, Nellie'*. The show was brief but memorable, both to those who watched and to Billie, whose 'show-business' career had been launched – however sketchily.

★ ★ ★

One day, Billie happened upon a hoard of gold coins in their storm cellar, a discovery which truly shocked her. Money was in short supply in the Cassin home, but the coins had spilled out of a money bag that she had found stuffed behind some of her mother's preserves. When she told Anna, her mother was so disturbed that there was a conference between the parents that evening, and the following day both Billie and Hal were shipped off to their maternal grandparents in Phoenix.

The children learned later that, while they were in Phoenix, their stepfather had been accused of keeping bail money which had been deposited with him in exchange for a woman's bail bond. It may have been rare for a charged criminal to pay in gold coin, tempting Cassin to hide the money away for himself and his family with no fear of recrimination. He must also have realized that it would be the woman's word against his – a suspected criminal's against that of a respected pillar of the community.

In her autobiography, *A Portrait of Joan* (1962), Joan wrote that her stepfather was 'cleared of any complicity in the matter', but it was more likely that he returned the gold and that the matter never came to trial. He was, however, 'convicted' over the party line – telephone calls which tied up the phone system for several days – while the family was shunned by most of its neighbours. Cassin's reputation in that small corner of Oklahoma was ruined. Joan's ability in later years to forgive human frailty was surely a grace acquired at the age of eight-and-a-half. She never got over her sense of guilt at finding the cache of coins in the cellar, precipitating the scandal that drove the family from modest circumstances into the degrading slums of a large city.

Cassin believed that he could make a fresh start in Kansas City, Missouri, where he was unknown except to booking agents in vaudeville and road shows. When the family first arrived, he invested the money from the sale of their bungalow in Lawton in a run-down hotel, the New Midland, near the city's tenderloin district. The family had rooms on the third floor, and Cassin and

Anna took turns at handling the front desk. There were too many deadbeats, however, and the hotel could only be run at a loss.

Kansas City was rapidly becoming a major metropolitan centre by the winter of 1913–14, when Billie first realized that they were stranded there and not likely to leave. The great Kansas City jazz artists such as Count Basie, Julia Lee, Charlie Parker and Lester Young had not yet begun their major contribution to American culture, but ragtime, chiefly composed by Scott Joplin, was in vogue. Ragtime musicians often practised in the New Midland lobby where Cassin allowed them the space free of charge, with the idea of entertaining the guests. Anna did not appreciate the gesture, but Billie, when was not at school, often danced around the lobby to ragtime, sometimes defying her mother's orders to 'go up to your room'.

Billie attended the nearby Scarritt Elementary School, where she was entered in the third grade with children at least two years younger than herself, much to her humiliation. She was subsequently transferred to a parochial school, St Agnes Academy, by her stepfather, who was a Catholic (Joan always maintained that *she* was Catholic until the middle period of her stardom, when she told the world via countless interviews that she had become a Christian Scientist).

Henry Cassin spoke with the Mother Superior of the Academy at some length, and then, on the way home to the hotel, he told his daughter that she would soon be living at the school as well as studying there. Cassin was not happy about this solution, but saw it as preferable to Billie being exposed to his own deteriorating situation and marriage back at the hotel. Eventually, with no money and his confidence gone, Cassin began to feel that he could never regain control of his affairs, and very soon drifted out of the family's life.

Billie was to learn of his departure in a devastating way. A few weeks after beginning her studies (and her work, for she was 'washing dishes, cooking for the entire establishment, making beds, waiting on tables – and trying to get some studying in between . . .'), she escaped from the Academy for a few hours and

walked all the way back to the New Midland Hotel to see her
Daddy, where she learned that he had gone – 'gone for good',
according to her mother. Billie was inconsolable.

Anna found work in a hand laundry, and she and Hal moved into
hovel behind the business, where Billie joined them on 'holidays'.
They shared one room and a bath at first, until Hal fixed up some
dilapidated rooms on the floor above, where they slept on pallets.

Billie discovered at the Academy that domestic manual labour
– scrubbing floors and toilets, washing dishes and kitchen
counters, making beds and doing laundry – was a kind of escape
from the classrooms which she still dreaded. Like many gifted
but undiscovered children, she was bored by rote teaching and
blackboard exercises, and would do nearly anything to avoid
them. In the workload at the Academy, which was heavy for such
a small girl, she could 'give her brains a vacation' – a practice
which threatened to become a permanent situation. Anna did not
seem concerned. Indeed, she was vexed that Billie was not with
her more often to help at the laundry.

In later years, Joan never failed to put down St Agnes in her
Hollywood interviews, and a nun who spoke with author David
Houston said:

'Some of the Sisters have been so upset and hurt by things
Lucille [Billie] said about the school. I don't know why she felt
she had to say such things. She was so successful, it's sad that
she didn't present a more positive image for your people . . .
Lucille was at St Agnes in about the fourth, fifth, and sixth
grades. She was never very truthful about her age. She was *not*
made to feel like a slave. The Sisters sacrificed to make her feel
loved and to teach her. They could see that she had talent, and
she was given singing lessons, dancing lessons, elocution,
drama. It was very common for there to be music and dance
recitals, and Lucille was often permitted to participate. She
never once credited the Sisters with that.'

Joan Crawford nearly always exaggerated or distorted events in
her earlier life (beginning with her birth), and her description of

St Agnes clearly falls into this pattern. Another grudge expressed was her treatment by other pupils because of her 'charity' status. At least half of the other girls at St Agnes were on work scholarships, and, as Sister Aquinas (a contemporary student of Billie's) has said, 'If her friends knew Lucille was [there] on charity, *she* must have told them.' There is in fact considerable evidence that Billie Cassin, the young vamp who became so popular at age fifteen, was well spoken and informed on current events, and attributed by most of her friends to her Catholic-school education – in other words, to the three years that she spent at St Agnes.

In the spring of 1918, at thirteen, Billie was allowed to help in the production of the Maypole dance in the annual recital given by St Agnes. The recital was performed that year in the old Orpheum Theatre, which would soon be supplanted as the major Kansas City vaudeville and movie-house by the Main Street Theatre. The old movie-house smelled of mildew, but much of its rococo splendour survived. Billie was allowed to assist in the direction of the Maypole dance and played the second lead as 'January', costumed in white.

Anna attended the performance, accompanied by a new lover, a Mr Hough, but Billie scanned the audience in vain for some sign of her beloved Daddy Cassin. She had searched for her stepfather for nearly two years. She looked chiefly at people's shoes as she moved among them on the pavements of Kansas City, knowing that Cassin's shoes were smaller than most men's and always had a shine on them. And then, one day, 'in the midst of those thousands of feet, I walked right into them! Daddy and I grabbed and kissed each other and talked . . . we had ice-cream sodas . . . he gave me money to ride home'. As she walked home, far too excited to ride the trolley, Billie dreamed of the day when they would all be together again. But that day never came, and in fact she never saw Daddy Cassin again.

★　★　★

Billie had begun sneaking out of St Agnes to meet boys in Budd Park, which was some distance from the school. As she reached puberty, sex became even more of an anodyne to her than scrubbing floors. Judging purely by her future behaviour in Hollywood, it seems clear that sexual contact with another person was more important than anything else in her life, excepting her fame and the career which had given it to her. Some of her future close associates would assert that she was 'oversexed', but, like Marilyn Monroe, Jean Harlow, Clara Bow, Rita Hayworth and a handful of other sex goddesses, Joan was the real McCoy.

The Sisters became aware of Joan's behaviour very early in her last year at the school, but did not expel her because they felt that, from what they had heard of her mother, Anna, the girl would become even wilder in her charge. Word of Anna's several lovers had reached the Sisters, and it would not greatly have impressed the ladies in black if Anna had told them that she planned to marry Mr Hough, with whom she was then living.

At least once during Billie's forays into Budd Park, she met a legitimate young gentleman who had no interest in love-making. His name was Ray Thayer Sterling, and he was then a senior at Northeast High School. Billie saw him first while he was playing an impromptu game of football with his peers. Later, Joan called Sterling 'my first beau, the confidant of my dreams. Ray was the one I called when anything went wrong, and I loved him with my whole fourteen-year-old heart. Ray wanted me to go out and get my dreams. Once I was in the process of realizing them, I lost him'. Smitten as Ray Sterling may have been with Billie, however, he must have seen how she flitted from one dancing partner to another on their dates, although she would sit out dances sometimes, 'just to hear him talk'.

Billie's park excurions finally became more than the Sisters could tolerate, and she was placed on probation. Billie retaliated by packing her things and running home to Anna and Hal and the (to her) offensive new man in her mother's life, Mr Hough.

★　　★　　★

Kansas City was a much subdued place in the autumn of 1918. America had entered the First World War in early April 1917, in order ' to make the world safe for democracy', in the words of President Woodrow Wilson, who had come into the White House on a peace platform. An influenza epidemic had swept all of the United States, and many Kansas Citians went about their business wearing face-masks. The city's splendid Union Station, the largest such terminal in the country, was now a place of departing soldiers and their weeping wives, girlfriends and mothers. In place of the flower vendors so prominent before the war, now the depot was crowded with the Red Cross canteens and their grey ladies handing out coffee and doughnuts.

As sugar began to be rationed, the temperance ladies were riding high on a crest of approval that would lead to the Volstead Act in 1919. This prohibition of alcohol was to last for more than a dozen years and brought about the speakeasies of the 1920s, along with the gangster era, as outlawed alcohol was, understandably, the province of outlaws.

At this time Billie was fretting about news, brought to her mother, that Daddy Cassin had died. Brother Hal obtained a work permit to assist his mother legally in running the laundry (he was then fifteen). Upon the heels of her angry flight from St Agnes, Billie was put to work in the laundry, no work permit being needed for a female child. Whenever she rebelled at the drudgery, she hastened to Budd Park, where she now had a reputation as the 'fastest girl' on that turf. Meanwhile, enrolled at Manual Training High School to learn a trade, Hal had his pick of the high-school beauties of the city. He was nearly six feet tall, very blond, and extremely handsome. If he had not had such a vapid personality, he might have become a film star when later he joined his sister in Hollywood.

Sometimes brother and sister would join up for an outing to Electric Park, an amusement park on the Missouri River which boasted the most thrilling roller coaster in the country. Billie wandered about eyeing the attractive couples while Hal rode all the rides, including the Steeplechase. At twilight they would watch the turning on of the magical lights which had given the park its name. The lights made the place literally glow, transforming it into a fantasy realm where the children could forget the laundry and their penury and think of themselves as fortunate to be standing there in such a magical place, surrounded by happy people.

It was in Electric Park that Hal discovered the exotic dancer, Sally Rand, who later would become a big attraction at the Chicago World's Fair in 1933. She was not yet known for her fan dance, but she was scantily clad and Billie became impatient as Hal lingered to watch performance after performance. Wandering around outside, waiting for her brother, she later wrote 'I felt more orphaned than Annie'.

In the spring of 1919, Anna told her children that Mr Hough had proposed and that she had accepted him, and that they would be moving into his Genessee Street home. Billie and Hal were never invited to attend a wedding ceremony, and Billie wondered whether it had ever really taken place. However, her home surroundings had improved. Genessee Street was middle class with trees and front gardens and was, in all ways, a step up from what the children had known even in Lawton.

No love was lost between Billie and Hough, and she later wrote that he was always trying to seduce her, but that she threatened to tell her mother. Perhaps it was a feeling of paternal obligation, or merely a hope to get this thorn out of his side, when Hough made enquiries about a school for Billie. Rockingham Academy, a private school which took toddlers in its kindergarten and went up to the twelfth year, needed a student-helper, and the headmistress, Effie H. Stuttle, told Hough that she would consider his 'stepdaughter' Billie for the position.

When Billie was accepted at the school and her mother escorted her there on her first day, Anna seemed contrite and wondered whether they were doing the right thing. Mrs Stuttle was a grim-jawed woman and made it clear that Lucille (she was never Billie at Rockingham) would be worked very hard with long hours. Billie was given a room under the attic eaves. Most of the students were, like herself, children of divorced parents, or so ungovernable that their behaviour had sent them on to this 'detention home', as Joan referred to it once in an interview. It does seem probable that Hough considered his 'stepdaughter' to be qualified in both categories.

The school was, in reality, a run-down mansion in a good neighbourhood. It consisted of fourteen rooms, all of which Billie had to clean. She also cooked, made beds and washed dishes. When her work displeased Mrs Stuttle, she was flogged or sometimes kicked with a sharp-toed boot after being dragged into the headmistress's office by her hair. She ran away several times and, once, she ran home to Genessee Street to find her mother gone. Anna had left Mr Hough and gone back to live above the laundry. Hal soon joined her there after a sojourn with his grandparents in Phoenix.

Now Billie had a choice: she could either return to Rockingham, and Mrs Stuttle's physical abuse (as well as some classwork), or she could go back to ironing shirts. She decided to return to Rockingham and, altogether, she was to remain there for four years, until her eighteenth birthday.

When Billie was fifteen, a boy invited her to a dance, and Mrs Stuttle, surprisingly, agreed that she could go. One of the other girls supplied her with a suitable dress, slightly faded but still attractive, and Anna helped her to mend and alter it. Of course, she danced every dance and was transported by the experience.

For more than a year thereafter, Saturday night meant that a Stutz Bearcat or some other expensive car would pull up in front of Rockingham and whisk Billie away to a country club or to Northeast High School for a dance. Mrs Stuttle felt that launching her charge in such social circles would help the school's reputation, and may not have guessed that Billie was anticipating the roaring twenties just as they were getting underway. Sometimes the janitor, in league with Billie, would let her in after midnight and say nothing to the headmistress.

In her last year at Rockingham, Mrs Stuttle put Billie in charge of the younger children. In 1928, Joan told an interviewer: 'The kiddies were worth going back for. They were practically orphans – neglected but not technically abandoned by their parents.'

In 1923, when Billie was eighteen, she left Rockingham, but only after receiving a phoney diploma from Mrs Stuttle, confirming that she had completed high school. She took the train to Columbia, Missouri, where she entered Stephens College, one of the most prestigious women's colleges in America which had a policy of admitting a certain number of working students, whose tuition and board would be 'paid' through work in the dorms and cafeterias. It was a desperate gamble. She was utterly ill-prepared, and knew the moment she entered her first classroom that she was out of her depth.

Billie was at Stephens for just under four months, and worked in the school cafeteria in exchange for her tuition and board. During this time she befriended the school president, James Madison Wood, whom she soon called 'Daddy' Wood. He took an instant liking to her, and recognized her great potential, as did others. When Billie entered a ballroom or gymnasium for a college dance, all eyes would be upon her. Even in her teens, she had a presence – a charismatic magnetism that made strangers wonder just who she was. Wood was to remain Billie's friend until his death.

Ray Thayer Sterling came down to see her at least once, but as she later wrote, 'There were glorious dances at the (nearby) University of Missouri and at the College Inn where Orville Knapp's orchestra played. Often we got home way past curfew.' Sterling must have been concerned about her blossoming on campus as a flaming flapper who danced every dance (while he sat them out and waited for an intermission when Billie would sit and talk with him about life and its possibilities).

When mid-term exams came up, Billie fled. She knew that she would flunk them, but Daddy Wood caught up with her at the station (and, according to one account, accompanied her on the train all the way to Kansas City, where he had an engagement). He gave her three rules for living, insisting that she never be a quitter and, from his own experience of life, informing her that no one else would be interested in hearing about her problems – in other words, 'When your problems are the deepest, let your laughter be the merriest.'

Wood also told Billie that, if she found she could do a job, she should go on to something more challenging. His philosophical advice might seem bromidic, yet Joan Crawford adhered to much of it in her later years. She rarely walked out on anything (except husbands); she was constantly improving herself and challenging her talents; and few heard her complain about the hand which life had dealt her, except to comment (to interviewers) about her own good fortune and how she had made the most of it.

Many years later, in April 1970, at the invitation of the administration of Stephens College, Joan was fêted at the school for her achievements as 'an actress, businesswoman, home-maker, mother and philanthropist'. 'My kids will never believe this,' she told an entranced audience, 'because I was a dropout!' She was at the end of one of the most celebrated careers in the history of film.

Mid-term in December 1923, Billie returned home to Kansas City where Anna and Hal were sharing a spacious apartment on Armour Boulevard, a good neighbourhood. Even though she had taken a secretarial course at Stephens ostensibly to learn typing and shorthand, her near aphasia in classrooms and similar environments rendered her incapable of taking on any office work. Relying solely on her personal charm and beauty, she quickly got a job in the millinery department at Kline's department store.

The dancing did not stop. Billie had young men lined up almost down the block for dates. She would go to college dances, speakeasies or road houses – wherever the music was gayest. She had learned the Black Bottom ('Black Bottom, and you twist it . . .') and the Foxtrot, and loved nothing better than to dance the night away. At the road houses, the musicians were sometimes black and played jazz, but at local college 'hops' the band was generally white. The two were not integrated until the 1930s, when Benny Goodman hired Teddy Wilson and Lionel

Hampton, and, in any case, Kansas City was a more southern than a northern city in nearly every way. People of a different colour or race – even Mexicans – were ghettoized. Billie moved throughout her years in Kansas City in a lily-white world.

Billie was no wilder than most of her female peers at those dances. 1923–4 was the first winter in the twenties when moralists really took alarm at the relaxation of morals which was happening all over America. Billie usually ended up dancing on a table-top, and as often as not in the bed or backseat of her dancing partner. Some observers felt that she had no moral values at all, but most did not know that her mother had never taught her any. Considering all this, the wonder is that Joan Crawford, the film queen, despite a continuing pattern of involvement with male partners, would become a kind of social arbiter within the film community, and that other stars would look to their manners when in her company.

★ ★ ★

When the Charleston was first performed in 1923 in a black revue (*Shuffle Along*) on Broadway, and took the nation and then the world by storm, it absolutely suited the times. The Charleston was a more raucous and acrobatic version of the Black Bottom, and Billie loved it. She had soon won a hundred trophies in Charleston contests, ranging from gold-plated cups (which were usually pawned) to giant teddy bears. Her partners were a mixed bunch. She wrote later that she really didn't mind when her partners were gay, because she would choose dancing over sex any time. There was also no room for romance in the master plan for her life which was then evolving.

During Billie's brief tour of the vaudeville circuits, she came into contact with Katherine Emerine, the producer of a second-rate revue which was often pulled together by an impresario of the day, Nils T. Granlund (who, by the end of the 1920s was producing his own revues for the vaudeville circuits). The Emerine Revue had a number of girls prettier than Lucille (she had put aside the name 'Billie', believing that 'Lucille' would look better on marquees), and at, five feet four inches she was also shorter than most chorines, but her ambition was so strong that she never hung back. Granlund observed her grit and determination, while Emerine was impressed with her self-confidence even more than her dancing, and, when the revue folded in Springfield, Missouri, Emerine told Lucille to look her up if she ever got to Chicago.

During this period, the situation at home in Kansas City had worsened. Lucille went to work once more as a shop-girl, this time at Emory Bird and Thayer's, and joined her mother in supporting the family as her brother Hal was fast getting nowhere and had taken to drink in his early twenties. [Doug Fairbanks, Jr told me that Hal was 'something of a bum. He always lived on hand-outs from Joan, and I think he was something of a crook in financial dealings with her'.] Her mother had taken in a new lover, which did not surprise Lucille, but his passes annoyed her so much that she was determined to get away from Kansas City as quickly as she could.

Within a few months, Lucille had the wherewithal to get to Chicago, and she took the train up there to accept Miss Emerine's offer of help. Emerine was out of town, but Lucille recalled the name of her manager and went to his office. The place was crowded with other young women, almost all of them, like herself, attractive girls seeking work. Just as she had done with Granlund, she did not hang back but pushed herself to the head of the line and, in front of the agent, Ernie Young, and his wife, sobbed out her tragic story — that she had no money to go home, that her good friend, his client, was out of town, and that she had to find a spot as a dancer. The Youngs gave her dinner and found her a job in a local nightclub.

Lucille's first club date was, predictably, in a low-life night spot in which she had to remove some of her scanty costume while doing a kind of shimmy. She played such dates for nearly two months, all of them booked by the Youngs. She then was booked with several other chorus girls to perform at a business convention in Oklahoma City.

It is an American tradition that girls brought into a convention as entertainment are invariably available after the performance, but this could not have distressed Lucille very greatly, promiscuous as she had been as recently as her stay at Stephens College the previous autumn.

Billie Cassin-Lucille LeSueur-Joan Crawford was raised in the belief that sex is as natural as getting up in the morning. She gained that reputation as an adolescent in Kansas City, during her brief college stay at Columbia, Missouri and then on the road as a chorus pony, and kept that reputation throughout her days as a film queen. She was quite forthright about this. Only Marilyn Monroe — more than twenty years her junior and as many years closer to the sexual revolution of the sixties — would look upon sex with equal candour, the difference being that, by Marilyn's time, Joan was projecting an image of herself as 'a lady' to her vast public.

Back in Chicago, it was more of the same. She was the same wild Billie that she had been in Kansas City.

Lucille was sent next by the Youngs to a large nightclub in Detroit, the Oriole Terrace, where she was one of more than thirty young women in the chorus. She remained there for two or three months — long enough to have become part of the more liberated faction of the chorus line. Some of the women smoked (although never backstage) and most of them drank. Nearly all of them either had beaux, if they were from the Detroit area, or would accept invitations for late dinners from the line of johns waiting just outside the stage door every night.

Lucille soon fell into the habit of picking up one of these johns and enjoying a free meal. Sometimes the man — often a salesman making the rounds of the mid-west markets far from home — would propose that they have a nightcap back in his hotel room. At first Lucille declined, but then, on reflection, she really saw nothing wrong with accepting.

On one occasion, Lucille had been in the man's room no more than half an hour when there was a sharp knock on the door. [Incident reconstructed from conversation with Beatrice Ames in

1974.] It was a house detective, and he had a street patrolman in uniform with him. Lucille was arrested on the grounds of prostitution and taken to the city jail, where she was booked along with another girl she knew from the Oriole Terrace. The girl 'knew the ropes', having been through it all before. She advised Lucille just to wait, and the backstage manager from the club would appear. She had already telephoned him.

Even though the manager arrived within the hour, it was time enough for Lucille to be shaken to the soles of her feet both by her brief incarceration and the fact that she now had a jail record.

Lucille's arrest record was later to disappear from Detroit's police files when it was forwarded to the FBI headquarters in Washington during the 1930s. Joan Crawford met FBI director J. Edgar Hoover at that time, and took the trouble to show him around the Metro-Goldwyn-Mayer studio during one of his visits to Hollywood. Hoover was known to be a fanatical movie fan and, in fact, kept long and comprehensive files on the sexual activities of some celebrities, as reported by his paid informants. Joan however, became a kind of friend to Hoover, and they maintained loose contact – mostly by correspondence – over a period of thirty or more years. In the end, Lucille's arrest file was apparently destroyed while in FBI hands at Hoover's request. Reading between the lines of the surviving documents, it seems fair to assume that this purging was undertaken by the FBI director entirely at his own initiative.

Another document in Joan Crawford's FBI file refers to a 'story from a high police authority' that, subsequent to her arrest, 'a motion-picture film of Crawford in compromising positions was circulated to be used at Smokers'. The pornographic movie referred to may well be apocryphal. No reliable person has ever seen it, and Joan herself wrote that it had been made by a failed actress years before her own career began. This sounds correct, because *The Casting Couch*, as the stag reel was titled, apparently was made in or around 1918, seven years before Joan ever reached Hollywood. Arthur Knight, critic and film historian, wrote:

'*Playboy* pays a lot of money to acquire pornographic films; you'd think that if a Joan Crawford stag reel existed, one would have been offered for sale. None has. Furthermore, I spent a week at the Kinsey Institute in Bloomington, Indiana, which has probably the largest collection of pornographic movies. I saw none with Joan Crawford. I don't believe such a film exists.'

The one troubling thing about all this is that the FBI file states that, during one investigation into the film, two postal inspectors were arrested. That would be a matter of court record, so there remains the possibility that Joan's studio, represented by attorney Bob Rubin, *did* have the matter investigated and that two postal inspectors *were* arrested during the investigation. There is also a record of Joan having to pay her film studio, Metro-Goldwyn-Mayer, $50,000 for her release from her contract in 1943. It is entirely possible that such an amount was demanded at that time *not for her release* (which had been mutually agreed upon), but to repay the studio in part for monies paid out years earlier to extortionists over this stag reel.

Apparently, *something* happened in Detroit before Joan's film career began, because the FBI files reveal no improper activity on her part once she arrived in New York (where she would remain several months longer than her relatively brief few months in Detroit), and yet three separate FBI documents repeat the allegation that she was arrested in Detroit. If she did get this terrible scare while there, it may explain much about her motives for the harshest treatment that her daughter Christina received at her hands, as described in the latter's famous book, *Mommie Dearest*.

If this episode is removed from the book, the whippings and tension surrounding Christina's life within the Crawford home do not quite make a horror story. The episode to which I am referring is the one in which Joan reacts to confirmation that Christina (aged twelve or thirteen) had become involved at Chadwick School with the captain of the football team, who had recently graduated. Christina tells us that 'like an answer to my prayers, I found Walter . . . When Walter asked me to go steady with him, I accepted happily . . .'

A year or two earlier, Christina had been stirred by sexual urges to have a rendezvous with a stable boy after dark, and the repercussions were several. The boy was expelled and Christina was forced to be examined for penetration, which a doctor asserted did not occur. Joan was near hysterical over the incident, and had now received word from the headmistress at Chadwick that Walter, who was even older, had returned to visit Christina. When Joan heard this, in Christina's words:

'. . . she went into a rage. In no time at all, she was screaming that I was not to be trusted and she was going to have to bring me home since I was causing Mrs Chadwick so much trouble . . . About ten o'clock that night, Mother showed up in the station wagon with her current secretary as companion. Since she'd been drinking, she at least had the sense not to drive by herself. Lately, she'd taken to putting her vodka in a plastic water glass filled with ice and drinking while she was driving.'

On the way home, Joan enquired about a liquor store. The secretary did not know the area, but Christina volunteered the information that there was a liquor store two blocks away once they got to the main street. Then, according to Christina, Joan slammed on the brakes, sending Christina halfway into the front and the secretary nearly into the windscreen. 'She slapped me across the face and yelled: "You *always* know where to find the boys and the booze, don't you?" As I opened my mouth to explain, she slapped me several more times and ordered me to shut up.'

It should be pointed out here that Joan's slaps and physical violence have become a leitmotiv of Christina's book. While there were certainly some 'whippings' of the children when they misbehaved, as daughter Cindy reported to me: 'Christina got more than I did or my sister because she got into more trouble.' As for the pattern of slapping, neither Cindy Crawford nor Betty

Barker, who came into Joan's employ permanently just three years after this incident, ever saw Joan slap any of the children. 'It was not in her to do that', Betty Barker told me.

Very soon in the text, Christina is calling her mother a liar for telling a house-guest that Christina has been expelled from the Chadwick School (this could not possibly have been true, as Joan had picked up her daughter from the school when it was not even in session. Joan had always been free with the truth, and sometimes declared that something was true or had happened so that she could use it as ammunition in an ongoing dispute).

Joan called Christina into the bar and – out of hearing of her guest – asked Christina why she always argued with her. Christina repeated her profound sense of outrage over Joan telling the woman that she (Christina) had been expelled, when it just was not true. This scene should, however, be viewed for a moment from Joan's point of view. She had come a very long way from her early show-business misfortunes, including her encounter with the law in Detroit. That trauma had been the result of her ignorance of the peril when anyone oversteps the bounds of normal behaviour – bounds never spelled out by her own mother, Anna.

It is, perhaps, reasonable to surmise that Joan would have been nearly out of her mind with anxiety upon hearing the details of Christina's escapade with Walter, and that, remembering her own out-of-control girlhood back in Kansas City, she would be fiercely trying to control these developments in her daughter. Even if this supposition is true, however, it provides no excuse whatsoever for the scene which followed.

When Christina told Joan that she thought 'that she was supposed to be the one who was more understanding since she was the parent and the adult', Joan completely lost control. As Christina wrote in her book, she:

'leaped off the counter and grabbed for my throat like a mad dog . . . like a wild beast . . . with a look in her eyes that will never be erased from my memory . . . I lost my footing and fell to the floor, hitting my head on the ice chest as I went down. The choking pain of her fingers around my throat met the thudding ache of the blow to the back of my head. She banged my head on the floor, tightening her grip around my throat . . .

'All I could think of was that my own mother was trying to kill me . . . She was trying to kill me and if I had the strength I would try to kill her first. She was terribly strong and all I could do was concentrate on loosening her grip on my throat.

'The next thing I knew, the new secretary burst into the small room.

'"My God, Joan . . . you're going to kill her," the secretary yelled. She tried to pull Mother away from me . . . Mother continued to hit me across the face . . .

'Finally Mother allowed herself to be pulled away from me and started crying.'

This is the worst abuse and the most terrible trauma described in *Mommie Dearest*. It is also the centrepiece at the feast of horrors in the film, although it is almost outranked by Joan's chopping down the rose garden, according to Christina, on the evening after Metro releases her from her contract. That release came in 1943 and Joan's rose garden had been removed in 1942 to plant a Victory Garden, according to eye-witness Betty Barker, so perhaps Christina is confused about the chronology. Christina also tells us that the gardener quit after seeing the destruction, but that, too, is inaccurate. Betty Barker recalled that when he left, it was for health reasons, and that his wife replaced him, remaining with Joan for some years.

So what really did happen during the writing of this book? Perhaps the first draft, which apparently was written while Joan was still alive to hear of it (and tell Betty Barker about it) was the most accurate. There is no question about Joan's inadequacies as a parent. She was simply too powerful a woman to make a good mother, and perhaps we understand now the truly pathetic attempts she made to relate to her older children, who were clearly more demanding than the twins.

There is perhaps a clue to what happened in the absence among the book's cast of characters of Cathy and Cindy Crawford, the two younger children who were very close to Joan. They are mentioned only in passing; they simply do not exist in the plot of this book. Christina seems never to have made any real effort to relate to her younger sisters, and today neither Cathy nor Cindy will have anything to do with their older sister because of *Mommie Dearest*. On the plus side, Christina has been drawn into the fight against child abuse and often speaks on the issue. *Mommie Dearest* is still in print (in 1994) sixteen years after its publication.

Whatever one may think of *Mommie Dearest*, its effect upon Joan Crawford's memory and reputation has been calamitous. In fact, the result has been to ensure that Joan Crawford will never become another Hollywood legend such as Marilyn Monroe, Clara Bow or Jean Harlow. Christina succeeded in this on a level that she may not have anticipated.

Joan's closest Hollywood friends, some of whom moved to New York soon after she did, naturally read Christina's book avidly, and their response was most peculiar. Helen Hayes MacArthur remained loyal to Joan immediately after her death, despite her telling me in an interview in 1973 (four years before Joan passed away) that Joan never should have tried to become a mother. In 1990, Helen Hayes published a final memoir, *My Life in Three Acts*, in which she confesses that Christina's book turned her against Joan.

Another lifelong friend to Joan who was turned against her by the book was Claudette Colbert. In addition, Anita Loos, who spoke at Joan's memorial service, cut Joan to shreds in an interview with *Newsday* some months later. (Anita Loos had, earlier, written a brief Introduction to this book, but faced with her remarks to *Newsday's* Jerry Parker, I felt that the honourable thing to do was to remove it from this text, as no longer reflecting her feelings about Joan Crawford.)

Just as many of Joan's friends were outraged by *Mommie Dearest*. Myrna Loy, who lived several blocks from Joan in

Manhattan, knew about the manuscript's existence long before it was announced for publication. She was so incensed by the betrayal that, when Christina walked into a room at the Academy of Motion Picture Arts and Sciences just before Joan's memorial tribute, Miss Loy saw her coming and walked out as quickly as she could. Mary Brian, Metro-Goldwyn-Mayer director George Cukor (who spoke eloquently of Joan at the tribute), Douglas Fairbanks, Jr (her first husband) and press agent John Springer all deplored the book.

Cesar Romero, a close friend of Joan's, also stood firmly by her after her death, in the wake of the accusations. Known affectionately as 'Uncle Butch' by all the children, he remembered that, when Christina was a married woman, settled in Manhattan with her first husband, he and Joan went to dinner at Christina's apartment. Mother and daughter seemed to have an affectionate regard for one another, and Christina expressed her love for her mother during the course of the evening. Romero was therefore puzzled by Christina's book, and questioned her motives in writing it just a few years later.

From the chapters which follow, many readers may conclude that Joan's memory has been ill-served by Christina's memoir, especially if it is taken into account that some of the continuity is wrong, and that there are critical omissions which would balance the portrait of the actress. As there is no effort made here to skew this new biography in any direction other than that in which the facts of her life take us, Joan's posthumous reputation should benefit from the corrections.

ALMOST PRESENT AT THE CREATION

Flight was becoming a pattern in Lucille's life. She had fled Rockingham Academy to go to Stephens College and, when that experiment failed to work out, she had fled Stephens to return to Kansas City and a job in a department store. Now she knew that she had to escape from Detroit as well.

J. J. Shubert, the Broadway impresario, had a musical 'breaking-in' at this time in Detroit with his production of the revue *Innocent Eyes*. The show starred Mistinguette, an ageing French music-hall legend who, eight years earlier, had sponsored the spectacular career of Maurice Chevalier. Joan later described the revue's star as having been: 'very beautiful when she was young and even now, when she was (to us) very old [in her fifties], she had a magic all her own'.

On the closing night of *Innocent Eyes*, which was just after Lucille's humiliation at the hands of the Detroit vice squad, word came back to the chorus girls' dressing-room that J. J. Shubert was in the cabaret audience. Lucille found a waiter friend who knew Shubert by sight, and asked him to point him out. Then, when the chorus line rushed out to do their high-kicking, fast-tempoed version of 'Runnin' Wild', Billie's twirling skirt brushed Shubert's table in a kick that knocked his highball glass into his lap. Glancing up as he brushed himself off, he met those enormous eyes and a big, frightened smile. Later, Joan would deny that it had been anything more than an accident, and claimed not to have known at the time just who Shubert was.

After the show, Shubert came backstage looking for the 'little fat girl with the blue eyes', and asked Lucille whether she would like to join his revue as a chorus girl. Without hesitation, she said 'Yes', and, when she learned that *Innocent Eyes* had completed its break-in engagement in Detroit that night and was leaving the following afternoon, she instantly agreed to go, failing to give the Oriole Terrace management any advance notice and jumping the show. This was an act that could blackball a performer in show business permanently, but Lucille had no reputation to protect. She was only a worried mid-western chorine, afraid of being fired by the cabaret's boss for splashing a customer. She was also euphoric about her future, her life touched by magic at that moment. Word of her breach of show business rules never caught up with her, as she was destined after her début in the Shubert revue and a brief run in *The Passing Show* never again to be a part of live theatre.

During the run of the latter, Lucille became friendly with singer-entertainer Harry Richman, who had hired her as a chorine and singer and gave her what became a big hit song of the twenties, 'When my sweetie walks down the street (All the little birdies go tweet, tweet, tweet)'. She became one of Richman's incredible number of sexual conquests, numbering thousands according to his memoirs. Despite his non-stop womanizing, Richman was one of the biggest cabaret stars of the era, composing some hits himself and introducing dozens of major hit songs by friends in Tin-pan Alley.

Richman also spent many months in Hollywood, commuting between the two coasts, and, within two years of his involvement with Lucille, fell seriously in love with a film star who was very much like Lucille had been before her arrest – Clara Bow. Clara had a long string of lovers in the 1920s, but Richman was determined to marry her and even put an engagement ring on her finger. To Clara, however, it was just something to show the next boyfriend. Within a decade, Clara had become 'burned-out' and suffered a breakdown – surely an omen to Lucille.

A fellow performer on Broadway at this time, Jack Oakie, remembered Lucille as a platonic friend – a relationship so new and remarkable to her that she gave the matter a whole paragraph in her autobiography:

> 'Ours was no romance. As a matter of fact, knowing Jack taught me that girls and fellows can be friends, that there is a wealth of sharing for two people who have a relationship uncluttered with coquetry. This is something every girl should learn . . . Girls who feel every relationship with the opposite sex had to be flirtation are missing a great deal.'

Lucille and Oakie often dined together at inexpensive cafeterias, rode the double-decker buses with their open-air seats up topside and talked of the movies and what their chances might be if they could get to California. Within three years of their meeting, both were starring in films, Oakie for Paramount and Billie for Metro-Goldwyn-Mayer.

Lucille's break came first. Harry Richman claimed to have been instrumental in setting up a screen test, for Lucille LeSueur, conferring with Nils Granlund (who knew her from the Emerine Revue) about her film potential. He also said that it was his idea to bring in Metro executive and aide to Louis B. Mayer, Harry Rapf, to look her over. Rapf apparently then gave her his card and told her to give him a call. Lucille's version of events was that, two days before *Innocent Eyes* broke for a two-week Christmas holiday, Metro executive Rapf and his studio attorney Bob Rubin caught the show. The only thing wrong with this story is that Lucille by then had gone into the chorus of *The Passing Show*. As neither Lucille nor Harry Richman had very great reputations for facts about their pasts, however, the truth about what actually took place remains unknown.

Later that same week, Lucille was given a screen test along with a dozen other girls. She was asked to return a few days later, and, this time, her screen test was not routine – she was the only one being tested that afternoon. Those present that day were Granlund, who had escorted her, Harry Rapf and Rubin.

In Douglas Fairbanks, Jr's autobiography, *Salad Days*, he hints that Rapf had dated Lucille prior to his arranging that special screen test. There seems, however, as much probability in that story as in Harry Richman's boast or Lucille's sanitized recollection in her own autobiography.

In this book, Joan suggests that she was not very enthusiastic about going into films. As a twenty-year-old, she saw all this as a diversion from her main goal of becoming a great dancer. She told Rubin that she was going home to Kansas City for the Christmas holidays (*The Passing Show* shut down for two weeks over Christmas), and that, if they wanted her, they could reach her there. In Kansas City, she could connect with her old life once again, seek Ray Thayer Sterling's always welcome and intelligent advice, and decide whether she wanted to remain on Broadway or to become a starlet who might or might not make it.

As soon as she was at home, she quickly fell into the old routine from which she had sought to escape – ironing shirts in the laundry. When she asked if Ray Sterling had called, she learned that her old boyfriend (and the one person whom she trusted to advise her, just in case Metro phoned or sent her a wire) had left Kansas City in pursuit of a higher education in law. She also discovered upon arrival home that her mother's lover had abandoned her, and that there was a new man in her mother's bedroom.

As Christmas approached, Lucille began to wonder why she had come home. Little had changed in her mother's life, and her brother Hal was now a married parasite. On Christmas Day, a telegram arrived from Metro telling her that she had been put on a five-year contract with a salary of $75 a week, and ordering her to leave immediately for Culver City, California.

★ ★ ★

An underling from Metro's publicity department met the train, and escorted Lucille to a third-class hotel called The Washington, which was near the station. Pete Smith was Lucille's first publicity director and a kind man, always cheering on frightened new arrivals. Some ten years later, well into the talking-picture era, Smith would become the producer and narrator of a series of

'Pete Smith Specialities' – short films on subjects ranging from dogs which had been taught to count to demonstrations of three-dimensional films.

In the mid-1920s, however, Smith confined himself to promoting Metro's contract players. With Lucille, he thought that athletic poses might be the best way to tone down her 'hoyden' look. She was therefore photographed swimming, sprinting and even playing football. Smith was later to do the same thing with Greta Garbo, but Garbo's first film was such a success that she baulked at further press exploitation.

Eleanor Boardman, a leading lady who had been at Metro for a year, was friendly to Lucille. Boardman married director King Vidor in 1925 and therefore had only a brief career, but she remained in close touch with Lucille (or Joan, as she then became) throughout her Hollywood years. Boardman said: 'When Joan first came to Hollywood, she was alone and didn't know anybody. I befriended her and invited her up to the house in Beverly Hills I had with [husband] King Vidor for Sunday swims and buffets. Then suddenly she was launched and she didn't need any further help from me, although we saw each other constantly.'

Boardman realized that Lucille was quick enough at acquiring enough social skills to get ahead. She was also aware that, slight as she was, Lucille did have a presence, and that heads would turn whenever she arrived anywhere. Boardman's advice to her was to go to Harry Rapf's office and talk to him about her future, as he was the one who had urged Metro to hire her.

Rapf had Lucille cast in a bit role in *Pretty Ladies*, and as a member of the chorus in *The Ziegfeld Follies*, an early film effort to exploit the popularity of that show. She was then given an equally small role in *The Only Thing*, an improbable Elinor Glyn romance with Eleanor Boardman and Conrad Nagel. [Malcolm MacGregor, a leading man at Metro from 1924–30, believed that Joan was not in Eleanor Boardman's *The Only Thing* in 1925, but, rather, that she was in the silent version of Maugham's *The Circle* in that same year, also starring Eleanor Boardman. When reached in 1970 and asked about such a possibilty, Joan agreed that this could be the case. 'I just went where they told me in those days,' she said. Existing stills from *The Only Thing* show only someone in crowd scenes who resembles Joan. She could not possibly have been given credit on screen for such appearances, although she may have been drafted to appear uncredited.]

It was after this in the middle of 1925 that Pete Smith decided to change her name, asking a fan magazine, *Movie Weekly*, to co-sponsor a contest to re-name her. The winning suggestion was 'Joan Arden', and some publicity went out on Lucille using that name, but there happened to be an actress already listed by that name who complained. The second choice was sent in by a woman in Albany, New York, and it was, of course, Joan Crawford.

Lucille hated her new name. By now, her closest friend at the studio was leading man William Haines, known as 'Willie' to his friends. Willie told her not to fret: 'They might have called you "Cranberry" and served you with the turkey at Thanksgiving.' Shortly before his death in 1973, Willie told me: 'We used to kid each other a lot. I called her "Cranberry" for years.'

★　　★　　★

Metro Goldwyn Mayer had opened its Culver City studio on 26 April 1924. The walled-in complex of studios and small buildings was just a quarter of a mile from the heart of the small town. Louis B. Mayer had merged operations with Marcus Loew's Metro Company, and their intention was to bring in Samuel Goldwyn (né Goldfish), chiefly because they coveted his Culver City studio. Goldwyn, however, had a strong wish to go independent at that moment. He was willing to sell Mayer and Loew the studio and even his company assets, but not himself, and so, in a most unusual move, Mayer and Metro took over the Goldwyn Company, officially becoming Metro-Goldwyn-Mayer in 1924, while Samuel Goldwyn moved to new studio facilities, which became the Goldwyn Studio.

Irving Thalberg, although incredibly young, had come into MGM as former Head of Production at Universal Pictures under the venerable Carl Laemmle, one of the founding fathers of the Hollywood film industry. The new company's chief rival, however, was not Universal, but B. P. Schulberg's Paramount Pictures, which was very much at the top of the movie studio scale. Mayer and Schulberg had been partners at the old Selig Zoo studio as late as 1924. If Mayer hoped that Schulberg would come into MGM as a partner, he was mistaken.

The bosses were, of course, only as good as their stars and directors. Schulberg had recently signed a contract to distribute the prestigious and commercially successful films of D. W. Griffith, and he and author James M. Barrie had chosen Betty Bronson to play the title role in *Peter Pan*. This was a major hit in 1925, with a beautiful young woman named Mary Brian playing Wendy. Brian and Joan Crawford became very close friends that year and, in 1926, both were nominated as Baby Wampas stars (female film players considered by the Western Association of Motion Picture Advertisers as showing promise on the screen).

Schulberg also had both Gloria Swanson and the inscrutable continental Pola Negri under contract. By 1926 he was starring the uninhibited Clara Bow, and she became perhaps the most talked-about and popular screen actress of that time. William Powell, who had been employed as a floor-walker at Emory, Bird and Thayer's in Kansas City a year or so before Joan had worked there, was also with Paramount. In order to compete, Mayer had to keep very busy scouting out new performers. In 1925, he had John Gilbert, who was then the highest-paid male star in films, Barbara LaMar and Ramon Novarro (Mayer's answer to Rudolph Valentino). He added two new stars that year — talent-search winners from the east, William Haines and Eleanor Boardman. By the end of 1925, MGM had matched Paramount's profits.

In Europe, Mayer had bagged one major director, Mauritz Stiller, and, at Stiller's insistence, his protegée, Greta Garbo. Mayer's roster of directors was a distinguished one, and included King Vidor, Rex Ingram and Fred Niblo. Irving Thalberg, whom Mayer had brought into his new company from Universal to supervise production of his films, was then twenty-six and in delicate health. He had brought with him from Universal the director (and actor) Erich von Stroheim. Von Stroheim, however, had justly earned a reputation for going way over budget on his films, and Mayer was lamenting the cost overruns on von Stroheim's version of *Greed*. Less of a problem to Mayer was Thalberg's actress protegée, Norma Shearer, who that year supplanted the daughter of Thalberg's ex-boss, Carl Laemmle, in his affections.

By the time of Joan Crawford's appearance in her first film role, Mayer had one of the most valuable stables of players in American films. In addition to all the Metro leading men and ladies already mentioned, he had also put Conrad Nagel under contract (for the rest of the 1920s, Nagel would alternate between the stock-company stage and Hollywood), and, briefly, Jackie Coogan, the child star of Chaplin's *The Kid*, as well as Renée Adorée, who supplied the love interest opposite John Gilbert in King Vidor's blockbuster war film, *The Big Parade*.

By 1926, Gilbert's place at the top of the box office champions would be challenged by Mayer's discovery, William Haines. Haines was that extraordinary phenomenon, a romantic *comic* actor, which made him more versatile than Gilbert. In an attempt to cover all bases, Mayer hired cowboy star Tim McCoy during this period. Comedian Buster Keaton had also been lured over to the studio by Keaton's brother-in-law, Joe Schenck.

This impressive range of leading players gave MGM the edge over the other studios. It was becoming the most desirable studio in Hollywood, both from a financial and prestigious point of view, for nearly everyone associated with American films.

Mayer's star and director roster was so impressive that, before the year was out, Metro was able to negotiate a deal for the services of the comedienne leading lady, Marion Davies, then number eight among film favourites in box-office standing. She came aboard in an elaborate barter exchange with her lover, William Randolph Hearst, the publisher whose love for Davies had brought him into movie-making. The deal was that Hearst would supply unlimited publicity and press exposure for all

MGM stars and productions in his chain of newspapers, the biggest and most successful publishing venture in the country, while MGM would finance, release and distribute all of Hearst's own films, called Cosmopolitan Pictures.

Equally important during the 1920s and early '30s when the public became alert to their film favourites being mere human beings who could get into as much mischief or trouble as themselves, were the studio publicity chiefs. Pete Smith soon left the field, leaving media control (meaning newspapers in most cases) in the hands of Howard Strickling. A big man with a loud voice and sometimes jocular manner, Strickling had a gift for persuading reporters to be lenient both on the stars and others on Metro's payroll who got into trouble. It was Strickling who kept the lid on the Paul Bern 'suicide' when Jean Harlow was his bride, and it was Strickling who soon became aware that protecting Joan Crawford from scandal was going to be a priority matter.

★   ★   ★

This was the company set-up when Joan was brought in to be groomed for stardom. Some of the stars in that silent era – such as Greta Garbo – could barely speak English, but others, including Marion Davies with her powerful sponsor Hearst, and Norma Shearer (soon to marry Irving Thalberg), made Joan quake a little as they passed, even though Marion, for instance, always gave Joan a smile and a wink.

Joan was essentially alone. She felt that she had no one in her corner, but knew that it was vital to find someone important in the MGM hierarchy to be her Hearst or Thalberg. She began working on her acquaintance with Paul Bern, a story and production aide to Thalberg. A German Jew who had come into the studio in its early days as a writer and director, and had moved up to become a power in production planning, Bern not only seemed smarter than most of the men around him, but was also more of gentleman than all the others, so it made perfect sense for Joan to latch on to him. She was hoping that he could help fill in some of her cultural deficiencies and, if he really liked her, that he could persuade Thalberg that she had some talent and was well worth developing.

The name Joan Crawford first appeared in film credits in a melodrama starring young Jackie Coogan, then nearly ten years old and the first male child star in American films. He had made a tremendous hit with Chaplin's *The Kid* in 1920. *Old Clothes* (1925), in which Joan played the ingenue, would be his last film until he became an adolescent and able to take the role of Tom Sawyer. Hearst Hollywood columnist Louella Parsons wrote that Joan had been discovered by Jack Coogan, Sr, which came as a surprise to Joan when she read it.

By her fourth film, less than six months after arriving at Metro, Joan was playing the title character of Irene in *Sally, Irene and Mary* (1925), and began to be noticed by large numbers of fans and critics. The other two starring roles in the film were played by Constance Bennett and Sally O'Neil. Connie Bennett was considered the major star of the film and was deferred to at every turn. She barely nodded at Joan except during their scenes together, but Sally O'Neil, who was in her first film, became a close friend.

Joan was still far from having the unique stamp of the superstar (such as that of Constance Bennett), and had not yet lost all the weight that she should have done. There was even some gossip about her character during this period which may well have been rooted in truth – Metro executive Harry Rapf, who had discovered her for the studio and with whom she had had an affair, still occasionally slept with her. An unattractive man, known around the studio as 'the anteater', he had a nose so long that, years later, Joan said that 'his proboscis concealed his genitals'. Nor was it simple 'casting-couch' sex, for Joan had her contract and had aroused some interest in Louis B. Mayer.

It would be almost impossible in that concentration of authority (in Mayer, Thalberg, Rapf and Mannix) for the other men not to know that Joan was granting sexual favours to Rapf, a married man. Mayer, however, had learned not to examine too closely the private lives of his stable of screen personalities. Film fans knew nothing about Harry Rapf, and, if they saw his face in a movie gossip magazine photo, they would be looking at an anonymous, uninteresting (to them) person. Mayer knew this about his fiefdom. Studio liaisons were tolerated if they did not 'frighten the horses in the street' or keep the fans away from the box office, and at twenty years of age, Joan knew with whom she could sleep and with whom not. Production head Irving Thalberg, for instance, was off-limits primarily for health reasons and also because there were three women very interested in keeping other females away from him – his mother, Henrietta, his sometime girlfriend, Rosabelle Laemmle (daughter to his former boss, Carl Laemmle, head of Universal Pictures), and Norma Shearer, who already had told fellow player Eleanor Boardman that she was going to marry Thalberg.

The truth seemed to be that, once Joan began being seriously groomed for stardom late in 1925, some of her intense obsession with sex – which had so absorbed her for the half-dozen years since she had first discovered its pleasures in Budd Park in Kansas City – was diverted by her all-encompassing ambition to become a fully-fledged film star.

William Haines was the leading man in *Sally, Irene and Mary*. He had become a kind of escort to Joan, and so she felt very much at home despite Connie Bennett's arrogance towards her. Willie took Joan to his home to meet his male lover, Jimmy Shields, who was even better looking than Willie. The trio saw one another constantly, and the men were instrumental in getting Joan invited to William Randolph Hearst's ranch at San Simeon, two hundred miles north of Los Angeles, where Marion Davies presided as chatelaine of the fairy castle.

On screen, Haines was brash, breezy and impudent, and he also exhibited some of these qualities off-screen. A big, good-looking man of well over six feet, he became like a brother to Joan. It transpired that Marion had this same 'sibling' feeling about Willie, which could have resulted in some rivalry between the women. Joan never expressed this to Willie, however, as she was fearful that he might turn against her.

Such fears were evidently grounded in reality, for Joan was never invited to San Simeon again as a single woman hanging on to Willie Haines's arm. Her next invitation would not in fact come until several years later, as Mrs Douglas Fairbanks, Jr. She frequently dined and attended parties at the beautifully decorated Haines-Shields home in Beverly Hills, however, a social connection which continued throughout the men's lives. In her autobiography of 1962, Joan called the men 'the happiest married couple in Hollywood', and she meant it.

In the winter of 1925–6, Joan was sent with Willie Haines to New York, where he was to star in a film called *West Point*. While they were there, Joan became involved in a brief affair with the third male lead, Edgar Allen Neely, known professionally as Neil Neely. In May 1926, Joan was named in a divorce action brought by Hannah M. Neely, who claimed that she had found a love-letter from Joan Crawford in one of her husband's suit pockets. In answer, Neil Neely told his wife that he had had many romances since they had been married, and that 'one more or less made little difference'.

As for Joan's sexual preference, she seemed to have little interest in straying from traditional flirtations and brief affairs with men. She had already met several bisexual actresses, including Ruth Chatterton, Lilyan Tashman and Natasha Rambova. The fact that the three women were married to George Brent, Edmund Lowe and Rudolph Valentino respectively, however, seemed to suggest that many Hollywood liaisons were not what they seemed.

As time passed on, and women stars began to dominate the screen in the 1930s and throughout the 1940s, leading ladies such as Ruth Chatterton, Kay Francis, Annabella, Janet Gaynor, Greta Garbo, Katharine Hepburn, Jean Arthur, Tallulah Bankhead, Claudette Colbert, Martha Raye, Rosalind Russell, Barbara Stanwyck and Nazimova (who had become a character actress in the 1940s), all figured in stories circulating in Hollywood which linked them romantically with other women. None of these stories (except Bankhead's, Nazimova's and possibly Garbo's) can be confirmed, but there seems to be some correlation between box-office strength – which these women all enjoyed – and the licence to be as different as they liked off-screen. [In 1994, at the age of seventy-six, Martha Raye said that she had had a serious affair with Joan Crawford when they were both involved with the USO. It is probably true.]

A suggestion that Joan Crawford might be among this not very exclusive circle of strong leading ladies came from her daughter, Christina, who wrote of her mother having been 'surrounded by homosexuals' as her career went into decline, which she considered part of 'the turmoil' existing in the late phases of her mother's career. Christina also wrote of a female member of Joan's staff locking her bedroom door at night because of Joan's alleged demands. There was, too, an occasion when Marilyn Monroe claimed to have been the object of a subtle 'pass' by Joan during a visit to her house. Whether or not such incidents were true, Joan certainly had many gay friends and was entirely tolerant of homosexual relationships, writing only in a positive way about them in her autobiography.

★   ★   ★

During the mid-1920s, when Charlie Chaplin, Harold Lloyd and Buster Keaton were all busy turning out their brilliant features, the silent screen fostered the golden age of comedy. With his baby face made up in chalk white, with sad eyes projecting the same kind of pathos as Chaplin (except that his character on screen was more vulnerable than Chaplin's), Harry Langdon produced his own features for First National from 1925–7.

Joan was loaned by Metro to Langdon for his very first independent production, *Tramp, Tramp, Tramp* (1926). Joan played the girl in an advertising campaign for a shoe company which sponsored a marathon cross-country walk. Langdon enters the marathon in order to win a $25,000 prize and the love of the girl in the advertisements. The legendary director, Frank Capra, was a gag writer for Langdon and was credited with the story for this feature. The film was a success, but First National complained that it went over budget and was too long. Langdon repeated this mistake several times before being forced out of control of his films and becoming a supporting player for the rest of his career.

In the following year, Joan made her most important film up to that time, *The Unknown* (1927). It starred the gifted and awesome Lon Chaney, who played a man who has his arms amputated in order to impress a circus girl with whom he has fallen in love. The movie was directed by the extraordinary Tod Browning, who had a penchant for the odd and bizarre. Joan was very excited to be cast as the love interest in a Chaney film, and told Norma Shearer how thrilled she was to be working with him. Norma said to her, 'Don't get overjoyed too soon — you may get a letdown, like I did. There's something strange about the man. He makes you glad he's self-involved, as he usually is, because it would be goose-pimply to be the direct object of that man's attention or interest.' Joan's excitement changed abruptly to apprehension, and she asked Norma what she meant, to which Norma replied, 'You'll find out soon enough.'

Joan may have avoided any close friendship with the 'man of a thousand faces', but she was mightily impressed with his total immersion in his role. It made her aware of film characters having layers of humanity that she had totally overlooked up until then, and she told a reporter just after *The Unknown* was released:

> 'I want the Joan Crawford I am this year to be only a building block for the Joan Crawford of next year . . . I want to be prepared for those years that come when youth is gone . . . I haven't done a thing, not a single thing, with which I'm content.'

And she was as good as her word.

THREE

THE RIVALS

Now that she had an image in films, Joan made an effort towards domesticity away from the screen. Her small bungalow in Hollywood, as noted by Paul Bern, was decorated with black velvet hangings on the walls with irradiated colours that glowed in the dark, and more long-legged French dolls than anyone could count atop chests, tables and in corners of the sofa. Mother Anna LeSueur had been brought west by her daughter to keep house, and her brother Hal and his wife, Jessie, had arrived shortly afterwards. Then, in 1927, when Metro realized that Joan was becoming one of their most popular leading ladies, with Louis B. Mayer's financial help she bought a seven-room house at 512 North Roxbury Drive in Beverly Hills.

Joan kept her first, smaller house, and her mother and brother, with his family, lived there for many years at her expense. What the new, more elegant house gave Joan — as well as a better address — was some distance from her family. It was the start of her successful effort to cut herself off from an immediate family of whom she felt ashamed. She did not want a snooping journalist to uncover her mother's colourful but embarrassing past, and she was convinced that Hal was simply waiting for a chance to exploit her new-found, glamorous friends. Moving away also meant that she could have her own car, and not have to share one with Hal, who managed to wreck every one that she bought.

Louis B. Mayer clearly saw more than just promise in Joan when he advanced her the money to buy a house. Mayer had a reputation as a shrewd judge of talent and potential. He saw beyond Joan's freckles (always concealed by make-up), her muscular legs, and her 'hey, hey' image, and ensured that she was groomed to be taken seriously as an actress of quality.

What Joan brought to this endeavour was an abiding belief in herself, and in her ability to vamp convincingly whenever she was compelled to behave as a cultured human being. Eventually, of course, she would become exactly what Mayer wanted her to be, and what she aspired to be – a lady of the cinema. No social pedigree or Bryn Mawr diploma could ever top that in her view. And she left nothing to chance. As early as the end of the 1920s, Joan hired instructors from the University of California to come in to help her studies in English, history and even French.

★ ★ ★

Timing is everything in the making of a star. When Joan had come on to the scene as a player in Metro's growing stock company, the age of the vamp (Theda Bara) was long over, and that of the swooning, delicate heroine (Dolores Costello, Corinne Griffith, Lillian Gish) was in its last days. The flapper was rising rapidly to dominate the screen (Clara Bow, Colleen Moore, Louise Brooks). Two great stars, Gloria Swanson at Paramount and Greta Garbo at Metro, were looked upon as 'originals' who could and would play any part without regard to trends. By her nineteenth film, or three years into her career at Metro, Joan was playing a flaming flapper (silently) in *Our Dancing Daughters* (1928). It was a role in which she was to be typecast in her next half-a-dozen films, and established on celluloid the first of several Crawford screen images – that of the frivolous, high-kicking party girl.

In an almost classic instance of the ill-timed promotion of a star, Joan's leading man in *Our Dancing Daughters*, Johnny Mack Brown, illustrates the heartbreak in the typical studio build-up and abandonment of, in this instance, a male star. Johnny Mack Brown was a handsome collegian whom a talent scout had plucked from the University of Alabama, where Brown had been a star football player. His first screen role cast him opposite

Marion Davies in *The Fair Coed* (1927), and he was then given a leading role in Garbo's *The Divine Woman* (1928). Metro seemed to be grooming him carefully to become a fully-fledged star along the lines of Gary Cooper, whose career paralleled Brown's most closely.

After playing opposite Joan in *Our Dancing Daughters*, Brown was impressive enough to be her leading man in *Laughing Sinners* (1931), originally called *Complete Surrender*. Brown played a Salvation Army officer who saved Joan from suicide. The box-office chemistry of Joan and Clark Gable in *Dance, Fools, Dance* (1931), however, which immediately preceded the Brown-Crawford vehicle, persuaded Louis B. Mayer to scuttle the original footage on *Complete Surrender* and re-shoot all the Brown scenes with Gable.

Brown must have been devastated. It seemed obvious that Mayer's personal loyalties were nearly always dictated by the profitability of any asset in his grasp, and he knew that he could exploit the team of Gable and Crawford. Johnny Mack Brown was a clean-cut expendable, and in Mayer's mind, easily replaceable.

In 1930, director King Vidor had cast Brown in the title role of his major western, *Billy the Kid*, at the suggestion of Irving Thalberg, who also seemed to have an eye on Brown. Wallace Beery, one of Metro's most popular stars, was given the key role of Sheriff Pat Garrett. The film (shot in wide-screen, its first major use in a Metro-Goldwyn-Mayer film) was a success, and came out several months before the re-shot *Laughing Sinners*. Depite all this, Johnny Mack Brown's career went into a decline in the 1930s. His personality was just too nice for the film world.

On 8 October 1928, a month before shooting began on *Our Modern Maidens*, Joan became engaged to Douglas Fairbanks, Jr. So much publicity was given to their love affair, and now its climax, that Mayer successfully borrowed Doug, Jr from his home studio (Warners-First National) to play opposite Joan in the new film. By the time the film was released in September of the following year, they were already married. The wedding took place at St Malachy's, an actors' church in New York, and, while

Doug, Jr's mother, Beth Sully Fairbanks Evans, and her future husband, musical comedy star Jack Whiting, were in attendance, no one from Joan's family was there.

Young Fairbanks had lived close to the peculiar heat and unnaturalness of the aura of his father for so long that he failed to recognise that Joan was fast becoming a sun of nearly equal radiance. Her cultural ignorance made her seem naïve, but that side of her was a sponge that soaked up everything that came close to it. Doug, Jr quickly realized that he was as much her tutor as anything else.

Joan did not make any special effort to cultivate the acquaintance of Doug, Jr's real mother. She was far more interested in going to Pickfair, the California home of his father and stepmother, Mary Pickford.

Doug, Jr explained the situation:

'She and Mike Cudahy were engaged for a time and his family disapproved. He was one of my best friends. He was tall, good-looking, athletic, but also "they" said, an alcoholic. They used to go to the famous Cocoanut Grove a lot together to dance. They were great dancers. At the time, I was going with Helene Costello, Dolores Costello's sister.

'When Joan first contacted me after the first night of the play *Young Woodley*, all I knew about her was that she had a reputation as being a hard and serious worker. It was said by many that she was going to be "very important" in films, though not necessarily a big star. Such things were, and still are, unpredictable. After all, who could have known that the girl in the barber shop in Stockholm, Sweden, was going to turn out to be Greta Garbo? Joan was much admired by all who met or worked with her. While we were "going together" in late 1928, I made *A Woman of Affairs* with Greta Garbo and John Gilbert.

'Once we were married, Joan's "in-law" problem was with my own mother, Beth, not my step-mother, Mary, and my father. The latter were always pleasant to her and found her attractive to have around. My mother would have resented any young woman who took me further away from her. But Beth did try to be pleasant around her, although she resented Joan's position as the young woman who took her son "away". My stepfather, Jack Whiting, the popular Broadway "song-and-dance" man, was only about ten years older than I. He could have become a big star. He was almost as great a dancer and musical comedy performer as Fred Astaire. He was very graceful, very good-looking. I think marrying my mother hurt him a lot professionally. She was so much older.'

Doug, Jr went on to describe his childhood:

'She also strained the purse of her second husband, James Evans, Jr, of Pittsburgh, so I began my career in films at thirteen. My father didn't react at all well to this, but my mother didn't want him to interfere with this because, although he left her a good deal of money, she went right through it. And I was at that time keeping about six or more other people – grandparents, an aunt, an uncle and a cousin, etc. Although my father didn't realize that all this was going on, it would have made him angry to have known that all that money had been blown away.

'My schooling was off and on, actually more off than on. I went to regular schools up to the age of twelve, had tutors after the age of thirteen and continued the equivalent of high school with tutors. Years later, I wanted to get a commission in the US Naval Reserve. The war in Europe began, and I was not anxious to come up through the ranks if I could help it. The US Navy insisted on a university education, which I didn't have. What I did was to take a correspondence course with the University of California, and got my degree that way. After that I was able to apply for my commission.

'Joan was largely self-taught, and I was "educated" at home, so we had that in common. She was very diligent about it – voice lessons; she didn't have a very good voice but she made it as attractive as she could. She studied and tried to improve herself in every way.'

What all this reveals is that Doug and Joan were far more alike than anyone could possibly have known. They both were supporting family members in their early teens and neither had what was called a 'proper' education by American standards and certainly not by European standards. Their ambitions however, were different. Despite his early success in films, Doug, Jr had no conspicuous ambition to be the greatest male star alive (as his father had been), while Joan very clearly wanted to climb to the pinnacle of movie stardom.

★　★　★

Talking pictures were simply another means for Joan of advancing her fast-moving career. When she first heard her own voice in playback, she thought that she sounded like a man, but that seemed to be preferable to sounding guttural like poor Vilma Banky or lower-class Brooklynite like Clara Bow.

Joan took lessons from a voice coach, because she needed to sound more refined and less nasally mid-western. The distinctive Crawford voice that emerged was queenly, even when she was playing a shop-girl. Her diction became impeccable, and a part of her that she could not abandon even at the grocery store or in a swimming pool. As each part of her persona was refined by Metro, she took it for keeps. It was her voice, deep and commanding, as much as anything else that later made her friends confide that she was always 'on' — that she was always Joan Crawford, the star.

When Norma Shearer married Metro production head Irving Thalberg, it became a policy of the studio not just to give her the plum roles, but also to nail down the film rights to any successful Broadway play which might suit her. This situation was a constant irritant to Joan throughout the late 1920s and '30s.

As a consequence, when Metro produced its first all-talking film in 1929, *The Trial of Mary Dugan*, Shearer was cast as Mary Dugan. The studios often filmed crime and courtoom dramas in the early talkie days. Metro had in their files an old Broadway play by Bayard Veiller, called *Within the Law*, which had been a silent film some years earlier. In 1930 it was dusted off, and dialogue was added as a vehicle for Norma Shearer. The heroine of the play has spent three years in prison for a crime she did not commit. Shearer could portray innocence extremely well, and she was looking forward to the production. Soon after it was announced, however, she became pregnant, and Thalberg was so overjoyed by the prospect of fathering a child that he informed the studio that Norma would be making no films for a year or more.

Mayer decided to go forward with the film, which soon became known as *Paid*, with Joan as the star. Her obvious popularity gave her the courage to play this serious dramatic role. The field of skilled dramatic actresses among the Hollywood stars at that time was not crowded. Metro had Ruth Chatterton, Greta Garbo, Helen Hayes and Norma Shearer. Paramount had Sylvia Sidney, Estelle Taylor, Tallulah Bankhead and Miriam Hopkins. Warner Brothers did not yet have Bette Davis (she was at Universal at the start of her career), but they did have Kay Francis and Mary Astor, Astor being a much underrated actress who played women with pasts capable of creating new futures for themselves.

Mary Astor was given a slightly wider dramatic range than Francis, whom Warner Brothers seemed more interested in giving something sensational to wear. This was also becoming true of Joan. In fact, as the early 1930s moved on, the studios' star assets became almost interchangeable – Francis could have replaced Joan in any of her films, and vice versa. Joan was dressed by Gilbert Adrian, and Francis by Orry-Kelly.

Metro designer Gilbert Adrian was in fact responsible for making broad (and even padded) shoulders popular in women's fashion. Joan had fairly broad shoulders to begin with, which Adrian decided to exaggerate. He also designed a 'Letty Lynton' frock for her, which, through copies made by Sixth Avenue manufacturers in Manhattan, became the most popular single garment ever made in America.

When Metro released *Paid* in 1930, critics and fans everywhere realized that the screen now had another strong dramatic actress with a considerable range. Joan's acceptance as an actress and not just another personality instantly changed everything for her. She could now complain personally to Mayer if a script did not suit her, and, while Thalberg still knew that Joan and his wife, Norma Shearer, were rivals, he kept quiet as the other studio executives sought new material for Joan.

By the end of 1930, Joan was listed as the number one female box-office favourite. To everyone's surprise, she had surpassed the 'It' girl, Clara Bow, in popularity. Surely it was no coincidence that the woman who edged out effervescent Clara, the reigning box-office queen during the late 1920s, was a glamorized reflection of the American woman who was going to triumph over all odds during those depths of the Great Depression. In *Paid*, she played a woman wrongly imprisoned. Even though she would not go near a gaol again for more than ten years (when playing a criminal in *A Woman's Face*), there may have been an element of timeliness in Joan's rising to the number one position with that particular film.

★ ★ ★

By 1931, following the film *A Free Soul* with Clark Gable, in which she played an heiress who felt compelled to kick over the traces, Shearer became far more saintly in her film roles. Joan profited by this canonization, falling heir to all the slightly wicked but well-meaning roles rejected by Shearer (and Thalberg). By this time, when the Depression was taking hold, Joan had as dedicated fans millions of shop-girls and secretaries. They swarmed into cinemas around the world; they wrote her letters and poured out their pitiful tales identifying with her screen characters. Joan considered the fans vital to her career and still answered all her fan mail personally. She was convinced that it was these fans who had elevated her to stardom – wrongly, perhaps, as some esteemed critics seldom found fault with her screen work even with weak scripts. While Joan had no Irving Thalberg, she did have Louis B. Mayer in her corner for nearly twenty years.

Joan rose above all her peers by the sheer force of her presence on the screen – through enormous will and kinetic energy she reached out to her vast audiences by way of her image. That ability to hold her audiences was enhanced by a face that was the most photogenic in Hollywood: she had no bad angles. Alone among film actresses, she knew exactly how she looked on the screen because she sat in on the rushes (the daily takes on her current production). She noticed immediately when a baby spot hit her face from above that the extraordinary planes of her face were sharply highlighted. She was forever afterwards hit by that baby spot with the resultant 'Crawford look'.

Joan was aided in her dominance by the availability of the fan mazagines. Most of the film monthlies were priced at a dime, although the most prestigious title, *Photoplay*, cost twenty-five cents. Here, she was seen as not only the most popular actress of the time, but also as a social arbiter and the mistress of one of the great Hollywood homes, where the famous gathered when they were not at San Simeon, Hearst's castle in the Santa Ynez mountains, or at Pickfair, where she was a frequent guest. In 1929, Joan bought a white-stucco mansion at 426 North Bristol Avenue in Brentwood, for $40,000. Over the years, the house would expand to twenty-seven rooms.

Joan's fans were not drawn to her films by her dramatic ability, nor by exotic glamour, which was then cornered by Marlene Dietrich; and, even though she was often called a 'comedienne' in the decade ahead because she appeared in several sophisticated comedies, she was never compared to Carole Lombard or Myrna Loy, or even Irene Dunne.

Joan was invariably thought of as the ideal American woman, who could not be pinned down to any region because her speech – perfected by the best coaches at Metro – was devoid of accent or dialect. If you had last seen her in one of her 'modern-maiden' films, you would be surprised to find her an heiress in her latest film. You might think of her as a flapper, but that image wore thin as the Great Depression ground on inexorably, and she became a shop-girl so that her audiences could either identify with her or fantasize with her.

In spite of this great success, Norma Shearer remained a thorn in Joan's side from the beginning of her Metro days until very near the end. In 1936 Shearer was cast as a very mature (thirty-six-year-old) Juliet in an ambitious film production of *Romeo and Juliet*, and in 1938 starred in her costliest film, *Marie Antoinette*, which was released at a time when Joan's reign as box-office queen at Metro was waning.

Strong-willed and with a massive ego, however, Joan was determined not to go down in her career. In 1939 she fought for (as Louis B. Mayer was opposed to her taking a supporting role) the part of the hard-edged Crystal in Anita Loos's adaptation of the stage success, *The Women*, written by Clare Boothe Luce, Crystal was a husband-stealer and gold-digger who has been having an affair with the husband of Mary Haines, played by Norma Shearer.

The rivals met on the set, and everyone was waiting for some disagreement to explode into a cat fight, but Joan was too composed for that. While Shearer played her emotional scenes (in the role of a victim, as she was often cast), Joan sat near the camera set-up knitting furiously. Only once, while they were shooting close-ups of Shearer, did this antagonize the actress enough for her to stop the action and cry out to Joan to 'please stop that knitting!'

A casual study of Shearer's attitude towards Crawford suggests that she considered herself 'a lady', whereas Joan was not. There was never any serious confrontation between the rivals, because Shearer inherited Thalberg's shares in Metro on his death in 1936, putting her in a strong position, while Joan Crawford was a major money-making element for the studio. Shearer probably had the edge on Joan in cold logic, however, as Joan was often governed by her emotions. When Joan insisted to Mayer that she should be Irene to Clark Gable's Harry Van in *Idiot's Delight*, for instance, Shearer knew that Joan would be miscast in the role. There was a helplessness in Irene which needed to be projected, and no one would believe Joan's Irene to be sufficiently vulnerable when she becomes stranded in Europe by Hitler's war.

Mayer was a shrewd man, and his strength lay in knowing

every little weakness of his people. He understood Joan's insecurity better than anyone, and now he exploited that insecurity and told her that Norma would be getting the role of Irene because 'it would be wrong for you'.

There was some irony in the fact that, although both Crawford and Shearer were hold-overs from the 1920s and early '30s, only Joan had the ability to change her image. Shearer never changed, and by 1942 was out of pictures. Joan, on the other hand – her career in almost as great a peril – left the studio and went elsewhere, still in the business with a third of her films yet to be made.

FOUR

NOT A SIMPLE AFFAIR

I n 1931 Joan was cast in a leading role opposite Clark Gable, who was to become a major figure in her life. In the film, *Possessed*, Joan played a paper-box factory worker who wants something more from life and moves to Manhattan. There she meets a brilliant lawyer, played by Gable, whose marriage exists in name only, and who takes Joan as his mistress. Although the script was adapted by Lenore Coffee from a play, the situation of the principals greatly resembled that of the two stars.

They had both come to Metro in the 1920s and learned their craft at the same time with the same coaches and directors, although Gable had already had some stage experience, whereas Joan was entirely trained on the sound stages of Metro. They were equally at ease with the crew around their sound stages, earning the friendship and respect of all the grips, gaffers and others who made up the lower echelon of film-making. While Joan had some pretensions towards becoming more genteel than she had been when she arrived, however, Gable had none. He had the wit to see beyond her flings into culture, and even to tease her about it.

The major difference between them was that Gable's screen presence, unlike Joan's, was almost a true reflection of his off-screen persona, as is so often the case among major film stars. The wonder is that he and Joan were so strongly attracted to each other, because Gable was clear-sighted enough to realize that she did not put aside her screen image away from the camera. She fell into her usual profanity, her love of gossip and her love-making, but certainly not as Lucille LeSueur or even Billie Cassin. She was the actress Joan Crawford, no matter what she was doing.

Joan's honeymoon with Doug, Jr was over by this time. Non-stop physicality in a new marriage or relationship can be deadly, and, after a year or more (in their case, nearly three years, when one counts the year-and-a-half in which they slept together before they married), the body sometimes rebels against further intimacies with that partner. It stops responding, and, in many a marriage, the result is long periods of asexual domesticity.

When Joan and Clark Gable first met, he was willingly trapped in a loveless marriage to an older woman (Ria Langham), who had underwritten his apprenticeship as an actor. There seems little doubt that, both during and after the production of their co-starring film, *Possessed*, Gable gave Joan what she later described in blunt terms as the best sexual experience in her life. In her sixties she was bleeped during a television interview with David Frost when she referred to Gable's 'balls'. 'He had 'em,' she insisted.

Gable never commented in print about his feelings for Joan, but they seemed clear enough to others. Doug, Jr knew from friends who worked with the two of them during the making of *Possessed* that they were alone together in the mornings and after work in the dressing-room trailer which he, Doug, had given her. That galled him more than anything.

Joan was quoted often enough as saying that Clark Gable was the great love of her life. This is remarkable when one realizes that the affair, which presumably was consummated many times over, was not reciprocal. Gable attracted women – nearly all women – and was involved with one or several, either on the side or by marriage, throughout his spasmodic relationship with Joan, which she insisted lasted from the making of *Possessed* in 1931 until Gable's death in 1960.

There was a kind of freeze upon the affair in 1937 when Joan turned down the co-starring role in *Parnell*, an historical movie about the Irish Prime Minister, to be played by Gable. As he also began living with Carole Lombard at about this time, it is hard to determine whether Gable turned cool towards Joan because of the relationship with Lombard, or because she refused the *Parnell* assignment. Joan's refusal was rare for her, but she had ample cause to be wary of the projects she took on, having been roundly roasted by the critics the previous year, when she had played Andrew Jackson's confidante and a romantic partner to several of his aides in *The Gorgeous Hussy*. Her instincts were right – *Parnell* flopped resoundingly.

The affair survived Gable's romance with Carole Lombard in 1938–9, and, with an intermission, his subsequent marriage to her. Speculation about the two of them centred on what kept them together as lovers through so many years, not about the sexual event itself. Of course, everyone knew that they came from similar, deprived backgrounds – faintly rural in his case, big-city in hers. Neither had finished high school, and he kidded her whenever she became the 'grande dame'. Both were overly sensitive to public opinion, and kept Howard Strickling very busy maintaining their untarnished images.

Joan liked popular music. She was also cultivating a taste for grand opera, and was even studying singing with a voice coach. With the exception of an interlude during his boyhood when he played with the town band, Gable, by contrast, rarely showed that he cared for music at all, and even resisted appearing with singing star Jeanette MacDonald, for whom he showed an abiding disdain when they co-starred in *San Francisco* in 1935. Beyond differences such as these, however, a factor in Gable and Joan's continued relationship may have been the fact that their careers continued their astonishing rise in the 1930s, with both of them appearing on the list of the ten top box-office favourites during the middle of the decade. Their union was a kind of mating on Olympus.

Neither of them had the resources – love of literature, good, serious conversation, a taste for gourmet dining, or an interest in museums or art in general – to consider any alternative to sex as the most satisfactory pleasure in life. Gable had his outdoors, of course, and Joan had her Brentwood mansion, where the social life never stopped, but both were self-obsessed takers (except with the less fortunate in Joan's case), who seemed insensitive to the feelings of those who loved them.

Joan was forever worried about her image, about how she was perceived by others. She was even more insecure about this than Gable. His personality on screen was essentially a refinement of the man he was off-screen – jealously guarding his manhood through countless sexual conquests, learning to shoot, hunt and fish, becoming a Mason, then a Shriner, and doing everything that a one hundred per cent heterosexual male believes certifies his maleness.

Gable was a homophobe, a characteristic which is, of course, acquired, not innate. In childhood, his father worried about his becoming a 'mama's boy' around his stepmother. More significantly, however, his hatred of 'nances' and 'fairies' did not seem to be in him when he entered the movies in small roles in the late 1920s.

At that time, the two biggest stars in Hollywood were John Gilbert and William Haines. Haines, as we know, was openly gay – the very first major star to be 'liberated'. On one occasion, after a party, Haines propositioned Gable, something he often did. His straight 'tricks' (a trick being a straight man or one known as such who has a sexual encounter with a gay man) were famous throughout Hollywood, while, at the time, Gable had a reputation for marrying older women who could help his career. Haines and Gable did have sex. Perhaps Gable's motive was his advancement in films, as no one in American movies was more successful than William Haines.

As far as is known, this episode was unique in Gable's life. No other such episode was ever gossiped about. It does seem unlikely, however, that Willie Haines would have resisted telling his best female friend, Joan, about the incident, especially after she confided in him about her affair with Gable while she was married to Doug, Jr.

'Well, Cranberry,' he may well have said, 'We've both had 'im.'

Gable was surrounded by a small percentage of men at Metro who felt the same way (and probably were prompted by the same unconscious fears) as himself — writer Johnny Mahin, directors Jack Conway and Victor Fleming, *but no other actors.* Actors generally accepted the gays among them without comment, as Joan certainly did. She was known for her tolerance, while Gable — immersed as he was in the company of macho males — adopted all their prejudices. He made anti-semitic remarks, and, when he realized that most of Carole Lombard's close male friends were either gay or super-tolerant, began withdrawing from that circle. In time, Lombard took up his friends to keep him happy, went shooting and fishing and played poker alongside them.

After the war, Gable would join James McGuinness's notorious Motion Picture Alliance for the Preservation of American Ideals, along with his friends Victor Fleming and Johnny Mahin. This was the far-right reactionary group most active in bringing about and institutionalizing the infamous Blacklist. His name appeared on the list of members of the executive committee as late as 1953, when the Blacklist had torn the movie industry asunder.

★ ★ ★

Louis B. Mayer, their boss, tolerated Joan and Gable's obvious on-set 'romance', and saw to it that, through Howard Strickling, nothing of the affair reached the media. (Strickling knew exactly how to handle the press, and was invaluable throughout Joan's career at Metro. While he was in charge, no Crawford story ever made the front page, with the exception of headlines about her marriages and divorces.) He understood, too, that it had become a necessary connection for both of them, and continued as their lives outside the studio moved along separately with marriages, affairs and divorces. Joan, of course, respected Gable. Since attaining stardom, she had never slept with a man whom she did not admire, and she admired Gable more than most of her other bed-mates.

It is probable that Joan would have married Gable if he had ever asked her, yet she knew that Lombard was the only wife he really treasured. Joan had got on well with Lombard, and, when the latter was killed in a tragic air crash during a war-bond tour in 1942, Joan asked to be loaned out to Columbia Studios to take over her role in a film almost ready for production, *They All Kissed the Bride*. She donated her entire salary for the film $125,000 – to the Red Cross. Taking it for her own use would have been unthinkable. When she learned that her agent, Mike Levee, whom she had inherited years earlier from Doug, Jr, had taken his usual ten per cent, she fired him.

In March, two months after the tragedy, Joan sent Gable a note at the studio saying: 'If you'd like to stop by and have a quiet dinner, I'll be home rather late tonight and all this week.' Gable stopped by that very night, and every night thereafter during the shooting of the film *Somewhere I'll Find You*. He arrived on that first night extremely distraught, having held in his feelings all day at the studio. 'Why Ma?' he asked over and over, as Joan stood mute nearby, gripping his hand. She knew that 'Ma' was his name for Carole, and had been ever since their marriage.

Even Joan could see that he was downing his drinks too fast. 'Clark,' she said. 'You've got to stop this drinking.' Then he put his head in his hands and wept. In a way, the two became even better suited as sex partners after the tragedy – Gable had withdrawn from any real feeling or passion, while Joan was the product of the Metro assembly line, both in and out of bed.

Gable did not stop drinking, however – not until that July, when he began to get in trim for his army enlistment. He joined up in early August and was shipped off with cameraman Andy McIntyre, who never left his side, to Miami Beach for training in the air force.

Joan and Gable continued their affair until his departure. It should be apparent by now that they were spiritual cousins when it came to sex, if that is not a contradiction in terms. To them, sex was a function as necessary as brushing one's teeth, and with no more commitment of the heart than that. Sex kept you looking your best and your life in balance. After sex, too, they shared their most private worries and discussed what could be done about them.

On the screen, however, Gable had moved beyond the possibility of co-starring with someone like Joan Crawford. Earthy film queens such as Sophia Loren, Lana Turner and Ava Gardner would be considered likely co-stars, but studio creations like Joan were no longer considered suitable to play opposite such a 'natural actor' as Gable after the late 1930s. They both knew this, although Mayer would give them a last hurrah in 1940 with the film *Strange Cargo*.

With time off for the war, their sexual interludes continued until Gable's marriage to Lady Sylvia Ashley (she was Douglas Fairbanks's widow and had therefore been Doug, Jr's stepmother for a time). Joan and Gable picked up again upon Gable's separation from Sylvia, and continued their liaison until he met and married Kay Spreckles, when the affair abruptly ended for good, possibly leading Joan to rush quickly into her own fourth marriage with business executive Alfred Steele.

BREAKING AWAY

There was a moment when Doug, Jr knew that the person he had married was no longer an insecure young woman, but a successful, self-confident and demanding film star. Even her old nickname, Billie, hung in the air betweem them like a rope-bridge that was gradually fraying, although he would never call her anything else.

It happened in late 1931. Metro was giving Joan very little breathing space between films now that she had moved ahead of all the studio's other actresses at the box office. She had just finished *Dance, Fools, Dance* and was beginning the all-star production, *Grand Hotel.* Doug, Jr saw what was happening between them, but would not concede that his first marriage was turning out to be a failure.

In order to understand just who Joan Crawford was as a human being, one should grasp this moment, when the transition from vulnerable and sensitive Billie to the full-time film queen that she became occurred right before Doug, Jr's eyes. Of course, it did not happen overnight, but it did strike him that she was different, and not in ways that were especially endearing. Some machine inside her had been turned on, and it was always ticking away. She seemed to be allowing herself so many minutes for Doug, Jr's idle conversation. She was running on a tight schedule – one to which she would keep for the next twenty-five or thirty years.

Accompanying Doug. Jr's disillusionment was the realization that Joan had fallen out of love with him. He knew that this happened in many marriages, but, naïvely perhaps, he had imagined that they were the exception. He had bought into some of the hype surrounding their union — Hollywood's perfect couple. The problem, of course, was that Joan knew she could not share everything she did or planned as 'Joan Crawford' with Doug. She had begun disappearing for whole days 'as a rest'. He wondered if it were a rest from him.

★ ★ ★

In *Grand Hotel*, the film which Joan was making at this time, she and Greta Garbo had no scenes together. They did have dressing-rooms in the unimposing building at Metro, where even stars of their magnitude had cubicles in a row one flight up. Joan always said 'Good morning, Miss Garbo' as she passed Garbo's open door, but she never had a reply. One day she decided not to say it and Garbo then came to her own door and called after her, 'Gut mornin'.' Then, when they met on the dressing-room stairs one day, Garbo stopped and said that she was sorry they had no scenes 'togedder'. Joan later said that seeing Garbo's face in the twilight from the window on the stairs was a moment when she wished she were a lesbian.

Most of Joan's scenes in *Grand Hotel* were with Wallace Beery, Lionel Barrymore, and his brother, John. The critical raves for this film were expected for the Barrymores, Garbo and Beery, but, when the critics accepted Joan as their peer in every way, she was finally established as one of Metro's most convincing actresses. When Joan's reputation as a mother was ruined after her death, ignorant commentators also condemned her work, speaking of her 'artificial, arch acting', but this was far from the view held by reliable critics when her film career was at its peak.

In the film, she played the role of Flaemmchen, a stenographer preoccupied with wealth and creature comfort who becomes involved with Preysing (played by Wallace Beery), an industrialist whom she finds unattractive but useful. John Barrymore plays a down-on-his-luck Baron who is plotting to steal the jewellery of a ballerina resident in the hotel, Grusinskaya (played by Greta Garbo). When the Baron actually encounters the ballerina, he falls in love with her and persuades her to go away with him to begin a new life together. This creates a problem, however: he will need money in this new life and he has none, so he attempts to burgle Preysing's hotel suite. Preysing surprises him and he is killed. Flaemmchen is in the suite at the time, but old Kringelein, a book-keeper with a terminal illness (played by Lionel Barrymore), saves her both from interrogation and arrest. For once, Flaemmchen is drawn to a man for his goodness rather than his money, and she goes away with Kringelein in search of a medical specialist who can cure him.

Joan's notices on *Grand Hotel* were all raves. She was not only Metro's most popular actress with the fans, but also with most of the critics.

Joan's next film project was the theatrical smash hit of the early 1920s, *Rain*. Lewis Milestone, known as 'Milly' by all his friends, had recently completed his greatest film – still a classic – *All Quiet on the Western Front* (1930) for Universal, and was finishing the film version of Hecht and MacArthur's *Front Page* (1931) for Howard Hughes. Milestone's first choice for the central role of Paul in *All Quiet on the Western Front* had in fact been Douglas Fairbanks, Jr, but Doug, Jr's studio, Warner Brothers-First National refused to release their popular young leading man to Universal.

Milestone was then asked by 'the front office', to direct the talking picture version of *Rain*. It was not a project about which Milestone could become excited. He considered the story fairly dated, although he agreed with the producers at United Artists that Joan Crawford would be an obvious choice to play the lead, having seen an early showing of *Grand Hotel*, Joan's latest Metro film. Like many others, including the critics, he had been much impressed with her performance as the stenographer Flaemmchen, and felt that it would be a natural transition for Joan to play an out-and-out prostitute in *Rain*.

Milestone already had a reputation for his skilful direction of actors, but it was generally felt that actresses were better off with a director like Edmund Goulding or (later on) George Cukor. Joan knew this about Milestone, but must have believed that her personality was aggressive enough to cope with this, and she was excited by the prospect of *Rain*, as Milestone told her his plans for the film. Somerset Maugham's South Sea island story, *Miss Thompson*, had been adapted for the stage by John Colton and Clemence Randolph, and had been performed on Broadway and elsewhere a decade earlier to tremendous crowds. It had been a triumph for actress Jeanne Eagels in New York in 1922 (Eagels had made three films, including Maugham's other South Sea classic story, *The Letter*, but she died aged thirty-five in 1929 and never won a large film-following), and had also been filmed as a silent picture with Gloria Swanson in the part of Sadie.

Bette Davis once said that her own best performances were filmed when she was in love. This was also true of Joan. When she was truly in love with someone, with all her deepest feelings stirred, it was easy to lose herself in a part. Lewis Milestone did not know this, but Joan knew it about herself, and knew that she was out of love at the time, and was taking extra precautions for *Rain*. She would simply have to work harder. As Doug, Jr later wrote, 'everyone else . . . [was] to just leave her alone on Catalina Island [where they would be shooting]'.

Doug, Jr also said of that period in their lives:

'I, too, wanted to get away from home life for a bit. I did not welcome Billie's preoccupation with work to the detriment of our personal life. As luck would have it, Bob Montgomery unexpectedly phoned me one day to suggest that if Larry Olivier and I were free and could find one more friend, we could charter C. B. De Mille's sailing yacht *Seaward* and split the cost four ways. That seemed a marvellous idea. I worked out the arithmetic and my share of the charter would be no more than what I would have been paying for Cielio Lindo [his home with Joan in Brentwood] and incidentals were I to stay home. As far as I was concerned, the deal was on.'

This was the first instance when Joan and Doug, Jr began to take separate paths. It was the winter of 1931–2.

When, during *Rain*, Joan discovered that she was pregnant, it was an ill-timed accident. Her marriage with Doug, Jr was dissolving, and she was in the midst of making a film which she considered perhaps the greatest challenge of her film career up to that point. Doug, Jr later commented:

> 'She was pregnant and she said that she slipped on the deck of a ship while shooting a scene and lost the baby. This is what she told me. Dr Branch was not very clear. If I thought I could afford to keep a child, I sentimentally would like to have had it. From a practical standpoint, probably not.'

On Catalina Island, Joan was refusing to take Doug, Jr's calls. 'Miss Crawford is sorry but she's rehearsing. May I take a message?' Doug, Jr recalled that she had answered every one of his calls before, and was angry and hurt. He decided to fly over to Catalina Island to see her. When he arrived, he found all his personal messages to her thumb-tacked to a bulletin board 'for the edification of others on the set or in the nearby hotel ...'
As he put it:

> 'My arrival that afternoon took her by surprise. She could barely control her irritation with me for "daring" to come over when I knew she was concentrating on the challenge presented by this part. I don't recall in any detail who said or did what, but it was unquestionably a taut and emotional, very private "scene".'

Joan made it clear to Doug that the best thing for him to do would be to take the next amphibious plane back to the mainland.

For the role of Sadie Thompson, Joan was dressed in a tight-fitting checked outfit and was garishly made-up, her mouth seeming even larger because of lipstick and her eyes heavily mascara-ed. She wore cheap costume jewellery, and in fact looked very much like the caricatures of herself then beginning to appear in newspapers and magazines.

Milestone had cast Walter Huston (father of John) in the role of the fallen minister, the Reverend Davidson. Huston was much in demand at the time as a character lead, and made eight movies for release in 1932, including his major role in *Rain*. A young and handsome William Gargan played the marine sergeant who falls for Sadie and, at the end, implies that they might have a future together after the suicide of Rev Davidson, who has walked into a stormy sea and drowned himself.

Critics were divided about Joan's performance. I am not. I have seen the film (on video tape) numerous times, and am always excited both by Joan as Sadie and by Huston as the errant preacher. Both are fairly primitive, raw but sincerely felt performances. Several critics lauded Joan in the film, and some felt that it was thoroughly bad. Many years later, Milestone told an interviewer: ' . . . Crawford wasn't up to it, and the picture didn't get off the ground – although there were a few things in it I liked.'

In time, Joan came to agree with her critics. She wrote in her memoir:

'. . . most reviews were written in acid and I grieved over them. I grieved over the letters that came in from fans hating my mouth make-up . . . I didn't even know then that you could work from the interior to the exterior. I was still working from the exterior . . . Oh, who am I kidding, I just gave a lousy performance!'

★　　★　　★

In the spring of 1932, while *Rain* was in its final stages, Doug, Jr was said to be 'on the prowl'. It began when he came back from his disastrous visit to Catalina Island. While he said that he did not know who 'stepped out' first, now he did not hestitate to do so himself, and his friends, including the Laurence Oliviers, David Niven and Robert Montgomery, all believed that his marriage was collapsing.

By the summer, Joan already had three big films in release that year. *Rain* was being prepared for release in the autumn. She was exhausted and very much in need of a vacation. Doug, Jr saw this, and immediately began making elaborate plans for a trip abroad for the two of them. It was a last chance to save their marriage.

To Doug, Jr's surprise, Joan 'now seemed delighted with the idea of a honeymoon in Europe, especially since our studios – for publicity purposes naturally – would foot most of the bill'. It was a much-delayed honeymoon after their marriage in 1929, but Joan had never been abroad, and the Laurence Oliviers (she was actress Jill Esmond) were also leaving at the same time, in Jill's attempt to save *their* marriage. Doug, Jr and Joan agreed with the Oliviers that the best ship for all of them would be the brand new German liner, the *Bremen*, due to leave New York in late June.

In New York, Joan was trying her best to fit in with her husband's friends and family. They stayed at the St Moritz Hotel on Central Park South, into which they had been booked by Metro and Warners, rather than at the Algonquin, where they had stayed on previous visits to the city and where the owner-manager Frank Case had taken on an almost familial role with Joan.

They went to see Doug, Jr's young stepfather, Jack Whiting, in the musical *America's Sweetheart*, which co-starred Harriet Lake (later known as Ann Sothern), and, in Jack's dressing-room afterwards, Joan raved about his performance. She seemed, in Doug's words, to be trying to get things 'on the rails' again, and endeavoured to persuade him that the tensions of the recent past were over. Doug, Jr's close family friend, Genie Chester, introduced them to her parents, and they much enjoyed their times together. Genie's father, Clare Chester (Chairman of the Board of General Foods) quickly fell for Joan, never imagining that she would tell Doug, Jr that he was sending her roses frequently while they were in Manhattan, along with accompanying notes indicating his romantic interest in her.

'The richest girl in the world' Barbara Hutton held a big party on the night before they sailed for Europe at the Casino in the Park, and Paul Whiteman's orchestra supplied the music for dancing. The next morning, during the panic surrounding their departure for the North German Lloyd pier in Brooklyn, Mayor Jimmy Walker phoned their hotel suite and told them he was sending some of his motorcycle 'gendarmes' to get them through the morning traffic to the Brooklyn docks in a hurry. They left the St Moritz through a crush of reporters, photographers and fans in the company of their studios' two press agents. As they climbed into their limo, they saw two or three motorcycle cops awaiting their departure, as Mayor Jimmy Walker had promised. Once established aboard the *Bremen*, Doug, Jr thought that his wife saw the whole ship as a huge movie set, with the other passengers as 'extras and bit players'.

Hordes of fans alerted by the press were awaiting their debarking in Southampton. Much to their surprise, they also found Noël Coward on the pier to greet them. They stayed at the Berkeley Hotel in Piccadilly, and Doug, Jr described their whole visit abroad as 'one happy haze'. On the first night, they were applauded by the entire house when they entered the Royal Box at the Drury Lane Theatre to see Coward's *Cavalcade*. Everything they did during the next few weeks stirred Doug, Jr's profoundly anglophilic heart.

Noël Coward threw a cocktail party for them at his Belgravia home, where even the future Duke of Kent, Prince George, youngest brother of the future King George VI, was an honoured guest. They then spent a country weekend dividing their time between the Kent countryside homes of actor-producer Ivor Novello and Coward's rambling Goldenhurst. When they moved on to Paris, Maurice Chevalier, already an international film star, attended a party in their honour, and they had their portraits painted by the fashionable Spanish artist, Beltran-Masses.

With all of this, according to Doug, Jr, Joan had no patience whatsoever. 'She hated it all!' he was to say. 'She put on a brave, well-trained, smiling face, said the right words of gratitude, but she was only peripherally interested. She felt, she confessed, like a fish out of water, gasping for breath, longing for something familiar to cling to.' She told Doug, Jr, that she would have been just as content to have read about the things they did, 'and anyway, the pictures she'd seen seemed better than the real things!'

To Joan, it was all a bad dream and she could not wait to get home to California – not only to their formerly beloved

Brentwood mansion but also to Culver City and the studio. As a result, they returned home ahead of schedule, and Joan did not return to Europe for many, many years.

Joan got off the train from the east almost delirious to be back home. Once in her house in Brentwood, she tore about like a long-lost puppy, reaching out a finger and touching the walls, and exclaiming: 'Jesus, I'm glad to be home again.' The servants had decorated the front hall with vines and gardenias (her favourite flowers) and in the middle of it all was a wreath they had chipped in to buy which said 'Welcome Home'.

Joan was to say years later that she and Doug, Jr came home from Europe because he had been 'summoned' to appear in a film. This was completely untrue, but, as we have already seen, Joan reworked her life experiences and those of the people closest to her into a history that she decided should be 'the truth'. As novelist and screenwriter Budd Schulberg pointed out, Joan re-created her life story as she lived it.

Once Doug, Jr and Joan were at home, it became clear that the only way they could remain a couple was to give each other space. Joan rented a hideaway cottage in then unspoiled Malibu Beach, and never told even Doug, Jr where it was.

★　★　★

In the relatively small world of Hollyood, Joan had very quickly become someone of consequence. Her long-time private secretary, Betty Barker, described her employer's effect upon others:

> 'Oh, wow! She had a tremendous presence about her. She was a star from the beginning. You would always notice her right away. She was always the most important person in anything, it seemed to me. Gracious and polite to everybody. I never saw her really be cruel to anybody, except some of the maids that she used to get angry with. Yes, she just seemed to have a star on her forehead and everybody kow-towed to her because she was so elegant and gracious and kind and so *important.*'

She was sought out by everyone who counted because her mere presence always generated excitement. Within the film colony, Joan had her own select friends, who were all loyal to her and remained so throughout her life. Among the men, besides Paul Bern and Willie Haines no one was closer to her than actor Cesar Romero. They met in 1932 when Romero was appearing on Broadway in *Dinner at Eight.* They both attended a party at the Manhattan home of motor magnate Walter Chrysler, and Cesar danced with Joan. She had come with Franchot Tone, who would later become her second husband.

A year later, Romero was brought to Hollywood by Universal Pictures, and soon afterwards went to dinner at the Trocadero Cabaret, where Joan was again escorted by Franchot Tone. Romero wondered whether she would remember their dance together at Walter Chrysler's, but, before he had a chance even to think much about it, a waiter brought him a note from Joan's table asking him if *he* remembered their dancing that night in New York. It was the beginning of a friendship which would last until Joan's death and even beyond, as Romero was one of perhaps a dozen of Joan's friends who valorously stood up for her memory in the wake of daughter Christina's vitriolic book about her mother, *Mommie Dearest.*

Having gained one friend, however, Joan was to lose another – her confidant and mentor, Paul Bern – when he married Jean Harlow in 1932. Joan bitterly resented Harlow for taking Bern away from her. Even though she had no romantic thoughts about him whatsoever, she had been close to Bern for half-a-dozen years, and felt protected by him. She had in fact dated him in the late 1920s, although there were clearly no sexual favours involved as it was revealed at his death that he was chronically impotent.

The sizzling career of Jean Harlow, Metro's platinum blonde, peaked when she married Bern, who had become increasingly her advocate, so much so that Joan realized that she was losing him and his influence and became a little desperate. She was often overheard blasting Harlow and her 'little vulgarities'.

Within months of the marriage, Bern was found shot to death in his home, which he now shared with Harlow. He left behind a 'suicide note' suggesting that their sexual relations 'last night were a comedy', for which he apologized. Some who have dug deeper into the case, however, have concluded that an embittered ex-wife may have shot him during an angry exchange over her own finances and his new wife.

Howard Strickling and Louis B. Mayer were among the first on the scene, getting there ahead of the police. Harlow was whisked away by a studio driver, and the story given out by Strickling was that she had stayed the night at her mother's home, where she now was 'devastated by the news'. In essence, the studio destroyed all evidence at a probable murder scene, and protected one of their most vulnerable star properties.

★   ★   ★

The Depression had deepened in 1932. There were foreclosures on houses and farms all across America, and families were doubling up as banks seized their properties. By 1933, the Dust Bowl in the Plains States was deserted, as this natural calamity had wiped out all the farmers who had not already lost their farms to the bank. Ironically, these were the years when Joan touched the peak of her popularity and success. She was now earning in excess of ten thousand dollars a week, at a time when a loaf of bread cost a dime.

Joan made it clear to everyone with whom she worked – from the make-up people to the gaffers, that anyone, without exception, who had need of emergency funds was to come to her. Hundreds and eventually thousands of dollars went out from Joan to these people.

It was also around this time that Joan established a wing at the Hollywood Presbyterian Hospital for indigent children and mothers. It cost several thousand dollars a week to run, but Joan routinely wrote a cheque for despatch to the hospital. Since acquiring her Brentwood home and a staff of ten (for a time during this period, her two butlers wore livery during her formal dinners), it almost seemed as though money was something which Joan could not bear to keep, and indeed it went out as fast as it came in.

Throughout her life prior to her success, money had meant dimes and quarters needed for survival. Dollar bills were treasures, to be slipped into the tops of stockings and saved for a new dress. Now that she was earning nearly two thousand dollars a day, having such riches seemed too surreal to grasp. They had to be spent.

It has been implied that Joan made her charities very public, using them merely as publicity vehicles. Those who were closest to her, however, know this to be untrue. She took two runaway boys off the street, for instance, financed their completion of high school and then sent them through college. When she became involved with the League for Crippled Children, she remained one of their most generous sponsors. Through her money and urging, hundreds of boys and girls received useful arms, legs or prostheses, and in one instance, a special saddle. When young Clover Kerr, who lost both legs and an arm in a traffic accident, expressed a wish to ride in the motion-picture polo tournament, Joan heard about it. She had a special saddle made for the boy within two days.

★   ★   ★

Meanwhile, Franchot Tone had been brought to the coast by Metro after starring in several successful plays mounted by the Group Theatre in New York. He was then twenty-nine years old and as handsome as he would ever be. He (and most of his Group Theatre colleagues) were far to the left politically. In time, this would work against his advancement in films, as he would be accused of biting the conservative hand that fed him.

Tone made his screen début in *The Wiser Sex* (1932), and he starred with Walter Huston in *Gabriel Over the White House* (1933), a surprise hit. Director Howard Hawks then cast him in a William Faulkner movie story (Faulkner was then under contract to Metro) entitled *Today We Live*, about a group of Britons bonded together by the First World War. Hawks and Metro believed that the story needed some love interest, and a leading role for Joan was written into the script. Franchot was cast as her brother, and they had several scenes together. The film was not successful, and most of the critics complained that Joan was mis-cast as an English girl. Franchot's notices were generally good, and Joan later wrote that he 'stole' the picture.

By the end of 1932, Doug, Jr's film earnings nearly matched Joan's, but now rumours of divorce were circulating. Doug, Jr still wanted the relationship to work. He had grown close to his father during the latter months of the marriage, and Pete, as he called Doug, Sr, thought that he and Joan should try to iron out their differences.

It was Pete to whom Joan went when she decided to divorce his son. She thought it fitting that her father-in-law should know before anyone else, including her husband, that she was going to give up on her marriage. They met at the Brown Derby, and she told him the sad news over lunch. 'Billie,' he told her, always using the name his son favoured, 'when two people are this unhappy, they shouldn't stay together.'

What she did not tell Doug, Sr or his son was that she had fallen in love with one of her three leading men in *Today We Live*, Franchot Tone. Early in their separation, Joan had told Doug, Jr that they would 'lead their own lives' from then on with an eye to discretion. What she was saying, of course, was that she would begin dating Franchot in a discreet way, and that Doug, Jr was free to do the same. She knew, or at least believed, that he was doing so anyway.

In March 1933, Doug, Jr was sued by a Dane named Jorgen Dietz for 'alienation of affections'. Mrs Lucy Dietz had been a dress extra at Warners, and, according to the suit, had become involved in an affair with Doug, Jr at the studio. When I asked Doug, Jr for specifics on this, he said, 'It wasn't me. It was my dresser at the studio, and he would drive my car to meet the lady during our lunch breaks.'

The scandal was 'handled' by Warner Brothers in such a way that eventually it broke in the press. Studio head Jack Warner was delighted to hear all the details of it. 'That guy Fairbanks has so many faggot friends that I was beginning to wonder about him, too.' Eventually, Warner Brothers paid the Deitzes a fraction of what they were demanding out of court, and, according to Doug, Jr, with a proviso that they leave the country and go back to Denmark. They did.

Joan was also very busy with other men, besides Franchot. Actor Ricardo Cortez, who had been one of her two leading men in *Montana Moon* (1930), escorted her about Hollywood, and she was seen at times driving her roadster with other young men in tow.

★　　★　　★

One night, Doug, Jr was filming a scene on a nearly full-sized mock-up of a ship being buffeted by a storm, which drenched him over and over again in retakes. It was chilly, so he had an electric heater going in his portable dressing-room, and plenty of scotch and hot coffee to ward off pneumonia. Even with all these precautions, he said that his teeth 'were chattering on the rim of my whisky glass' when his agent, Mike Levee (who performed the same chores for Joan) knocked on his door. Doug, Jr told Levee that he would be glad when the scene was done and he could go home to his warm bed in Brentwood, whereupon Levee said: 'That's what I came to talk to you about. I'm sorry to bring you this news . . . but . . . er . . . but you're going to stay at the Beverly Wilshire Hotel tonight, not at home.'

Doug, Jr was puzzled, and asked whether the house had burned down. Levee told him that Joan had booked a double room for him at the hotel, and that his German secretary, Joan's maid and Levee's own secretary had spent most of the night packing all his belongings in whatever they could find, and moving them to the hotel. Joan also had changed her telephone number and did not want him to have it. In other words, without prior mutual consultation, Joan had thrown him out of her house.

While plotting and directing this brutal eviction, Joan was also trying to manage the great news break that this decision

ABOVE: Joan (second from left) in a lineup of starlets at Metro-Goldwyn-Mayer during her first year there, in 1925. Note the huge bow on her skirt, and the anklets on the 'college girl' on the right.

BELOW: Film still from *The Understanding Heart* (1927), one of Joan's early films. Francis X. Bushman (at the door) confronts Rockcliffe Fellowes as Joan looks on.

ABOVE: Joan does the Charleston and stops the crowd cold in *Our Dancing Daughters* (1928).

LEFT: Joan with Douglas Fairbanks, Jr, in 1929, when they only had eyes for each other.

RIGHT: Early in her career, Joan appeared on many fan magazine covers. This one dates from 1929, her bobbed hair reflecting the fashion of the Charleston era.

Motion Picture

MARCH   25 CENTS

Joan Crawford

MARLAND — STORE —

BELOW: The Metro-Goldwyn-Mayer hierarchy in 1929. Louis B. Mayer sits with the legendary production supervisor Irving Thalberg at his right.

RIGHT: William Randolph Hearst and Marion Davies, with their cosmopolitan production unit at Metro-Goldwyn-Mayer, gave Joan her first big break with *Our Dancing Daughters*, released in the United States in October 1928. Here they are seen in a rare photograph together in Germany, 1929.

LEFT: In one of her last pure publicity shots, Joan 'lights' the largest firecracker in California, July 1932.

RIGHT: Joan with Fred Astaire in the Tyrolean number during production of *Dancing Lady*, 1933.

BELOW: Joan at lunch with William Haines and comedian Benny Rubin (left) at the Hollywood Brown Derby, January 1933.

ABOVE: Joan with Clark
Gable (left) and Stuart Erwin
in *Chained* (1934).

RIGHT: A publicity shot for
Chained. The famous 'Joan
Crawford' look is finally
achieved (1934), and would
remain thus for at least
twenty years.

ABOVE: Another shot of the Joan Crawford face. Here, one eye is kiddingly made to look natural, while the other is emphasized with more mascara, longer lashes and a wider, darker eyebrow. Joan liked this schizophrenic look.

LEFT: Myrna Loy came to Metro-Goldwyn-Mayer around the same time as Joan, and they remained firm friends until Joan's death. Loy bitterly resented Christina Crawford's book *Mommie Dearest.*

LEFT: Everyone at Metro adored Jean Harlow, seen here in a 1934 publicity still. She married a Thalberg associate Paul Bern, which probably led to Joan's distaste for the platinum-haired star. Thereafter, Joan insisted she could not stand Harlow. The relationship did not improve even after Bern was found shot dead.

ABOVE: Norma Shearer, circa 1936. She won the heart of Irving Thalberg and thus became Joan's chief rival at Metro-Goldwyn-Mayer.

RIGHT: Greta Garbo, along with Joan, was one of the few great film stars who were created and given their persona by a studio. The most interesting contrast between them was their reading habits: Joan cultivated a taste for the classics and good contemporary books, while Garbo – despite her aura of mystery – preferred movie magazines, which she devoured in quantity. Here she is seen with John Barrymore in *Grand Hotel* (1932), in which Joan also appeared.

generated. More than a month earlier, she had given the news to the fan-magazine reporter, Katherine Albert, a freelancer at *Modern Screen* who had become one of her close friends. [Joan and Katherine had a falling-out on one occasion, when Joan arranged for Katherine's daughter to marry in her living-room after Katherine had sent her there for Joan to talk some sense into her.]

'Nobody knew it but me,' Mrs Albert said. 'He [Doug, Jr] didn't know it. I don't know how I conned her into letting me do this, but I did. It was the first time in history that a magazine has beat the dailies . . . It was at least thirty days in advance. It was a big scoop.'

In spite of this, Hearst Hollywood columnist Louella Parsons insisted that *she* had scooped *Modern Screen* by inveigling the truth out of Joan two days before the magazine appeared and then rushing the story into print first.

Doug, Jr told a reporter: 'I'm going to try mighty hard to win her back. I'm going to send her flowers and I'm going to make dates with her. And I'm going to try to prove to her she is the only thing in the world that really counts.' He also added that he wanted the world to know that Joan had not deserted him when he was in trouble (over the suit brought against him by Mr Dietz). No one particularly believed him, but everyone thought of him (as they should have done) as a terribly gallant young man.

In May 1933 Joan won her divorce on the grounds of 'quarrels, arguments and differences', which she claimed had caused her to suffer a nervous breakdown (she had in fact spent two weeks in a Connecticut sanitorium during the previous year). Lawyer Jerry Geisler, known as a show-business attorney, handled the divorce for her. Joan's cosmetician Syb Jones testified under oath that she attended Joan several times a week, and observed that Joan would cry when her husband cross-examined her about her lunch partners and 'where she was at certain times – times when I knew she was working'. Joan's sister-in-law, Kasha LeSueur, who was her stand-in at the studio and the mother of little Joan LeSueur, whom Joan entertained at weekends, was also on hand to add her testimony, but the judge said that he had heard enough and granted the divorce.

Joan's insensitive handling of her separation and divorce from Doug, Jr was the first major instance when she rode roughshod over those close to her. Hal LeSueur, her brother, and their mother, Anna, might have said that they had been rudely shunted aside, but children often break away from parents and siblings, and Joan had been extremely generous to them financially. In any case, the break did not mean that Anna could not come on to Joan's movie sets, for she often did, sometimes bringing some home-baked goodies with her, and, just as often, Joan would tell her secretary to phone Hal and see how he was, if she were too busy to do so herself, as was usually the case.

It should not be forgotten, however, that her studio knew without doubt that she was their biggest asset, and they treated her accordingly. Every little detail about her films was discussed with her in advance, and had to meet with her approval. It was impossible for Joan to shut off this total control over her daily activities at Metro when she came home to Brentwood. She frequently scolded the maids for failing to clean part of her house properly, and, just as often, they either left or were fired.

Doug, Jr may have continued to believe for a number of months that he would be an exception to this total control that Joan implemented on everything and everyone around her. When he learned that he was wrong, he plunged into another movie for Warner Brothers and then, as soon as he could, left America for his beloved England.

Upon Doug, Jr's return in June aboard his and Joan's honeymoon ship, the *Bremen*, he came down with pneumonia in New York. It is probable that the stress of the recent upheavals in his life lowered his resistance. He lay critically ill in Doctors Hospital, while Joan agonized in California over his condition, some of her agony undoubtedly being caused by guilt. She put through three calls to her young ex-father-in-law, Jack Whiting (Doug, Jr's mother's husband) and offered to go to Doug, Jr's bedside, although she made it clear to everyone that her willingness to be with him did not mean that there would be a reconciliation. Beth Whiting was there at the hospital, of course, and never left her son's side while his condition was critical. By the end of June, he was out of danger, and by mid-July he was able to leave hospital.

★ ★ ★

Throughout that summer of 1933 and into the autumn, Franchot Tone and Joan were together almost constantly. Joan promoted him as the lead in David O. Selznick's *Dancing Lady*, in which Broadway star Fred Astaire was making his screen début. Joan played the role of Janie, a burlesque dancer with Broadway as her goal. Tone took the role of a playboy who is infatuated with her and offers her a job as a chorus girl in a Broadway musical he is backing. The show's dance director, Patch Gallagher (Clark Gable), is determined to make the show a success. Joan tells Tone that she will marry him if the show is a flop, so he attempts to sabotage the production. He nearly succeeds, but Gallagher brings it off and makes the show a hit, whereupon he and Janie go into a clinch for the finale.

Today, *Dancing Lady* is revived chiefly because of the début of Fred Astaire and one song, which has become a great standard: 'Everything I have is yours'. The presence of both Tone and Gable in the cast caused Joan some worry, but she found Gable quite tolerant of Tone, even though he hated his leftist political views. Franchot may well have said something to Joan about the Gable matter. In fact, one suspects that Joan had Franchot chosen as her co-star for this and several other films simply so he could see that she was not fooling around with Gable on the side.

★ ★ ★

When Irving Thalberg and his wife, Norma Shearer, arrived home from an extended vacation in 1933, he knew that his power had been taken from him, in the name of conserving his waning energies because of his heart condition. Thalberg was no longer the creative genius behind all the more prestigious Metro films, including those of the major MGM stars such as Joan Crawford, Clark Gable, Marie Dressler, Wallace Beery and Greta Garbo. In other words, his power and influence in Hollywood had been wrested from him. Mayer now would supervise all production at the studio with Nick Schenck's backing. Thalberg would, however, be allowed his own production unit within the studio, and within that unit, there would be no company interference in what he did. Mayer excluded Norma Shearer from his takeover.

Thalberg allowed himself to be convinced that the new order would work, but, when he proposed that he should use Joan Crawford for a film that he had in mind, Mayer told him that Joan would not be free of other commitments for over a year. It then came home to Thalberg that his wings had been clipped rather barbarously and, given his delicate health, that he must resign himself to the coup that had taken place in his absence.

Joan was then working on *Dancing Lady*, scheduled for release that autumn. Thalberg knew about this film in progress, but he thought that she would be free afterwards. He was informed, however, that producer Lawrence Weingarten had secured her for the title role in *Sadie McKee*, scheduled to follow *Dancing Lady* almost immediately, and that producer Hunt Stromberg (who had always looked upon Thalberg as his mentor) had secured Joan and Clark Gable as the stars of *Chained* after that.

Joan would be tied up for nearly two years, so Thalberg had to fall back on his own resources. He would star his own wife in his first independent production – a re-make of Michael Arlen's *The Green Hat*, which was released in 1934 as *Riptide*. Thalberg also secured for her the rights to a Broadway hit starring Katharine Cornell, *The Barretts of Wimpole Street.*

Joan must have been secretly elated when she heard that Thalberg had wanted her but could not have her. She was one of the top ten box-office stars in 1933, as she would be over the next three years. In his pursuit of her, it would seem that Thalberg was finally placing commercial value above prestige.

★ ★ ★

Joan had proposed Tone for the male lead in *Sadie McKee*, which was released in 1934. This was a typical Crawford vehicle in which she played a maidservant at a mansion where Tone is her employer. Tone and Robert Montgomery alternated in such playboy parts at Metro, both of them looking at home in top hat and tails. Joan had this type of character engrained in her by this time, and breezed through the production easily.

During the making of the film, Tone moved into a rented house near Joan's in Brentwood so that they were within walking distance of each other. He had already proposed to her, but she was uncertain about another marriage. In fact, she told journalist Edwin Schallert that 'An actress should not marry. I am sure of that.' Her final divorce decree from Doug, Jr was only weeks away, and she added: 'It is better to say no, and cause a small hurt now, than to say yes, and cause a great hurt later on. It is simply the oft-told tale that a career and marriage do not mix.'

This was in the spring of 1934, while Joan was in the throes of enlarging her estate. She added a small and exquisite theatre in which she and Tone could rehearse and take on stage roles that she would never attempt elsewhere, a bath-house and a new swimming pool. She now counted Tone as one of her 'five closest friends'. Those friends also included actress Jean Dixon (who was in *Sadie McKee*); actor Francis Lederer, who wrote one-act plays which were presented in Joan's little theatre; Lynn Riggs, who wrote the basis for the great American musical, *Oklahoma*; and Jerry Asher, who was Joan's close confidant and originally in Metro's costume department before being 'promoted' to the fan mail department. The six of them would get together every Saturday night 'for talk well into the morning' and that, Joan insisted, was the sum of her social life.

As for her feelings for Doug, Jr, and any possible regret about the past, Joan said that she had heard that he was planning to marry Gertrude Lawrence in England, and that she was 'hoping for his happiness'. She went on:

'I am not mourning the past. The suggestion that I still love him in the sense of being heartbroken is wrong. After all, it must be remembered that I took the step towards divorce, and that would never have happened if I had loved him to the extent that I could not bear to be separated from him. No, that is past, and I am not eating my heart out. I tried to make that marriage a success, tried perhaps too hard. It doesn't pay to force romance. That I have really been in love, I doubt. That I can ever be here in Hollywood, I question. Hollywood itself stands in the way of any great, true love. If a woman, an actress, is in a position where she can give up her career, wed and give her husband children, she can be happy here. But the career must become an incident. If two people are in the profession, they both should leave it if they want to marry, and then they could, perhaps, be happy.

'I am no diplomatist about my feelings. I cannot conceal my moods. That's too difficult in married life, especially if one's husband is in the same profession as oneself, and that profession is acting. I don't think it's fair to the man, and I don't want to go through life causing unhappiness . . . Hence a refusal of marriage now is better then consent, followed by heartbreak and divorce. It doesn't pay to take the risk.'

All of this must have been Joan's way of telling Tone not to propose again, but, of course, he did, being the individualist he was (at least in Hollywood). In the Group Theatre back in New York he and his fellow actors had always fought against the odds to put on a play, and to raise money for the survival of the Group. He was not about to abandon his pursuit of Joan in the face of lesser odds. She had become his girlfriend and everyone (including Gable) knew it. He would not rest until she was also his bride.

★　★　★

During the summer of 1935, Tone was away on location on Catalina Island for *Mutiny on the Bounty*. He had not been back for very long when Metro told him that they were loaning him to Warners for the male lead opposite Bette Davis in *Dangerous*. Unusually handsome in an off-beat way that would fade early in his forties, denying him any further romantic roles, he was later described by Davis as 'a most charming, attractive, top-drawer guy. He really was'. In fact, Davis told fellow Warners star Joan Blondell that she had fallen in love with her leading man. As Blondell had done the same thing with Dick Powell and then married him, she should not have been surprised by this news, but she was. Davis was married to a musician, Ham Nelson, a handsome 'hunk' of a man too good-looking to stray from.

'I thought she was kidding,' said Blondell. 'And furthermore, I didn't think she went in for that kind of thing – for sound-stage romances. It's not that she was a Holy Mary; she wasn't. Her career always came first. So I kidded with her, saying that we all get crushes on our leading men from time to time, and they passed although I wasn't the one to prove it.'

Davis then became very angry with Blondell, and said: 'Joan! I am *not* a schoolgirl. I don't *get* crushes. I am in love with Franchot and I think he's in love with me.' Then Blondell recalled thinking, but not saying: 'Boy! If Joan Crawford gets wind of this, there is going to be war.'

Davis and Tone began having 'rehearsals' in her dressing-room. She was playing an actress in *Dangerous*, and she said that she felt Tone needed some additional input from her on her character in the film. Tone's scenes began to expand as Davis continued her 'input'. Joan was anything but taken in by this sudden magnification of his role. She tried not to be jealous. But then, when Tone – flattered, no doubt – hinted at Davis's interest in him, Joan suddenly took the intiative. She told Tone that she had reconsidered her position about never marrying another actor, and that they should consider themselves engaged.

Hearst star reporter Adela Rogers St Johns was invited one morning to accompany Joan to visit the set of *Dangerous*. Joan had not been at the Warners Burbank studio since the early days of her marriage to Doug, Jr, when she would drop by to pick him up for some social event. To the best of Adela's knowledge, Joan and Bette Davis had never been formally introduced. On the *Dangerous* set, Joan did her gracious lady routine, while, as Adela recalls: 'Bette did her best to ignore her, keeping those huge eyes of hers fixed like a bayonet on Franchot.'

Joan and Adela then stood on the sidelines while Tone and Davis performed what was becoming known as a Bette Davis climax. In the scene, Davis visits Tone in his office and tells him (just as she had told Leslie Howard in *Of Human Bondage*) that he was a sap to believe she had ever loved him. 'You! With your *fat* little soul and smug face. I've lived *more* in a single day than you'll ever *dare* live.' Adela remembers it as a powerful scene, and that the contrast in style between Davis and Tone was striking. 'I could sense Joan standing to attention beside me. She knew that Davis could never compete with her sexually, but talent-wise? That was another horse race indeed.'

★ ★ ★

Meanwhile, as had happened in Joan's alliance with Doug, Jr, her constant off- and and on-screen association with Franchot Tone was generating speculation by gossip columnists and fans that she was in love again and about to marry.

Tone wanted to introduce Joan to his Group Theatre friends in New York, especially since *Men in White* had been produced by them and he had put up some of the money (from his film earnings). They travelled east on the Super Chief to Chicago, then changed on to the Twentieth Century Ltd, which took them into Grand Central Station. Joan insisted that they should not leave the train together, so she got off first and encountered the biggest crowd of fans, reporters and photographers ever to have greeted her. One insistent reporter asked: 'Are you engaged to Franchot Tone?'

Joan smiled at the question, then seemed at a loss for words. She did not want to commit herself publicly, but she knew that Tone would be getting off the train soon after she had done and that someone in Grand Central was sure to see him. She would never deliberately lie to a fan or reporter, although she did embellish a few facts and distort others. There was a *Western Union* boy in his late teens on the fringe of the group closest to her, and he shouted over a couple of heads: 'Tell them "Time will tell".' Joan thought this a brilliant response, sighed in relief, and said: 'That's right, time will tell.'

The *Western Union* boy was Dore Freeman. He was already on her master list of super-fans in New York, as well as a recognizable face to her. That week, Joan sent Freeman a gold watch inscribed: 'Time will tell, Love, Joan Crawford.' In one of his letters to her, Freeman indicated that he would like to make a career in a Hollywood studio. Joan got him a job as an office boy at Metro, where in very short time he became a fixture in the publicity department, and where he eventually became an executive in the stills department.

Joan had received her final divorce decree from Doug, Jr in April 1934, but she delayed fulfilling her commitment until the summer of 1935. They were together in New York once again, and Tone took her backstage to meet the legendary theatrical couple, Alfred Lunt and Lynn Fontanne, in their smash-hit production of *The Taming of the Shrew*. Joan was charmed by the Lunts and they remained in touch for many years, but she was also impressed with the fact that they were both 'in the profession', which she had so arbitrarily told Franchot was death to a marriage.

Nick Schenck, who was then president of Loew's, Inc, the owners of Metro-Goldwyn-Mayer, arranged a quiet wedding with the help of a friend of his, Herbert Jenkins, the mayor of Englewood Cliffs, New Jersey. It was 11 October 1935. The married couple then returned to Manhattan, where they dined and drank with other celebrities at the Stork Club, telling no one but columnist Walter Winchell their secret. At that time Winchell had a Sunday night radio show of gossip items and he announced: 'Good Evening, Mr and Mrs North America and all the ships at sea: Joan Crawford and Franchot Tone . . .' It was his lead item, and, the following day, the newspapers in America and abroad had pictures of the couple, or of Joan by herself, accompanying lead stories.

They spent their brief honeymoon in the Waldorf Astoria Hotel. According to Hollywood reporter Bob Thomas, Joan was phoned there by a stranger who once again attempted to blackmail her over her alleged pornographic movie, *The Casting Couch.* FBI files state that she was married to Franchot Tone when a quarter of a million dollars was paid out to this blackmailer to suppress the film completely. [There is a great deal of opacity in the matter of *The Casting Couch* and its possible connection with Crawford. The FBI document on the subject mentions a possible pay-off to a blackmailer by Metro-Goldwyn-Mayer as far back as 1931.] If this statement of the FBI is accurate, Tone's family fortune as well as Joan's earnings must have been tapped. *Someone* must have been paid off, because Joan never again had to cope with that particular kind of extortion; she only had to deny enquiries about it over the years.

AN ERA PASSES

When Thalberg died suddenly after Labour Day weekend in 1936, Hunt Stromberg, one of Thalberg's favourite producers, and a kind of legend himself as a pyromaniac (he once set Dorothy Parker on fire with a tossed match which missed the wastepaper basket and caught in Parker's skirt) came up to Albert Hackett and his wife, and handed them some tickets to Thalberg's funeral service. Hackett protested, saying 'We didn't know him very well,' while his wife, Frances Goodrich, corrected him, telling Stromberg, 'We didn't know him at all.' Stromberg dismissed their excuses, and handed them the tickets, saying, 'Well, he liked you.' So they went to the funeral.

The Synagogue B'nai B'rith in Los Angeles was crowded. Clark Gable was prominent among the ushers, as was Joan's former father-in-law, Douglas Fairbanks, Sr. Joan and Tone sat about halfway back in the temple, in a section of pews reserved for the studio's stellar assembly. Norma Shearer Thalberg, the widow, was concealed from the other mourners at the front.

The Hacketts were among a crowd of writers at the funeral. Thalberg had been much respected by screen-writers because he listened to their ideas, so they were out in force – Frances Marion, Anita Loos, Moss Hart (who was an usher), Talbott Jennings, Herman Mankiewicz and his brother, Joe Mankiewicz and George Oppenheimer. Missing were F. Scott Fitzgerald (who was soon to be under contract to Metro, and would write, on the side, a fictional portrait of Thalberg called *The Last Tycoon*) and Charlie MacArthur, who was closer to Thalberg than anyone else, but who was too grief-stricken to attend. Louis B. Mayer was supposed to have said: 'Isn't God good to me,' as he was driven away from the service, but in truth he was a stricken man who cried very real tears.

At the services, Joan received a reassuring pat on the shoulder from Hunt Stromberg, who, she assumed, would be taking over some of Thalberg's personal projects including *Marie Antoinette*, on which he was already working. The touch was perceived as it was meant: Joan would still be queen of the 'A' films at Metro, while Norma Shearer would be given the lead in big, special films tailored especially for her.

★   ★   ★

In their spare time, Joan was working very hard with Tone on classic repertory plays in the little theatre behind her house. In June 1936, she told reporter Harrison Carroll of the *Los Angeles Herald:* 'Franchot and I have finally manoeuvred so that our contracts terminate at the same time . . . It is my firm intention to go into stock companies and get a year's experience to prepare me for Broadway.' Carroll was a little sceptical, and asked whether she thought she would be able to step down from the glamorous position she now held, but Joan startled him by asking, 'What's being a movie star?'

Harold Clurman, the fabled director and a leading founder of the Group Theatre, visited Hollywood several times and recalled going to Joan and Tone's Brentwood home on Sundays for brunch, which was always followed by theatre talk and reminiscences by Tone of the Group. It seemed obvious to Joan, and she said so in several interviews, that he was happiest when talking about his days in the New York theatre. Clurman believed that Tone suffered from an 'ambivalent conscience', and that his defection from the stage (especially the Group stage) was a fall from grace. Clurman, too, had overheard Tone comment, after contributing a thousand dollars for an ambulance for the Spanish Loyalists in their Civil War, 'Foolish, wasn't it?'

Clurman gives us an honest but slightly formidable view of Joan. She was, he avers, 'an iron rod of ambition'. He recalls that he once came upon her standing on her head in the patio area of her Brentwood home, whereupon she explained that she was strengthening her neck muscles and preserving her figure. He had also heard about her voice lessons. He deprecated her dominating influence on Tone. 'When I sent Franchot a copy of Stanislavski's *An Actor Prepares*, she grabbed it and read it first; her bold markings covered its pages.'

It was Clurman's opinion that Tone liked women 'whose minds were not as good as his own so he could educate them'. Joan, however, told Clurman a sadder story about her life with Tone. She said that he boasted to her – to prove that it was all her fault – 'that he laid a girl extra in his dressing-room on the set every night before going home to her'.

Rather astonishingly, Clurman once predicted that Joan would one day run Metro-Goldwyn-Mayer. He admitted that he had been wrong in that prediction, although she did wind up as, in his words, 'one of the heads of the Pepsi-Cola Company', a common fallacy spread by the tabloid press. More insightful is his last recollection of Joan: 'She always made me think of a Léger painting in which people are depicted as machines. Yet many years later she came up to me in Sardi's and, thinking I had forgotten who she was, introduced herself: "I'm Joan Crawford."'

★　　★　　★

In his retirement from the screen, Joan's old friend and studio pal, Willie Haines, was having his own problems. On 1 June 1936 he and his lover, Jimmy Shields, were spending a quiet day in their beach-house, a little bored, when Jimmy suddenly got the idea that he would dye their white poodle purple with vegetable dye. Although their next-door neighbours at El Portos Beach were hostile and referred to them within earshot as 'those fairies', their six-year-old son was friendly and sometimes played with the poodle. Jimmy thought the boy would enjoy watching the dog turn purple in the small tub of dye. So he came upstairs, as he had done dozens of times, and was appropriately amazed by the transformation.

As the boy was leaving, Jimmy gave him seven cents for an ice-cream cone, and that was his undoing. The boy's parents wanted to know who had given him the seven cents, and the boy told them, 'Mr Shields.' They wanted to know why, and the boy said, 'For watching their dog turn purple.'

The neighbours found this story incredible, and insisted to their son, who seemed not to know what they were talking about, that he had been molested. They phoned the sheriff, but the lady deputy who came out to talk to the boy went away a little puzzled. She did take the time to see that a purple poodle was sitting on the deck next door.

The following night, an ominous mob of men dressed in white sheets with eye-holes gathered on the beach in front of the Haines-Shields house yelling for the occupants to come out 'like men, if you can manage that'. Willie recognized the voice as that of his next-door neighbour. He opened the front door, which was on the second floor up a steep flight of stairs. Standing on the top landing and peering down at them, he warned them to go away or he would call the police. With that, several of the 'Klan', as they disguised themselves, rushed up the steps, grabbed him and dragged him down to the beach. Others ran upstairs to find Jimmy Shields. Jimmy was assaulted there in his own living-room – kicked and beaten about the body. Willie was severely beaten about the head, blacking both his eyes and giving him a concussion.

The gay-bashers, obviously led by their next-door neighbour, fled into the night, and Willie dragged himself upstairs to phone the police. They came out, searched about and found nothing, but Willie and Jimmy realized that their lives were in peril, and, taking their dog, drove to a nearby motel for the rest of the night. When Marion Davies learned what had happened, she immediately made arrangements for them to go to San Simeon, which was secure in every way.

Willie and Jimmy's other friends, including Kay Francis, Don Stewart and his wife, Bea Ames, Charles Boyer and his wife, Pat Patterson, Claudette Colbert, and, of course, Joan, insisted that

the men file charges against their next-door neighbour. Marion
Davies sounded out Hearst about pressuring the District Attorney
to do something, but Hearst thought that discreet support was
best. He was already helping Willie get started in the antique
business and was still his best customer. So nothing official ever
happened, but Willie and Jimmy never returned to El Portos
Beach and the house was sold.

Very little of this scandal reached very far beyond Hollywood.
News from the film community was dominated all through 1936
and '37 by what was happening with David O. Selznick's planned
production of *Gone with the Wind.*

When Selznick was negotiating to purchase the screen rights
to the film in 1936, Louis B. Mayer urged him to cast Joan
Crawford as Scarlett O'Hara, Maureen O'Sullivan as Melanie,
and Melvyn Douglas as Ashley Wilkes. Selznick told his father-
in-law (Mayer) that they would all be miscast. Joan did not
consider herself out of the running, however, because earlier
Selznick himself had spoken with her about it, and had even
wired his New York agent, Kay Brown, that 'I believe I would buy
it now for some such combination as Gable and Joan Crawford.'

Once he had plunged into the project, Selznick had a very clear
idea of who should play Scarlett. Paulette Goddard was under
consideration right until the end, although ultimately of course,
the role went to Vivien Leigh. As late as 23 November 1938,
Selznick wrote a memo saying that he had looked at the new
Goddard test 'practically daily since it arrived . . . and I must say
that each time I see it I am more and more impressed.' There
were, however, people writing to the Selznick Studio with
complaints about using Goddard, mostly from the conservative
religious right who considered her a sinner because she lived with
Charlie Chaplin. (Chaplin claimed that they were quietly
married, but it was never documented.) Such disappointments as
this for an actress who considered herself as much a lady as the
next woman, must have given Joan pause to reflect upon her own
risky amorous connections.

★ ★ ★

In 1937 the famed conductor of the Philadelphia Symphony
Orchestra, Leopold Stokowski, came to Hollywood to appear in
two films: one at Paramount Studios, *The Big Broadcast of 1937*,
with Burns and Allen, and another at Universal, *100 Men and a
Girl*, with Deanna Durbin. The film colony was in a state of
excitement about the maestro's presence among them. Joan and
Tone gave a reception for him at the Ambassador Hotel – the
Bristol house could accommodate forty for dinner, but their
Ambassador reception had all of Hollywood in attendance. It was
a social pinnacle of sorts, as it seemed only proper for the Tones,
the cream of society in the film community, to introduce to it this
titan of classical music, Leopold Stokowski.

No one questioned the propriety of this. It seemed a pre-
destined affair, and of course it cemented relations between
Stokowski and the Tones. He heard of their operatic ambitions
soon enough. After all, they *had* been studying voice and opera
with Signor and Madame Morando and, later, with Romano
Romano, the Metropolitan Opera's diva Rosa Ponselle's coach.
Joan felt confident enough about her voice to record some songs
at the studio, singing duets from *La Traviata* and *Don Giovanni*
with the baritone Douglas MacPhail and ensuring that Stokowski
heard them. When Stokowski said nothing about her tremolo, she
was emboldened to perform for the maestro, with Tone, in her
little theatre at a Saturday night dinner just a few weeks after the
Ambassador reception.

Stokowski congratulated her after the performance, but it was
not until the following day that Joan came down to earth long
enough to phone her good friend, Anita Loos, to tell her the
exciting news that Leopold Stokowski, the most famous
conductor in the world after Toscanini, 'was wild for me to give
up the movies and study to be an operatic diva'. Later that week,
when Romano Romano told her that it would take ten years of
constant study for her to be ready for an audition at the
Metropolitan, she stopped talking about the possibility. Soon the

duets became a thing of the past, as first her marriage and then her film career deteriorated.

Earlier, Joan had been blinded too much by her own success at Metro to notice that Tone's film career was in jeopardy. He had gone from his great success in *Lives of a Bengal Lancer* (1935), on loan to Paramount (where he was considered a major star), to a walk-on – twenty-six lines in Joan's *The Gorgeous Hussy* (1936). Had Tone not been so much in love with Joan, he might have seen that his value in Hollywood was being short-changed by Metro-Goldwyn-Mayer, to whom he was contracted. Both Paramount and Warner Brothers (he had co-starred at the latter with Bette Davis in *Dangerous* in 1935, which won her an Academy Award), valued him more highly.

Joan went to Louis B. Mayer and complained about Tone's casting in *The Gorgeous Hussy*, but, as she wrote, 'Mr Mayer was adamant'. Franchot's character in the film was that of John Eaton, Andrew Jackson's war secretary whom Joan's character, Peggy O'Neal, finally marries, so, in Mayer's opinion, John Eaton had to be played by 'an important actor'.

Unlike Doug Fairbanks, Jr, who not only had the luck to play the romantic lead opposite some extraordinary women in their early films (for example, Kate Hepburn in *Morning Glory* [1933] and Danielle Darrieux in her American début, *The Rage of Paris* [1938]), but had formidable allies in the British film industry as well, Tone seemed to be boxed in, and his character was to adapt himself to a situation rather than to change it.

★   ★   ★

In March 1937, a spread on Joan appeared in *Life*, the most popular magazine in America, which stated that:

'By the almighty standard of the box office, the young lady whose signature appears at left and whose person appears on the beach chair above is the first queen of the movies. In the previous years she was No. 7 on the list of box office champions. Those who ranked above her were four men (Clark Gable,

Robert Taylor, Joe E. Brown, Dick Powell), one child (Shirley Temple) and one team (Astaire & Rogers). Before Shirley Temple was born, Miss Crawford was drawing a star's salary as a sexy prototype of the then flaming Younger Generation. Now she makes $241,000 a year as a sophisticated comedienne . . . She has risen to stardom as the Shopgirl's Dream.'

Life's story on Joan accompanied a much-coveted selection by the magazine of her latest film, *The Last of Mrs Cheyney* (1937), as their 'Movie of the Week'. One would think that Joan's position in films was assured, but, despite huge box-office grosses, the critics were mixed about her performance in this film. Joan herself was also unsure of what she had done, as her director, Richard Boleslavski, had died before the last scenes were shot.

The Bride Wore Red, which followed *The Last of Mrs Cheyney* into the cinema within seven months, was directed by a woman, Dorothy Arzner. Unlike *The Last of Mrs Cheyney*, however, the film was 'a bomb', by Joan's own admission, even though Arzner had done with the film what no male director could have done as well: she fashioned its thin plot around costumes, or the way Joan dressed – a tactic perhaps appropriate to a film career as dependent upon what the star wore as upon the story or her performance.

It was not just bad films which seemed to plague Joan in 1937. For the first time in her career, she was getting a bad press, and, being as she was the American equivalent of the British Queen, this was close to sacrilege. One unfortunate incident occurred when Dorothy Rogers, one of Joan's most ardent fans, whom she had invited into her home and sometimes used for errands or chores, suddenly claimed that Joan had used her influence to have her fired from her job as a stenographer at RKO Studios. In her legal complaint, Rogers stated that a male friend of Joan's had persuaded her to make Rogers's employer fire her. She further stated that she had written a polite letter to Joan asking why she had done this, but that Joan's answer was to inform the Sheriff's department that Miss Rogers was giving her trouble.

On 10 August 1937, Dorothy Rogers filed a lawsuit against Joan for $50,000 damages. Within two days, Joan had invited Rogers and her lawyer to her home to try to reach an understanding, and Rogers's lawyer announced the following day that the matter had been settled. Joan had secured the woman a stenographic position at another studio.

★ ★ ★

Throughout the second half of 1937, Joan worked very hard on a film which would come closer than any other of her films to reflecting the agony of the Depression. *Mannequin* is the story of a woman of the tenements, and Joan wrote: 'I took one look at those poor Delancey Street sets and knew I was back home.' She was back on East 10th Street in Kansas City, even though the script set her in Manhattan.

Perhaps her strongest studio-contrived film, *Mannequin* portrays Jessica Cassidy, a working girl in a Manhattan buttonhole factory. She is in love with Eddie, a handsome, low-life boxing promoter (Alan Curtis), whose boxer, Slug McGoo, never wins. The film was redeemed from sordidness by producer Joe Mankiewicz's insistence on believability. No sentimental solution to a problem ever intrudes upon the unremitting wretchedness of the slums.

Jessica begs Eddie to marry her and take her away from this misery. Without telling her that it is only temporary, he borrows someone's vacant apartment and this becomes their honeymoon bower. Jessica believes that it is theirs to keep, and vows that she will work until she drops to keep the place. Eddie soon becomes involved in another shady deal, however, and he is arrested. Jessica bails him out by borrowing the money from a shipping magnate called Hennessey (Spencer Tracy) who falls for Jessica when he sees her after her marriage to the no-good Eddie.

Jessica and Eddie are immediately evicted from their honeymoon bower when the leaseholder reclaims it, and they find themselves back in a slum, exactly like the Delancey Street slum she left. Jessica listens to her mother (Elisabeth Risdon), and walks out on her husband and the wretched life she is living. Here, however, the film reflects its Hollywood origins. The sombre believability vanishes, and Joan turns up in an elegant wardrobe three months later with a new job as a mannequin in a department store. Hennesey sees her there, and asks her to marry him. The film also features one song, 'Always and always' (I'll go on adoring), sung by Joan, which, in advance of the film's run, became the number one song in America.

Mannequin has some flaws. Joan, for example, speaks her unaccented, perfect diction even in the tenement, and we never learn just how she frees herself of tenement life and becomes a model in a department store. Depression-mired audiences may have allowed Jessica considerable latitude to rise from the slums in such an inexplicable manner, however – after all, they wanted to believe that America still offered such opportunities. There were many fairy tales like this told on the screen it the 1930s, and all the film-makers got away with them. *Mannequin* does have one great redeeming quality: it shows Joan Crawford at her peak as a leading lady in a tailor-made vehicle, with a memorable actor (Spencer Tracy) opposite her. He taught her how to keep her own identity in a scene – even one with an actor as powerful as himself.

Away from the set, Tracy was a polo player. He taught Joan how to play, and even gave her one of his favourite polo ponies, Secret. She liked the game so much that she bought a second pony, but then Secret threw her when she pulled up short, and Joan turned a somersault, landing on her rear end. Typically, she climbed back on, rode the pony for forty minutes, and then rode him again the next day. She then said, 'Sell 'em,' meaning both the ponies – oblivious to the fact that Tracy had given Secret to her and just might want him back.

Mannequin opened at the Capitol in New York on 21 January 1938, and did brisk business during its opening week. Crawford fans were thrilled to hear Joan singing in her own contralto voice, and not dubbed. To ordinary filmgoers, however, even with Spencer Tracy, who brought his stolid, manly, good humour to the film, she was to the viewer less exciting than Tracy finds her.

Joan's acting style in *Mannequin*, while predictable, was of a calibre to match any other leading lady's of her day. She knew that she was carrying this film on her shoulders, yet the burden scarcely showed. A few critics considered her too grand for a 'slum princess', but they were surely missing the point of Joan Crawford's appeal, as she shows us from the opening scene that she is capable of lifting herself out of this Hester Street tenement by the elegance of her speech and her iron will.

In the wake of this film's success, Joan made an additional film with Borzage, *The Shining Hour* (1938), whose script was adapted from a mildly successful Broadway play. Margaret Sullavan was signed to play her rival in a love triangle, and their work together developed into a lifelong friendship between the women.

On-screen, however, Sullavan's presence led to a calamitous change in Joan's box-office standing. Sullavan's husky voice had won her many a male fan, and she had been climbing steadily in popularity since her movie début in *Only Yesterday* for Universal. Just after Joan's film, *Mannequin*, opened, Sullavan's best-remembered film, *Three Comrades*, from Erich Maria Remarque's novel, came into New York. The films' runs were less than five months apart, and *Three Comrades* was an enormous hit, quite in contrast to the ordinary business which *Mannequin* had done. Some influential cinema-chain operators concluded that Sullavan brought crowds to the cinema, while Joan merely brought out her fans.

Joan followed such trends closely – far more closely than did any of her peers – and she knew immediately that *Three Comrades* was a sensation. She already had found out that the screenplay had been written by F. Scott Fitzgerald, which surprised her because her own personal experience with him had pegged him as a drunkard.

Joan had been close to the production of *Three Comrades* because one of the 'comrades' was her husband, Franchot Tone. She had not, however, been prepared for the scale of the film's success, as she and Tone were drifting apart and she had convinced herself that it was her superior career which lay at the root of their domestic difficulties. As a consequence Tone never discussed with Joan the merits of any of the films in which he was cast.

It was during the standing-room-only run of *Three Comrades* in New York that Harry Brandt, a movie-chain owner in Manhattan and Brooklyn, wrote in *The Independent Film Journal* that Joan, along with Fred Astaire, Katharine Hepburn, Marlene Dietrich, and others, were stars who were 'box-office poison'.

One of the reasons for Joan's enormous success until then had been her prescience; she knew what to do with her career before any event could derail it. In March of 1938, before *Three Comrades* was released, Joan decided that something must be done, so she went to Hunt Stromberg and told him that she wanted F. Scott Fitzgerald to write something for *her*. Fitzgerald looked upon films as a challenge, and, in a strange reversal, relied upon his novels and short stories to sustain him while he tried to secure a reputation as a great screen-writer. He had failed to do this previously, but, with the success of *Three Comrades*, he was finally being hailed as the fair-haired boy in Metro's Thalberg Building (the writers' building).

Fitzgerald had drifted back east after being fired in 1931 over *Red Headed Woman* and replaced by Anita Loos. He was still obsessed with writing a successful story for Joan Crawford, and said as much to the lady herself when she invited him to one of her Saturday night parties. She recalled later that he had spent all evening in her kitchen 'getting sloshed on scotch'. It was easy to forget all that now, however, as Maggie Sullavan was being hailed as the most sensitive leading lady in American cinema. Joan always had believed that a great film could only come from a great script.

Stromberg was equally enthusiastic over Joan's request, and, a couple of months before the critical and box office excitement over *Three Comrades*, Stromberg asked Scott to adapt a story called *Infidelity* for Joan. It was planned to be one of four films starring Joan and produced by Stromberg.

Fitzgerald wrestled the project through several drafts. In all of them, Joan was to be a liberated woman of the world who marries her beloved and comes home unexpectedly to find him in bed with another young woman. Scott was careful not to show the adulterous couple in bed, but the Code Censors (the moral police then governing content and much else in American films) said that, content aside, the title, *Infidelity*, was out of bounds.

Neither Joan nor Stromberg gave up, and Scott kept working on new drafts. After months of revisions, however, Joan herself finally turned down the script, and the project died. It had become a parody of all her society-lady films. Still, Stromberg told Joan that Scott had mastered the sort of crisp dialogue which she delivered better than anyone else, and until his death in 1940 at the age of forty-four, Joan was Fitzgerald's champion.

Fitzgerald's keen interest in writing for Joan was not simply because he was a fan of hers. He knew that – almost alone among the American film stars – she attracted serious, intellectual film-goers to her pictures. Doubtless, her boss, Louis B. Mayer, had been apprised of the fact that, in addition to shop-girls and housewives, Joan and Greta Garbo had an almost exclusive hold on the intelligentsia. They lined up down the block to see anything in which Garbo appeared, and even flocked to Joan's performance in *Rain*, despite the mixed notices. Their films became essential cocktail-party topics in New York. After Fitzgerald's death, Crawford continued to fascinate this same audience in *A Woman's Face* (1941), *Mildred Pierce* (1945), *Humoresque* (1946), *Possessed* (1947) and *Sudden Fear* (1952), *Johnny Guitar* (1954) and *What Ever Happened to Baby Jane?* (1962). This hold she had on the serious thinkers, including many film critics, was to span a period of thirty years.

So, in a sense, Joan came to grips with the fact that she would not always be the most popular of film stars because she knew that she had her own special audience. From then on, she sought riskier projects because she knew that her fans were no longer just gum-chewing, slang-speaking shop-girls and hausfraus, but poets, painters, musicians and big-time executives.

As for being 'box-office poison', Joan had been at the very pinnacle of her profession for well over a decade. The criticism of one man should not have mattered. Katharine Hepburn was on the same list, and her career actually improved after being labelled – she moved from the financially shaky RKO Pictures to Metro, where she remained throughout the 1940s. Garbo was also on the list, yet her greatest financial and critical success, *Ninotchka*, was made nearly two years afterwards. Only Joan really took it to heart. The fans and the critics had made her a star – no one else. Now one of them had spoken out and the queen's throne began to tremble.

★ ★ ★

Joan had retained former husband Doug Fairbanks, Jr's manager, Mike Levee, to represent her in contract negotiations, and in May 1938, Levee informed the newspaper-wire services that Joan had signed a deal with Metro that which would earn her one-and-half million dollars over a five-year period. In an unusual move, the studio had deleted the option clause so that they were irrevocably bound to the star for that five-year period. In addition, because of her promise to Tone to attempt a stage career, Joan's new contract permitted her to take two years off to appear on the stage, with the two years being added to the length of her contract. Levee told the press that, if Joan did take off the two years, the contract would not expire until 1945, and that she had first signed with Metro in 1925.

The contract called for three pictures a year, or a total of fifteen, at a salary of $100,000 per film. Before Levee's negotiations, Metro was offering to pay Joan $400,000 annually under an option deal, but she was willing to take $300,000 under the no-option agreement. This was because the latter deal gave her security, and also because the tax burden on the larger amount would have nearly cancelled out the additional $100,000 involved. With this move, Joan was on a par with the most valuable stars in American film – in the same financial league as Bette Davis, James Cagney, Paul Muni, Janet Gaynor, Clark Gable, Robert Taylor, Myrna Loy and Carole Lombard.

The contract was Mayer's answer to Joan's sudden decline in popularity in 1938, and to the 'box-office-poison' label. Recalling her spread in *Life* magazine back in 1937, when she had been crowned in print as 'the first queen of the movies', Joan was hard to reassure.

So, just as Joan became the highest-paid film star under contract to a studio, she sensed doom over the horizon. Her role as a pillar of Hollywood society no longer seemed very important; her Brentwood mansion's landmark status no longer warmed her heart as bus-loads of fans stopped to stare at it.

The story was also starting to be heard about town that Tone was unhappy. Later Joan would write: 'Franchot's and my love cost him his rightful career in pictures.' Yet hadn't she insisted upon those two years away from film-making to attempt a stage career – all for him? Film commitments continued to bar her departure from the screen, however, even for a summer stock engagement. Then all those plans began to unravel. Joan should have written in her autobiography: 'Franchot's and my love blocked his way out of pictures back to the stage, where he wanted to be.'

In the spring of 1938, right on the heels of Brandt's attack in the *Independent Film Journal*, rumours were circulating that Joan and Tone were about to part. Both of them denied this at first, but then the stories began to be coupled with word of Tone's disaffection at his home studio. If he had only gone to another studio – to Warner Brothers or to Paramount, where he was highly prized – he could perhaps have become as big a star as John Garfield, whose Broadway background was similar, but he did not.

Tone developed a growing sense of hopelessness. He turned to drink, and sometimes, while drunk, became abusive. Clarence Brown, who had been Joan's director on *The Gorgeous Hussy*, dropped in at the set of *The Shining Hour*, Joan's only film in 1938, one day, and noticed bruises on her cheek and around her eye. He knew at once what had happened. Such behaviour directed against the actress who had saved Metro from sinking during the worst of the Depression was intolerable, and, when Brown told Mayer, as he most certainly would, it was inevitable that the studio hierarchy would turn against Tone.

Almost everyone was advising Joan to leave him, and he had no friends at court to mediate on his behalf, quite unlike the situation when her marriage to Doug Fairbanks, Jr was in trouble. And when Joan found Tone with a starlet in his dressing-room at the studio (one can imagine Joan having spies on movie sets to alert her), she instantly made the decision to separate.

It was a replay of the scene in which Doug, Jr had been told by agent and manager Mike Levee, while at work on a film, that his belongings had been moved to a hotel. Tone was evicted in much the same way while he was away from the house, but his most valuable possessions – such as the heirloom silver-plate which he had contributed to the household – were retained by her with no apologies. [According to Betty Barker, Joan's private secretary, the silver-plate was later given to Tone's son, Pascal 'Pat' Tone.]

Also at this time, probably with Tone gone from the scene, Joan had a curious sexual encounter with former child star Jackie Cooper. He was seventeen years old and was eager to satisfy his own curiosity about Joan's alleged sexual appetitite. Cooper had heard around their studio (Metro) was that she was a wild woman in the boudoir.

After a small party around her swimming pool, the youth declined to go home. 'You had better get out of here, young man,' she told him. But he refused to go and then made an obvious pass at Joan. She then closed all the drapes to the pool house, and in Cooper's words:

'I made love to Joan Crawford. Or, rather she made love to me.

'Over the next six months or so the performance was repeated eight or nine times. After the first time, however, it was always late at night. I would set a date with her, then manage to sneak out of the house after my mother and stepfather had gone to sleep. I would roll my car down the street until I was far enough away so I could start the engine without waking them. And I would drive to Joan's house.

'She was a very erudite professor of love. At the time I suppose she was in her early thirties [she was thirty-three] . . .

She would bathe me, powder me, cologne me. Then she would do it over again. She would put on high heels, a garter belt, and a large hat and pose in front of the mirror, turning this way and that way.'

He thought she was crazy, but that she was an extraordinary performer and that she was teaching him things which most men didn't learn until they were much older. 'There was never any drinking or drugs with her. It was all business . . . When I left, she would put me on her calendar for the next visit.' Finally, one night, she said that was the last time, and that he was not to call again. 'And put it out of your mind. It never happened.' After kissing him goodbye, she said, 'But we'll always be friends.'

Cooper kept his 'magnificent secret', partly because he knew that no one would believe him. He did not see Joan again until thirty years later in the 1960s, when he was a guest star on Peter Falk's *Columbo* detective series at the Universal studio. 'By accident,' Cooper remembered, 'I happened to run into her, and she took my hand, looked in my eyes, and, I think, remembered.'

★ ★ ★

Within a year of the final decree of divorce from Joan in 1940, Tone married Jean Wallace and they had two sons during their ten years of marriage. Franchot's first son's name was Pascal (his own given name was Stanislas Pasqual Tone), and they then had a second son, whom he named Thomas Jefferson.

Tone and his two wives (after Joan) spent far more time in the east than in California. He had a long and successful stage career, but he went out to the coast on a freelance basis, and half of his film career came after his divorce from Joan. He was very good in three thrillers: *Phantom Lady* (1944), *Jigsaw* (1949) and *Man on the Eiffel Tower* (1950). Between his marriages, he was sometimes a serious alcoholic, and suffered a facial injury during a bar-room brawl with actor Tom Neal.

By the 1950s, Tone had lost his unusual handsomeness and was forced by his appearance to take character parts. He remained active as an actor until his final illness. He and Joan never lost contact, and she saw all his films and attended all his plays. In 1966, he convinced her to vacation with him at Muskoka Lake in Canada, and she managed to spend a week with him. When he developed lung cancer, Joan would have him over to her East Side apartment for dinner, and when he was well enough, which was not often, they would dine at Joan's table at 21. Tone had aged prematurely, while Joan still looked like a woman fifteen years younger than her biological age, but she felt a strong loyalty to him which had little to do with how old either of them looked. When he died in 1968, Joan had him cremated according to his wishes, and then had his ashes scattered over the Canadian lake where he had vacationed all his life.

SEVEN

'MOMMIE DEAREST'

By 1939, Joan began to sense that her heyday as a favourite in the court of the roaring lion was ending. Lana Turner was being groomed for bigger things, in precisely the way that Joan herself had been in the middle and late 1920s. Joan was becoming more of a clothes-horse for Adrian than a film actress of significance. Invariably, she was given two leading men and a weak script for all concerned to overcome, and as a favour to Harry Rapf, her early protector, she consented to star in *The Ice Follies of 1939* with James Stewart and Lew Ayres. It was a mistake.

She was now a year beyond her label as 'box-office poison', but not nearly enough was happening in her career. Inside gossip reported that, on a transcontinental train ride from Hollywood, Marlene Dietrich and Kate Hepburn had got into a friendly argument as to which one of them should top the list of box-office failures. Dietrich insisted that she should do so, as Paramount had just paid her a large sum of money *not* to make another Paramount film, while Hepburn said that statistics could prove that her films had earned less at the box office than anyone else's, and that she should therefore deserve the top position. Joan did not see how they could joke about it. She was hurt more than anyone on this wretched list. While she knew that film scholars considered her one of the all-time 'greats', she seemed to be losing her bourgeois audience which had made her a star. She saw that as a tragedy.

Worst of all for a woman like Joan, there was no man in her

life. Alone in her Brentwood home one Saturday night, she felt so lonely that she telephoned George Oppenheimer, a screen-writer at Metro who was gay and always available, and told him that she needed some company. He was caught in his rented house, unshaven and wearing his old clothes, but she insisted that that did not matter. Oppenheimer recalled that they sat in her over-sized kitchen, which she said was the most comfortable room in the house, and talked at length about life in general and about her present misery in particular.

Joan was so devastated by what was happening that she rarely left her Brentwood mansion, and brooded for weeks. She consulted a Christian Science practitioner, who quoted Mary Baker Eddy: 'Though the way is dark in mortal sense, divine Life and Love illumine it, destroy the unrest of mortal thought ... and the supposed reality of error.'

It was then that Joan made a bad error – she decided that what she needed was a family. After her divorce from Franchot Tone in 1940, she made an effort to adopt a child, but single parents were not allowed to do so in California. She asked her lawyer, Greg Bautzer, who was a frequent escort, to canvass other states where this was permitted. Bautzer had no luck either, but eventually a baby broker (an illegal-adoption agent) found an infant girl. It was in this way that Christina began her life in the Crawford household. Joan was then thirty-four years old.

Joan's close friends knew why she felt compelled to be a mother as well as the most dedicated film actress of all time. She was seeking perfection in her life as well as in her art. She had control of her career; now she could create the perfect family with none of the flaws of the LeSueur-Cassin tribe. She had already taken her niece, Joan LeSueur, into her home and virtually raised her until she was three years old, when the child's mother, Kasha, her stand-in at the studio until 1934, divorced Joan's brother, Hal, and took her daughter east to live in New York.

Christina was to become one of the best-known children in Hollywood. The reason for that is fairly simple. 'Joan Crawford' was created for a vast film-going public, and Joan shared everything with that public. It was privy to her romances, her separations from her husbands, her divorces, her illnesses, her vacations. This makes it altogether unlikely that Joan would conceal such an important addition to her family as a baby, for all the months that Christina later claimed she was secretly in the home.

Christina made many other claims, too, in her famous book about her life as Joan Crawford's daughter, *Mommie Dearest*. Christina was named Joan, Jr, so she tells us, for a very brief time. She states further that her adoption took place in 1939, a few weeks after her birth in June of that year. This is in conflict with news reports by columnist Jimmy Fidler, a man who knew Joan well and followed her activities closely, as well as news stories with the headline: 'Joan Crawford Adopts Baby'. The date was May 25, 1940.

Christina explains this discrepancy by saying that eleven months went by before Joan officially adopted her, but the news stories about Joan adopting this baby girl all state that the adoption took place in New York City. Fidler also writes of getting the news from Joan directly, during a long-distance telephone conversation from New York. The news stories record the baby's chosen name as Christina, and say that she was taken from 'an eastern foundling home'. Christina writes that she was born in Hollywood Presbyterian Hospital, an institution which knew Joan very well as a generous friend and patron.

The great mystery here is how an astute reporter such as Jimmy Fidler could be so easily duped by Joan, as well as all her friends, several of whom were in her home frequently during the year in which Christina maintains she was in the nursery in Joan's Bristol Avenue home in Brentwood. If this was true, no one had any idea that she was keeping a baby there throughout those eleven months.

★　　★　　★

Alone in her mansion with her small daughter, Joan felt more than ever the need for some male companionship. Her gay friend

Cesar Romero had been one of the first to call following her divorce from Tone. 'Let's go dancing,' he had proposed, and they did. This had become a weekly ritual with them thereafter, but 'Butch' Romero was obviously never a prospect as a partner. Like Willie Haines, Butch was a surrogate brother, and a delightful one.

He also helped Joan through the heartache which followed her romance with a New Yorker, businessman Charles McCabe. The relationship was doomed because it was becoming very clear that McCabe would never be able to get a divorce from his wife. However, the easterner, an outdoorsman, taught Joan to hunt and fish in the Pocenos, and also introduced her to politics and big-business affairs. She taught him in turn to be considerate of others, especially his co-workers, citing her own close rapport with the crew on her films. She said that he already had this quality in him, and that it only required some encouragement to bring it out.

In the subsequent void, Joan consoled herself by writing verse.

> Where are you?
> My heart cries out in agony,
> In my extended hands
> I give my heart with
> All its cries – its songs – its love,
> But it's too late.

A little pretentious perhaps – doggerel certainly – but it gives us a clue that, at thirty-four, Joan felt that it would soon be too late to find the soulmate who had in the end eluded her in her attempts with Fairbanks and Tone. In 1939, to many of her friends Joan seemed a genuinely lonely person.

She even pursued a handsome leading man, Glenn Ford, new in films that year. He had considerable boyish charm and an ingenuous smile. In the little gem of a theatre next to her pool, they would run her films (his first film would not be out until 1940), as well as brand new ones fed into the no-charge Hollywood star circuit.

Ford soon confided to a mutual friend that Joan was too

ABOVE: Studio boss Louis B. Mayer, Paulette Goddard, Joan, and producer Hunt Stromberg in the lobby of the theatre where *The Women* was premiered in 1939. Directed by George Cukor, the film also starred Norma Shearer, Rosalind Russell and Joan Fontaine.

BELOW: A still from *Susan and God* (1940). Joan and Fredric March look troubled across their adolescent daughter, Rita Quigley. Again, Hunt Stromberg was the producer, with George Cukor directing and a screenplay by Anita Loos.

ABOVE LEFT: In *A Woman's Face* (1941), Melvyn Douglas, as the greatest plastic surgeon in Sweden, shows his work to Anna Holm (Joan), while his worried wife (Osa Massen) looks on. Anna had come to blackmail his wife before she encounters the good doctor.

LEFT: A scene from one of Joan's greatest films, *Mildred Pierce* (1945), for which she won the Academy Award for Best Actress. The film was nominated on four counts: best film, best performance by an actress (Joan) and best supporting portrayals (Eve Arden, Ann Blyth).

ABOVE: Another still from *Mildred Pierce*. Here, Joan is shown with Jack Carson and Ann Blyth.

RIGHT: Joan with her second husband, the actor Franchot Tone whom she married in 1935.

RIGHT: Joan presents the
annual Pimm's Cup at
Larue's restaurant in
Hollywood, 1951. Receiving
the award is Bill Gargan,
Joan's leading man from
Rain, a film they had made
together twenty years earlier.
Douglas Fairbanks, Jr's
stepfather, Buddy Rogers, is
on the right.

BELOW: Joan with her
husband, actor Phillip Terry.
They surprised Hollywood
by marrying just six weeks
after they had met. Joan
reported to the Metro studios
the day after the wedding to
continue work in her latest
starring vehicle, *Reunion in
France*.

BELOW: Hedda Hopper
(right) was one of
Hollywood's leading gossip
columnists. She was the first
to predict – just weeks after
production had begun – that
Joan would win the Academy
Award for *Mildred Pierce*.
Here she is shown with
Marion Davies in 1959.

ABOVE: Louella Parsons was Hollywood's most celebrated gossip columnist and Hedda Hopper's chief rival. She claimed to be a close friend of Joan's, and Joan gave her many exclusives, but the friendship became strained after Joan became a widow in 1959. Here, Louella is shown in 1942, greeting Tyrone Power, with his wife and Gary Cooper beyond.

RIGHT: A family portrait, taken in a dressing room/bungalow on the Universal-International lot during the shooting of *Female on the Beach* in 1955. Joan is with her son, Christopher, and her twin daughters, Cathy and Cynthia. Upon completion of the film, Joan became Mrs Al Steele.

ABOVE: Joan being fed some birthday cake by her twin daughters at their eighth birthday party. Cathy and Cindy were adopted by Joan as infants in 1947. From the very beginning, they were closer to Joan than the two older children would ever be.

BELOW: Joan cutting the wedding cake with her fourth husband, Al Steele. Joan was fascinated by Steele when they first met. A successful business-man, Steele was the kind of strong father Joan felt her children needed. They married in 1955.

LEFT: Joan with her oldest daughter, Christina, who would later write a shocking and much-publicized biography of her mother, *Mommie Dearest.*

Joan shown enjoying a happier moment during her troubled
relationship with her daughter, Christina (at her left). Her twin
daughter, Cynthia, is on her right. Although she was even closer to her
mother than Christina, 'Cindy' never saw any of the abuse alleged by
Christina in *Mommie Dearest*.

ABOVE: The last major Crawford hit, *Whatever Happened to Baby Jane?* (1962), was so successful largely because of the total lack of traditional movie-star vanity in its two key performances. Note the many freckles on Joan's hand and arm, which were not masked out for this shot, although those on her face — which were just as numerous, were always concealed to keep her from looking freakish.

LEFT: Joan, aged fifty-nine but looking many years younger, dancing with Glenn Ford, eleven years her junior.

aggressive and too intent on getting him into bed, yet he still found her interest useful, and he, Joan and a Brentwood neighbour of hers, J. Watson Webb, Jr, went to premières together. Then Ford met actress-dancer Eleanor Powell, and, within weeks, they were married.

Many years later, in 1964, J. Watson Webb, Jr gave a dinner-dance at a local hotel ballroom honouring Annabella, the gifted French star who had returned to Hollywood for a visit. Glenn Ford was by that time some years beyond his divorce from Powell, and Joan flirted with him openly and had his dinner place shifted next to hers. They danced all evening and became re-acquainted.

★ ★ ★

In early 1940 Joan was asked to replace Norma Shearer in the film version of a Broadway hit (which had starred Gertrude Lawrence in the title role) Rachel Crothers's *Susan and God*. At a party in New York given by playwright Moss Hart and his wife, Kitty Carlisle, Joan met Fredric March and his wife, Florence Eldridge. March was leaving for the coast that weekend to play the alcoholic husband of Susan, opposite Shearer. Joan secretly coveted the role of the foolish society matron who has embraced a new European theo-philosophy and meddles with her own family (a husband and daughter) so that they become totally estranged and dysfunctional.

The following week, Joan's telephone rang in New York. It was Louis B. Mayer, calling from the coast to inform her that Norma Shearer had refused to play the mother of a fourteen-year-old girl (Norma was then forty years old), and that George Cukor, the director had asked whether Joan would be interested in the role. 'I'd play Wally Beery's grandmother if it's a good part!' she told Mayer, and she left for the coast that night.

Susan and God received mixed notices. *Variety* gave Joan a rave review, and the other critics were impressed with her dramatic skill in blending a silly woman with a dawning intelligence which ultimately saves her family, but most of them saw it as a stepping-stone to a new and more versatile future for her, rather

than as a *fait accompli*. What the film did, however, was to impress
Louis B. Mayer and the Metro hierarchy with Joan's value as an
actress (as well as to ensure that Norma Shearer's tenure as a
great studio asset was coming to an end).

★　　★　　★

In the summer of 1940 Joan was drawn into her last significant
film for Metro, *A Woman's Face*. The screen-writer was Donald
Ogden Stewart, whose work she had always admired, and whom
she knew well socially as his former wife and now the Countess
Tolstoy, Beatrice Ames, was one of her closest friends. Joan had
met Bea Ames and her husband at the King Vidors' house in the
autumn of 1925, when Stewart was brought to Metro to write
Brown of Harvard for William Haines.

The script for *A Woman's Face* had been adapted by Stewart
from a French play by Francis de Croisset, which had previously
been filmed in Swedish with Ingrid Bergman. Joan had seen the
Bergman movie, and had been so impressed by it that she insisted
that Metro should acquire it for her.

George Cukor, the director, who had done well with Joan in
Susan and God, and whom she much admired and saw often at
Willie Haines's house (he was part of the Haines's circle of
successful gay men), was critical of her performance in *A
Woman's Face*, in Gavin Lambert's study, *On Cukor:* '. . . when she
becomes pretty (after a sympathetic plastic surgeon – Melvyn
Douglas – has removed the hideous scar from her face), she
becomes . . . Joan Crawford . . .' Cukor claimed that the picture
failed because it was interesting in the first half when Joan is
disfigured and a criminal, but then later in the film, as Cukor
continues: 'In this kind of situation you can still watch the actress
for touches of the movie queen sneaking in – artificial eyelashes,
lifting the breasts, all that kind of nonsense.'

Joan's character, Anna Holm, is so embittered that, when she
talks about her past, it is in a dead voice with a tinge of bitterness.
Cukor set her up for this moment by telling her 'to recite the
multiplication table by twos' until, as she put it, 'all emotion was

drained and I was totally exhausted'. Joan also later wrote that 'I say a prayer for Mr Cukor every time I think of what *A Woman's Face* did for my career.' It was certainly Joan's dramatic breakthrough – she received the best notices of her career up to that time for the film.

Joan knew that Don Stewart, the film's screen-writer, was very liberal in his views, but then so was she – or so she had thought ever since her immersion in liberal politics with Franchot Tone. Stewart, however, was further to the left than Joan could ever go, although he had enlisted her help with money and her name in the 'Anti-Nazi League', and she had commiserated with him when Bea Ames left him in 1939 to become a member of the White Russian aristocracy as Countess Tolstoy.

During the production of *A Woman's Face*, Joan had conferred with George Cukor and Stewart on several occasions, and afterwards Stewart had persuaded her to become more active in the Hollywood movement against fascism, which had become the chief liberal cause in the film colony at the time.

Stewart would be kept away from harm when the 1947 House Unamerican Activities Committee investigation of Hollywood took place, but his days at the studio were numbered from then on. Before the 1951 bloodbath could take away the remaining great Hollywood talents (Charlie Chaplin, Charles Laughton, the Fredric Marches, writers Dorothy Parker, Ring Lardner, Jr and dozens of others being either imprisoned or driven into exile in New York or Europe), Stewart went to England to live, where he would remain until his death more than thirty years later.

Joan herself earned a hundred-page dossier in the FBI for her 'subversive' activities – mostly under the sponsorship of Stewart – but she was never called by the HUAC. Unlike Robert Taylor, Louis B. Mayer, Gary Cooper and other Hollywood luminaries, she refused publicly to denounce the communists or to recant, nor did she ever imply that she had been duped.

Interestingly, Joan often saw Doug, Jr at these anti-fascist affairs and at any event to do with Russian War Relief. During the Hollywood witch-hunts, Doug, Jr was so incensed by what the blacklisters were doing that he phoned the House Committee (HUAC) and dared them to put his name on their list. He was not called to testify either.

★　★　★

In 1941 Joan adopted a thirteen-day-old boy, who was blond and of French and Irish descent. She named him Christopher, but, in a press release, made the mistake of mentioning his birthplace and birth date. His natural mother read the story, and realized immediately that the boy she had given up had been adopted by the great film star, Joan Crawford. When the boy was not quite six months old, there began a series of threatening letters from the boy's mother. They were wild, rambling and frightening. Joan gave the boy back to the agency (baby broker), and he was returned to his mother, who sold him within two days for $250. Joan was devastated by what had happened, but could see no other remedy.

Despite this painful surrender of the little boy, his mother seemed obsessed with Joan. In early 1944, she suddenly appeared at Joan's front door and informed Joan's secretary that she wished to see the Crawford children. When told that this was not possible, the woman forced her way into the foyer and attempted to go upstairs to the bedrooms that were occupied by the children. The secretary phoned the police and the woman was placed in the psychopathic ward of the Georgia Street Receiving Hospital in Los Angeles, from which she was subsequently released.

Joan continued to receive threatening letters from the woman. One letter, dated 11 January 1945, reads:

'I would write you a *threatening* letter — *if I knew how* to do it & *yet please God!*

'I will threaten you this & *it* is acceptable to God — that I shall kidnap my baby, if I *get the chance* & I shall work & wait for the chance — with all my mind, soul, & strength — until the chance comes!

It is written that *he* that doesn't take care of *their own* is worse than an infidel & denys [*sic*] the faith of God.

So to please God I must get my baby & take care of him! I do not fear you, nor none like you, nor all of your kind put together!

Do you doubt me? Try & see!

You are a perverse wicked woman full of sins and yet you think yourself above the poor!

Doesn't the same kind of _____ (obscene) come from your bowels as does come from mine? Or is yours wealthier?

Is your _____ (obscene) more refined than mine?

These above sentences are *clean* in the sight of God, for (obscene) & _____ (obscene) are the works of God!

I am poor & none to help me but God, but with His help, I shall prevail over you all! You mean hard-hearted vipers with wealth!

Joan contacted her studio's attorneys and explained what had happened. They in turn called in the FBI, and the mother was arrested by a US Marshal on 16 January 1945. Bail was set at $5,000, which the woman was unable to raise. No prosecution was sought because the United States Attorney, Charles Veale, decided that her letters were the work of a diseased mind. She was eventually institutionalized.

★　　★　　★

Joan still had no man in her life, and she confided some of her woes to press agent Harry Mines. The actor Phillip Terry had recently mentioned to Mines that he would like to meet Joan Crawford, and it struck Mines that he should bring the eager and good-looking Terry to his forlorn friend's Brentwood home. Terry was a former college football player who was now under contract to Paramount, where that summer he was featured with Eddie Bracken in *Sweater Girl*, a collegiate film notable mainly for one of its songs, 'I Don't Want to Walk without You'.

At six feet, Terry had a rugged build and a probable hidden agenda. He hoped to advance in films, but knew that this could not happen if he continued to be cast in second and third leads. It seems likely that Terry felt that he had nothing to lose by becoming involved with Joan, who was still very much a significant figure in Hollywood despite her current 'rough patch' at Metro.

Mines introduced them, Joan nodded her approval and Mines left them alone. Terry was naturally well-mannered and bright – in fact, reminiscent of Doug, Jr – but he did not come with a pedigree. He told Joan that he had studied at the Royal Academy of Dramatic Art in London. They did not go upstairs that first night except to look in on Christina, so, of course Joan said that he was 'shy and reserved'.

Reserved he may have been, but within six weeks, on 21 July 1942, they were married in a civil ceremony in Hidden Valley, under their legal names Lucille Tone and Frederick Kormann.

Joan's spirits picked up remarkably during the first year of her marriage, and she felt strong enough emotionally to take on Louis B. Mayer. Her films in 1942 and '43, *Reunion in France* and *Above Suspicion*, both set in Europe during the Second World War, which was then going on, had been savaged by the critics. In late 1943 she went to Mayer and asked to be released from her contract. She had been with Metro for eighteen years and there were risks in taking this step, but she felt compelled to leave and start again. Mayer pretended at least to be upset, but the management back in New York at Loew's Inc evidently baulked at the idea, because Joan's films still turned a profit. However, Mayer told them, 'She wants out, and I think perhaps she's right.'

Joan complained later that no one had said goodbye to her when she left Metro. She may have been exaggerating a little, or perhaps she departed so quietly that few of the people working around her knew that she was leaving.

Joan and Louis B. Mayer never lost touch with each other. Betty Barker could see that any discussion of Metro's activities or her part in them prompted a gentle nostalgia in Joan. She said: 'Joan always felt that her years at Metro were the best of her life. She thought L. B. Mayer was her friend, and she always said nice things about him.' This contradicts Christina's premise as she was later to assert in her book, *Mommie Dearest*, that her mother's life fell apart after she left Metro, and that she felt a lasting betrayal by Mayer and others. The truth was that, with the exception of *Grand Hotel* (the film in which she had starred with Greta Garbo in 1932), Joan's greatest movie triumphs came after she left Metro.

Phillip Terry had signed a contract with RKO Pictures that same year, so they still had a 'bread-winner' in the family even though Joan paid the expenses on the house and staff. Phillip saved face by buying all the groceries.

They adopted a little boy, who was known for a time as 'Phil, Jr' before becoming Christopher Crawford. Phillip never legally adopted Christopher or Christina, so they both belonged to their mother. It seemed likely that Joan did not have sufficient confidence in her new marriage to take the risk of having her third husband signing adoption papers, even though she was still trying to make the marriage work.

Joan's perfectionism was beginning to tell on the two children as they moved out of the toddler stage. Their social presence in the house before guests was carefully scripted by Joan, the niceties of their behaviour in front of guests a little too obvious.

If Joan's own childhood had not been so wretched, and she had formed some real attachment to her mother, Anna, things might have been different in Joan's household for her own two children. She herself had always been beaten with saplings whenever she misbehaved or did something to displease her mother, but the child Billie was tough by nature, and virtually unbowed by all that discipline. In fact, while Joan publicly stated that she had a Dickensian upbringing, her memories of her childhood suggest that she did enjoy much of it, including the drudgery. It would seem wrong to conclude that, when she disciplined her own children harshly, she was simply repeating what had been done to her.

Even after moving to California, Anna never had a close enough relationship with Joan to be a refuge or a moderating influence in her grandchildren's lives. The most she could do was occasionally to bake cookies or cakes for them and slip them through the kitchen door at the Brentwood mansion. Cesar Romero tried to help bridge the chasm between Joan and her mother by introducing Anna to his own mother. After that, the two women became ardent members of the Motion Picture Mothers Association, which held frequent meetings. Its purpose seemed to be a general basking together in the radiance of their offspring's fame. Anna had another close friend in the organization, Patia Power, mother of Tyrone, and the three women, Mrs LeSueur, Mrs Power and Mrs Romero, often shopped together, gossiped by phone and kept each other company for many years. Joan knew about this, and it may have served to ease her conscience.

Once Joan had been released from Metro and would be at home a great deal, Anna may have thought that there would be a thaw in their relations, but in fact it was the opposite. Anna could no longer even sneak in cookies to the children for fear of being caught by Joan.

All this aversion for her mother was not quite hatred on Joan's part. It was more an avoidance of bitter past memories, which had little to do with her life in Hollywood. Everyone who met Anna actually found her quite agreeable. Betty Barker, who sometimes spoke with her by phone at Joan's behest, found her mother 'a settled, sweet lady. She was small but stout. She had the same oval face and great big eyes as Joan. She was an awfully nice lady when I knew her'.

EIGHT

SALVAGING THE FUTURE

Terry made three films for RKO Pictures, and Joan was telling everyone that the management there was planning to build him into a combination of Cary Grant and Clark Gable. Within a year, however, RKO dropped him with little warning. He was not even close to becoming a leading man by then, so he switched careers temporarily and took on a job in a war plant. Joan would make up his lunch every night and put the lunch-box in the refrigerator. The next morning, after breakfast, there would be a little ritual of Joan handing him the lunch-box, and embracing and kissing him. She was now a housewife and apparently enjoying it, and for a little while did not seem to miss the studio life.

She was not aware of the perils of total independence from a studio at first. When she called in her business manager, however, and asked him exactly where she stood financially, his response shook her profoundly. She had been spending nearly as much as she was earning on additions to her house, formal dinners with liveried footmen, birthday parties for Christina, hundreds of pairs of shoes, dozens of designer dresses, house staff and Franchot Tone, her ex-husband who was in need of financial help despite his earlier wealth.

Before her first week of idleness was over, she received a call from Jack Warner, who offered her a contract at Warner Brothers. At the time, this was the third most prestigious film company, after Metro and Fox, and slightly ahead of the financially unstable Paramount. For two pictures a year, Warner Brothers would pay her a third of what she was making when she left Metro.

Rumours circulated that Jack Warner really wanted to use Joan as leverage in his many disputes with Bette Davis. Davis had recently sued Warner Brothers while she was in England, in an attempt to get her contract set aside, but had lost the case and was now back in her old pattern of rejecting scripts right and left. Joan had script approval too, of course, but nothing ever came her way that she liked and her idleness – which she had begun to detest – continued.

★   ★   ★

More than a year passed without Joan appearing in front of a film camera. Finally she accepted a cameo role playing herself in *Hollywood Canteen* (1944). After her single week of shooting for the film, she fell into the same routine of idleness, and eventually became so upset about being paid her substantial weekly salary that she asked Warner to take her off pay until he found a film for her. During her eighteen years at Metro, she had made forty-three films, averaging out to nearly three a year. The work ethic was strong in her, and she felt that it was dishonest to be paid for work not performed.

Lew Wasserman of the powerful MCA management company had been involved in Joan's career for years, and she now asked him to be on the lookout for a film that she could do at another studio, on loan from Warner Brothers. The word was out: look for a Joan Crawford-type picture. The word came back: there are none.

Joan was obviously going to have to try something new. She would have to find a strong script demanding an actress of power and range – someone who did not require the services of Adrian or Helen Rose or Jean Louis to dress. Then, early in 1945, after both Bette Davis and Barbara Stanwyck had turned down the role of Mildred Pierce, in the film of that name, the producer Jerry Wald learned that Joan was interested.

Everything seemed set for Joan to return to the screen – minus the glamour – playing a hash-house owner who expands her business into a mini-empire. There was a problem, however, with the director, Mike Curtiz, a Hungarian with only a minimal grasp of the English language. He had been signed to the production, but refused to accept Crawford in the lead, wanting someone who was convincingly real. Joan agreed to do a screen test, and proved that she was right for the part.

Once she was signed to the picture, Joan hired Henry Rogers, perhaps the best-known press agent in Hollywood at the time and a partner in the firm Rogers and Cowan. From the first days of shooting, Cowan plunged into a campaign to plug Joan as 'best actress'. He had told producer Jerry Wald that it was not too early to begin touting Joan's performance for the Oscars. Wald reluctantly agreed, and Rogers phoned Hedda Hopper with the news that Joan was giving an Oscar-calibre performance in *Mildred Pierce*. Hopper dutifully included the news in her column the next day, and then others picked it up. The result was that, as soon as production had finished, everyone in town was eager to see Joan's Academy-Award-level film. By the time the nominations were announced, Joan was virtually a certainty for the Award.

Mildred Pierce was charmed in every respect. It not only received rave reviews from the critics, but also generated long queues in front of cinemas in New York, London and other places in which there were serious film-goers. The following March, Joan won her Oscar for the film, in spite of competition from Greer Garson, Jennifer Jones, Gene Tierney and Ingrid Bergman.

Despite Jerry Wald's pleas, Joan refused to attend the Award ceremonies, insisting that she did not expect to win, and she remained at home that evening with her 'on-command' slight temperature. When Wald and Curtiz brought the Oscar back to the Bristol Avenue house for her, they found that Henry Rogers had already alerted all the press, and that there were about fifty reporters and photographers at the house. Joan allowed Christina to hold the statuette for several minutes before placing it in a special niche which had been empty for years, waiting for that moment.

That winter, she took her small family east and commuted between a house in the country and her Manhattan apartment on the East River. Everywhere she went, there were effusive greetings and congratulations. Hers was the biggest comeback story in show business at that time, matched only in 1953 by Frank Sinatra's astounding breakthrough into film and concert superstardom, beginning with *From Here to Eternity*.

When Joan returned to Hollywood, tragedy struck her good friends and Brentwood neighbours, the David Nivens, when Primula Niven fell down some basement steps during a party at the Tyrone Powers's home. She lay unconscious in hospital for several days, and then died. On the night of the accident, Joan offered to take in the Niven children, and they were with her for a fortnight. In this kind action, 'Ma Crawford', as she was known in that Brentwood circle, was far from being any 'Mommie Dearest' and Niven was eternally grateful. [The reader will find no mention in Christina's book, *Mommie Dearest*, of the fortnight during which the Niven children were looked after by Joan Crawford.]

★　★　★

When Joan and Phillip Terry went to New York to attend the wildly acclaimed première of *Mildred Pierce*, it was very reminiscent of Joan's first trip to Europe with Doug Fairbanks, Jr in 1933. Everyone around them could see that they had not come for a much-belated honeymoon, however, but to round off four years of marriage with a civilized finale.

Joan divorced Terry in April 1946. While her career had taken off again and was soaring, he was suffering career setbacks. He was given the role of Ray Milland's brother in the film version of *The Lost Weekend*, for which, of course, Milland won the Oscar for his performance, so that few people even remembered that Terry was in the film. He then played the third male lead in *To Each His Own*, and Olivia de Havilland won an Oscar for her performance in that. Terry lost heart after the divorce, and within a year was out of pictures.

In the same year, Joan was able to return to a 'Crawford-type' role in Fannie Hurst's *Humoresque*. She played a neurotic, wealthy woman who falls in love with a young violinist (John Garfield). She fosters the musician's career with her money, until he becomes very successful, and then, true to her unstable character, and unable to handle or properly respond to his own love for her, she kills herself. The film received the same rave notices as *Mildred Pierce*, and, once again, Joan was made to feel that she was a film actress of skill and importance. No longer did Jack Warner send her Bette Davis rejects.

Producer Jerry Wald then had a script crafted especially for her, called *Possessed*, her third major film for Warner Brothers. (Joan's first film of that title in 1931 was a typical Crawford vehicle of the 1930s in which she played a factory worker in a small town.) The new film was about a woman nurse who becomes involved in an unrequited love affair with an engineer (Van Heflin). Her employer (Raymond Massey) looks on in dismay as she keeps returning to his home emotionally bruised by her encounters with Heflin. When Massey's wife, a patient of Joan's, misguidedly believes that her husband is in love with Joan and kills herself, he turns to Joan in his grief and confusion, chiefly out of pity and loneliness. Heflin is hired by Massey as an engineer, and then nastily begins making up to Joan while becoming engaged to Massey's daughter. Finally, Joan crumbles mentally and shoots Heflin. She is incarcerated in a mental institution, while Massey awaits her recovery.

One upset occurred during the making of *Possessed*, in December 1946. A lawsuit against Joan, Warner Brothers and a Pasadena sanitarium was filed by attorneys on behalf of a Mrs Pauline McKay, asserting that Joan Crawford and three Warner employees from the screen-writing department had watched while Mrs McKay underwent electro-shock therapy. Joan was gathering material for her role as a psychiatric nurse in *Possessed*, which was about to go before the cameras. Mrs McKay was seeking $200,000 in damages.

Jerry Wald, the producer, insisted that no one had done anything wrong. He said: 'Our visit to the sanitarium was all perfectly legal. It was arranged through a doctor. We went there after we visited Los Angeles General Hospital. Raymond Massey, who plays opposite Miss Crawford, was also in the party.' Mrs McKay claimed that they were there without her consent. In February 1947, Joan denied even being present during Mrs McKay's treatment (in fact, she had turned her back in distaste while the electrical charges were going into Mrs McKay's brain). Eventually, the suit was settled out of court for a lesser amount than the $200,000 demanded, but Joan had to endure months of unfavourable publicity because of it. Unfortunately for her, there was no Howard Strickling at Warner Brothers to control the press.

The finished film, however, was worth all the trouble. Two years ahead of *The Snake Pit*, this was the first film seriously to dramatize a mental breakdown, and it did so in such a stylish way that it became something of a sensation. It also gave Joan a new audience – the art-house devotees. It was the first of her films to cross over from the mainstream of film-making to that special audience which preferred French, Czech, Swedish and Italian films, but would accept major American films if they were distinguished and sufficiently off-beat. *Possessed* was also extremely successful with its mainstream audiences, and so, unusually, it generally played in the major cities in two contrasting locations – both the big, centre-of-town cinemas and the little art houses near universities and in other areas foreign to the mainstream film world.

★　★　★

In other words, although *Possessed* was distinctly a Crawford vehicle, harking back to *A Woman's Face* (1941), it brought Joan right up to date. Her image had changed once more – she was the contemporary heroine at home among Freudian obsessions. Once again, she was nominated for an Oscar, but Loretta Young won in what was a considerable upset, as Susan Hayward had been widely expected to win it for her performance in *Smash-Up*.

The post-war era also marked Joan's own peace 'with honour' in her private war to regain her supremacy as a superstar – a war which had been raging parallel to the world conflict since her departure from Metro in 1943. While Joan may well have been affected by the war indirectly, she was never drawn into it, however, as was Martha Raye, for example. Of course, she was still going regularly to the Hollywood Canteen as a hostess, and she invited dozens of servicemen to her mansion for Sunday-afternoon buffets. She knew, of course, that Clark Gable had asked to be discharged as a Major in the Air Force a full year before the end of the war in Europe, but that Doug Fairbanks, Jr, whose life and career she still followed avidly, had been an officer in the United States Navy as a very highly placed liaison between the Americans and the British until the last shot was fired in the Pacific in 1945.

Joan liked to believe that she was very patriotic, but her real commitments to the American soldier and his needs would not consume all her energies until the 1960s, when she had left Hollywood, and there was an entirely different kind of war – a hateful war in most regards – which would draw her into an almost full-time commitment to the USO.

Meanwhile, throughout 1946, she had tried (not very successfully) to show an impartiality towards actors who had come home from long wartime service, as opposed to actors who, for varying reasons, did not serve at all and usurped the roles of leading men throughout the long years of the Second World War.

She was very cynical, for instance, about the on-screen heroics of super-macho John Wayne, who became a much bigger star during the war, while his peers were risking their lives. Privately, she viewed such men with contempt, but in the winter of 1946–7, she asked for Dana Andrews, who did not serve in the war, to play one of her leading men in Otto Preminger's *Daisy Kenyon*, along with Henry Fonda, who very definitely did.

Joan was borrowed by Twentieth-Century Fox for the production of *Daisy Kenyon*. She had complained to anyone who would listen that Warner Brothers was falling into the same fatal pattern as Metro had done, designing her films to a stereotype which bored her, and had let it be known that she wanted to be loaned out to other studios. Otto Preminger at Twentieth-Century Fox had made the necessary arrangements.

Daisy Kenyon was typical Crawford fare, with Joan playing a commercial artist who falls in love with a married corporate lawyer (Dana Andrews) and must keep the romance in its proper 'back-street' perspective. Then Henry Fonda, who has no other ties, enters her life. Circumstances in Andrews's marriage worsen and he gets a divorce, but Daisy (Joan) rightly chooses to resist him and to stay with Henry.

Henry Fonda was unhappily married at the time to a socialite (and the mother of Jane and Peter), who would kill herself within two years in a fit of depression over her husband's affairs. Dore Schary, Metro's new production chief and a celebrated raconteur, told the story that Joan found Henry very attractive, but was getting nowhere with her flirtation on the set. Finally, she asked the wardrobe department to make up a jock-strap with rhinestones, gold sequins and red beads. She had it handsomely gift-wrapped and then gave it to Henry on the set early one morning. He opened it and turned it over quizzically several times until it dawned on him what it was. The next scene required Henry to carry Joan up some stairs, and she whispered in his ear, 'How about modelling it for me later?' Henry, flustered, nearly dropped her.

★　★　★

Joan made two more films for Warner Brothers at the end of the 1940s, both of which had her typecast in roles that she was no longer interested in playing. In *Flamingo Road* (1949), she is a carnival dancer stranded in a southern town, where she finds herself up against a political boss (Sydney Greenstreet). His deputy (Zachary Scott) is weak-willed but decent, and falls in love with Joan. Greenstreet manages to get Joan into prison on a trumped-up prostitution charge. After several turns of the creaky plot, Joan, released from prison and determined on revenge, takes a gun and, in a confrontation with Greenstreet, kills him. The film ends with Joan in prison again, but hoping for an appeal in her favour, while Zachary Scott tells her that he will be waiting for her.

In *The Damned Don't Cry*, made in late 1949, Joan was, once again, carrying the picture. She is in every scene, and it is clearly a star vehicle. Her impassive style drains away some of the drama in certain key scenes, such as the accident which claims the life of her only boy. Her wide eyes simply become wider as a huge truck rolls over him and his bicycle (off-screen), and she literally walks through the picture.

It does not help that her co-star, David Brian, is stiff-necked and super-macho in his role as head of a criminal mob. The script is so predictable that some of the scenes are simply talked about rather than being enacted, as they have been done on the screen so many times before.

The film comes to life very near the end when Ethel (Joan) meets an upstart gangster (Steve Cochran) and has a brief affair with him. If Joan herself were not having an affair at the time with the film's director, Vincent Sherman, it would seem likely that she and Cochran would have had a mild fling at the very least.

For Crawford fans, the film is a medley of all her familiar routines, and she plays them with her usual competence. From a biographer's point of view, Joan can be seen in some of her films much as she was in life – keeping her emotions at a low boil, and seeing life as mostly harsh so that her personal defences are visible.

Warner Brothers' intention was obviously to repeat Joan's success in *Flamingo Road*. As with Metro eight years earlier, Joan was becoming far too much a Warner Brothers asset, which the studio was afraid to alter in any significant way. It was more than apparent to her that her days there were numbered. She would have to make a graceful exit.

Joan's romantic life away from the screen was also busy. Following her divorce from Phillip Terry in April 1946, she had had a brief affair with Don 'Red' Barry, a cowboy actor in Republic westerns. The wire services covered the romance as though it were serious news. Joan seemed to be much taken with Barry at first, and he in turn was so overwhelmed by her interest in him that he went out and bought her a white mink coat and several valuable pieces of jewellery, all on credit. He also conferred with agent Charlie Feldman about buying the rights to the hit Broadway play, *Anna Lucasta*, for Joan, as she had expressed an interest in making it into a film one day. This was what ended the romance, however – Barry had promised to 'deliver' Joan as the star in a production deal he was building around *Anna Lucasta*, and Joan rebelled. Barry did not have the $200,000 required to purchase the play, and was trying to raise the money through his connection with her. Joan promptly announced that the romance was at an end. She kept some of his gifts, completing their purchase herself, and returned those for which no payment had been made.

A redeeming legacy of Joan's involvement with Barry was her memory of Greg Bautzer, the Hollywood attorney 'to the stars'. Barry made a crack about Joan in a bar, and Bautzer gallantly defended her reputation by taking a swing at him. Bautzer lost several front teeth in the ensuing fracas, and Joan, touched by the gesture, paid for the dental work required to replace them.

NINE

EMBATTLED LOVERS AND THE SECRET TWINS

Greg Bautzer had telephoned Joan the week after she won her Oscar for *Mildred Pierce* but she refused his call. When he bribed Joan's studio secretary and found out that Joan was going to the La Quinta Hotel in Palm Springs for the weekend, he followed her there and confronted her: 'Look, Joan. I can't break through that telephone guard of yours in town. You're either busy, or not in, or not talking. But I'm here, you're here. It's a beautiful night. Let's go dancing.' They danced until dawn and remained together for the entire weekend, swimming, playing tennis, and 'recovering' in bed.

Bautzer showered gifts on Joan, including a gold charm-bracelet with one gold heart and a gold key, and a gold cigarette case encrusted with rubies and engraved: 'Forever and Ever' – words from the song, 'Always and Always', which Joan had sung in *Mannequin* back in 1938. He listened to her long, long telephone calls as though he had all the time in the world, when, in fact, other callers were getting impatient.

Joan's old friend Willie Haines approved of the match, and told Greg that, to be Joan's beau, a man had to be a 'combination of bull and butler'. Rosalind Russell said of them:

'He treated her like a star. When they entered a room, he remained a few steps behind her. He often carried her dog or her knitting bag – she was always knitting – and, at the dinner table, Greg did everything but feed her. Joan expected her escort to place her napkin in her lap, light her cigarettes and open doors for her. Not many men would put up with it. Greg did all these things without losing his masculinity. He made it seem as if it were the natural thing to do. They were nuts about each other.'

After having completed production on *Possessed* early in 1947, Joan went to Las Vegas to conclude the adoption process for two infant girls. While one of these adopted daughters insisted to me that they were indeed twins, as Joan always referred to them, newspaper reports at the time suggest that Cathy and Cindy – as she named them – were really born several weeks apart to different parents.

While in Las Vegas, Joan ran into Bautzer, who was there with Billy Wilkerson, publisher of the *Hollywood Reporter*. Joan was immediately aware that Bautzer was as attractive as ever, and very soon their on-again, off-again relationship was resumed. In her view, he had stood the test. Joan clearly believed that, if a lover could not stand up to slaps and physical punishment, then the affair could not be worthwhile. Once again, we must look at her role as a mother and wonder whether she were not practising the same sort of 'slug 'em and love 'em' philosophy here, too, as Christina and Christopher grew out of the cute toddler stage, because their mother treated them much as she did Bautzer.

As for the twins, what is most interesting about them is that, from the very beginning, they were closer to Joan than Christina and Christopher could ever be. While the older children seemed to behave only from a fear of discipline, Cindy and Cathy never misbehaved. To an observer, the situation ranged from one extreme to the other – the younger children rarely strayed far from Joan's side, while Christina and Christopher seemed locked in a never-ending struggle to escape their mother's tyranny, whether real or imagined. Christopher often ran away – certainly a clue to his unhappiness – and Christina also ran off once or twice. When they were old enough, they were both sent off to boarding school – Christopher to a military academy and Christina to the fashionable Chadwick School in Palos Verdes.

From Joan's point of view, she felt that she had done everything possible to be a good mother. Every year, for instance, she took time off to escort the girls and Christopher to Pebble Beach at Carmel, on the Pacific coast, and away from Brentwood, she was far less harsh and demanding. The young twins grew up remarkably free of any threat of punishment, and never came to hate their mother as Christina and Christopher were to do.

The rumour that Cathy and Cindy Crawford were *not* twins had begun to circulate early in their life at the Brentwood mansion. Joan was aware of it, and everyone around her had heard the story. As her secretary, Betty Barker, explained:

'I knew they were twins, but I never asked Joan because it was none of my business. I figured if she wanted to tell me, she could tell me. I think that's what most people felt. They didn't want to ask her . . . I think Joan didn't mind that the rumour was [around] that they were not twins because she was afraid that she would lose her kids like she lost the first Chris.

'But they *are* twins and Cathy found out all the details of her birth and her sister's birth, and their mother died when they were five days old.

'Cindy is [now] divorced [from her Iowa-based first husband] and lives down in Memphis.'

★   ★   ★

There had been a three-year interlude in Joan's affair with Greg Bautzer. In 1949 Bautzer began dating first Merle Oberon, and then Ginger Rogers. He had been irked by Joan's temperament, and by an incident in which Joan had asked him to check for a possible flat tyre on the way home from a party. While he was checking the tyre she drove away, leaving him stranded miles from his apartment.

Bautzer's affair with Rogers was serious – at least on her part – and on one occasion, in order to retaliate, Joan invited producer William Dozier to escort her to a dinner-dance thrown by Louis B. Mayer for Henry Ford II. At the Beverly Wilshire ballroom, they encountered Bautzer, who danced by with Rogers's cheek pressed close against his own. Joan pretended not to see this, but within half an hour she had disappeared from the party.

When Dozier telephoned Joan to find out whether she was all right, she was sobbing, so Dozier agreed to go out to her house to calm her down. When he got to the Bristol Avenue mansion, the maid told him that she had retired. The next morning, he walked into his office at the Columbia Studios and found it filled with flowers, with a note saying, 'Dear Bill, Please forgive a poor, frightened little girl. Love, Joan.'

Bautzer and Joan finally called it a draw and went their separate ways, although she continued to call on him from time to time for legal advice. His role in the centre ring at the Brentwood mansion was assumed by Vincent Sherman, a director at Warner Brothers, who for two entire years was in charge of Joan's career and her bedroom.

Sherman had been an actor, and first appeared in a supporting role in John Barrymore's film, *Counsellor-at-Large* (1933), but he really wanted to direct. In 1936, when the WPA Federal Theatre was at its peak, he was chosen to direct the New York production of the stage version of Sinclair Lewis's *It Can't Happen Here* (which, in an unusual move choreographed by the Theatre's head, Hallie Flanagan, opened simultaneously on the same day in fifteen cities across America).

Sherman then returned to Hollywood as a screen-writer, and wrote three forgettable films before directing a horror film entitled *The Return of Doctor X* (1939). Although only a year younger than Joan, he rapidly advanced to the forefront of house directors for Warner Brothers, directing Ida Lupino, Bette Davis, and, finally, Joan. His best-known films with Davis were *Old Acquaintance* (1943) and *Mr Skeffington* (1944), and, with Lupino, *In Our Time* (1944). With Joan, he directed *The Damned Don't Cry* (1950) at Warner Brothers, then *Harriet Craig* (1950) at Columbia (at Joan's personal request, as he had to be borrowed from Warner Brothers), and finally *Goodbye My Fancy* (1951), again for Warner Brothers.

Sherman was a compactly built man with the look of a middle-weight fighter. His nose had been broken at some point, and he greatly resembled the boxer, Max Baer, except that Baer was a taller and bigger man. Sherman caught Joan's interested glance before they ever worked together, and they began an open affair, despite the fact that Sherman was married. Joan and Sherman's wife sometimes spoke on the telephone together, and, at least once after a quarrel, Joan phoned his wife and told her 'You can have him' and sent him packing.

The best of the Vincent Sherman films in which Joan starred in the late 1940s and early '50s was *Harriet Craig* (1950), a re-make of George Kelly's play, *Craig's Wife*. It was the first of six pictures that Joan would make for Columbia during the 1950s and '60s.

Those who knew Joan realized at once that there were elements of her own character in Harriet. She was playing a wife whose one great obsession in life is with her immaculate house – she will not even allow cut flowers in her living-room because they are messy and drop petals. She drives everyone away from her until finally she is left alone in her house, her husband having seen the hopeless and sterile character of his wife at last. Joan was not blind to the parallels, but she drew on her own resources for every role she played, and this was no exception.

In the film, she allowed only her dark side to show. She knew that she had this self-obsessed drive in her, but always had the intelligence to know that it could offend. As Harriet, however, Sherman (who knew her intimately, of course) urged her to repress her tendencies towards generosity and her need to be liked (if not loved), and to allow her streak of meanness – which she knew she had possessed at least in her early years of climbing to stardom – to dominate her characterization. [When stardom was assured, and she relaxed in her new role as queen of the movies, a 'nice' Joan Crawford was the image promoted in all of her press releases.]

George Kelly's trump card in writing the play twenty-five years earlier was the way in which it had ended, with Walter

Craig smashing his wife's favourite porcelain antique and walking out on her, leaving her absolutely alone in her empty house. In the version updated for Joan, at producer Bill Dozier's request, the screen-writers left this intact. Conceivably, the same thing could have happened to Joan in real life, and both Doug Fairbanks, Jr and Franchot Tone must have seen the irony if they watched the film.

Joan's affair with Vincent Sherman, like her relationship with Bautzer, was marked by crude brawls in which Joan would be battered to the point where her screams and the blows drew daughter Christina to rush into her mother's room to stop the mayhem. As this had also happened with Franchot Tone and then with Bautzer, it seems logical to assume that Joan was drawn to abusive men (although in Tone's case, one is tempted to believe that he came into the affair and marriage with an idealization of Joan, and never struck her until he was either goaded into doing so or *asked* to do so).

In 1951, the affair with Sherman ended abruptly, soon after Joan's 'rescue' by Christina. She reconciled with Bautzer and, because they were seen so constantly together, gossip resumed about their possible marriage. They still had their differences, but seemed drawn to each other. He was a lot like Clark Gable — a 'man's man' — and he was easily provoked to raise his fists in a bar-room or someone's home. He often drank until he could barely stand up, and he gambled frequently. Joan, on the other hand, seldom quarrelled in public. She could hold her liquor amazingly well, and she never gambled on anything. They were opposites except in their sexual behaviour; they both enjoyed 'rough sex'. Joan occasionally gave friends such as press agent Henry Rogers hints about the status of her relationship with Bautzer. One Saturday morning, Rogers ran into her at the Farmers' Market off Fairfax in Hollywood, and she pulled him aside and lifted her oversized dark glasses to show him a very black eye — an old-fashioned 'shiner'. 'He loves me,' she said by way of explanation.

After an all-night poker game, drunker than usual, Bautzer

ploughed his car into a lamppost and mailbox on Wilshire Boulevard. He made the front pages of the newspapers the next day, and Joan pretended at least to be so shocked that she broke off with him once more. Bautzer, in turn, pretended not to care and began romancing his favourite leading ladies. Joan, enraged, packed her bags, took the children and went east to stay at the Hampshire House hotel in New York. According to Henry Rogers, she went with four trunks and she came home with eleven, all loaded with gifts from Bautzer.

Naturally, however, the affair could not last. Joan's spies told her that Bautzer had had lunch for two days running at the Columbia Studio with Rita Hayworth, and Joan broke off with him again by changing her telephone number and taking up with handsome Peter Shaw, the Irish actor and writer (who married Angela Lansbury in 1949). Shaw, however, was too strong a personality to remain long as prince consort to the queen of Hollywood, and they soon parted. Bautzer made the first move to resume their long-running affair.

Whenever Bautzer and Joan appeared in the foyer at a party, a definite hush silenced the guests and all eyes became fixed on the entrance to the room. Bautzer and Joan loved such moments and made the most of them. They would smile at their entranced 'subjects', before gliding into the room. Then, as if on cue, everyone resumed what they were doing before their majesties arrived.

The couple exchanged expensive gifts. One evening, before they were to go out to a formal party, she gave him a pair of diamond cuff links from Cartier's to wear with his dinner jacket. Bautzer was always curious to know the value of their romance to Joan, so this time he went into Cartier's and asked how much they had cost. He was told $10,000.

Shortly after this, they had another of their all-night brawls. It was over their unfaithfulness to each other. Joan had been told that Bautzer was seen having lunch with Lana Turner and even holding her hand. Bautzer, in his turn, shouted that he knew that Joan had been seeing Charles Martin, a screen-writer and director

(*I'll Be Seeing You*; *Death of a Scoundrel*), and that she was introducing him as her new beau. [Housemaid Senta Vincent told me that Charles Martin lived in Joan's house for a long time, but that Joan was not in love with him. 'He was ten or fifteen years younger than she was,' she said. 'He was also very lazy.']

Bautzer became so angry that, as he was leaving, he ripped off the diamond cuff links and gave them back to Joan. She, in turn, was so infuriated by this gesture that she stormed into the bathroom and flushed them down the lavatory. Then she suddenly sobered up enough to cry, 'Oh my God! What have I done?' She forbade anyone to use the lavatories until a plumber could come the next morning. Once he had found the cuff links in the bend of a pipe and retrieved them, Joan paid his $500 charge happily. Meanwhile, Bautzer had left the house in such a blind rage that, on the way home, he smashed the black Cadillac which Joan had given him into a brick wall.

Such behaviour in Hollywood meant that a romance was more than just a temporary affair, and Henry Rogers was besieged by the Hollywood press corps for specifics about Joan and Bautzer. 'Are they getting married or not?' Rogers would ask Joan what to tell them, and she invariably said, 'Check it out with Greg.' Joan knew, of course, that Greg had never proposed. Cautious lawyer that he was, he was not about to commit himself to a roller-coaster life with anyone as mercurial as Joan.

Rogers and others were convinced that if Bautzer ever proposed to Joan, she would quickly agree and that would be that, but he could never bring himself to do so. Instead, whenever asked about possible Crawford-Bautzer nuptials, Bautzer would say, 'I wish I could be that lucky.' Henry Rogers, for one, thought the response was brilliant and asked Bautzer how he came up with it. Bautzer told him, 'I've been trying for a long time to think of something that would make Joan come off like a queen and still make me look good. With that quote, it makes people think that I want to marry her and she won't have me, but my friends know the truth. They'll laugh and say, "Bautzer scored again."' Hedda Hopper, for one, laughed at Bautzer's comment, and told Rogers,

'That son of a bitch can really come up with those one-liners.'

The relationship reached a climax one night. Joan was asleep on her unheated sleeping porch (one of her spartan habits towards her well-being), when, as she told Henry Rogers:

'I heard noises outside one of my windows. I quickly identified them as footsteps and thought immediately of pushing the alarm next to my bed, but I decided it must be one of the security guards who patrol the grounds at night. Then the noises got louder. It sounded like branches of bushes and trees creaking and breaking. Someone was climbing the tree outside my window and the lattice-work on the side of the house. I heard a scrambling of hands and feet, grunts and inaudible cuss words coming from whoever it was out there. I was terrified and paralysed with fear. I knew I should scream and push the alarm, but at that very moment there was a horrendous crash. Someone had smashed one of the windows and was climbing through. It was Greg. His hands were bleeding. He had smashed the window with his fists. I was still terrified and I watched him take off his clothes, charge toward me, throwing off my covers, tearing off my nightgown and then the sonovabitch raped me!'

'"Oh, come on now, Joan," Rogers said. "He didn't rape you."

'"Of course, he didn't. But it sounds better that way. I'll never forget his grabbing me with his bloody hands. In a moment his blood was all over my body, all over the bed . . . And I want you to know, Henry, it was the most exciting sexual experience of my life!"'

While Joan seemed to be self-sufficient emotionally, she still needed the ears of friends whom she could trust during this critical time in her life when she was shoring up her renewed career as a top-grossing star. She confided in Cesar Romero, Willie Haines and Henry Rogers. She showed all of them her gift to Bautzer, which she presented him just after she had received her first big cheque from the earnings of *Sudden Fear* in 1952 – a black Cadillac convertible (the car which he subsequently crashed into a wall on the night of the diamond cuff links incident). When Bautzer protested at the gift, she told him: 'I'm a producer now. I can afford it. Shut up!' She had recently signed a deal to co-produce other films with Joseph Kaufman (the producer of *Sudden Fear*) for RKO Pictures.

Bautzer worried constantly about Joan overspending. He knew about her permanent rooms at the Hollywood Presbyterian and then the Cedars of Lebanon Hospitals, which she maintained for film people and indigent newspapermen. He also knew that she had given a huge sum of money to the Texas Theatres' Crippled Children's Fund, towards the expansion of their Warm Springs Foundation, as well as making a promotional trailer to be shown in cinemas for donations.

In the autumn of 1952, Noël Coward visited Hollywood. Joan had first met him when she was married to Doug, Jr, and knew that the two men were close friends. Joan gave Noël a formal dinner at Le Pavilion and invited two hundred guests, including two of her ex-husbands, Doug, Jr and Franchot Tone. Bautzer was Joan's co-host, and they were arm-in-arm throughout much of the evening. When asked what he thought of Bautzer, Coward later said: 'Too many teeth.'

It was quite an evening. Jack Benny played the violin, and Noël performed a party number with Celeste Holm. Willie Haines decorated the main banquet room, converting it into a small garden of Versailles with showers of pink gardenias. Tony Martin and Dinah Shore sang. Other famous guests in attendance that night included Anne Baxter, Clifton Webb and his mother, Maybelle, Gene Tierney, Irene Dunne, Robert Taylor and his wife, Barbara Stanwyck, Jane Wyman and Marlene Dietrich.

TEN

THE QUIET REVOLUTION

Hollywood in the 1950s was slowly becoming a different place from the town conquered by Joan in the 1930s. As television continued making inroads on the film business, the studios had to divest themselves of their chains of movie houses by Government edict. This was the beginning of the end for the old studio-peonage system. The independent film-makers also came into their own, and no longer had to look to United Artists for financing and distribution. *All* the studios began to release films like United Artists, scouring the world for films or 'packages' (a deal involving a director, one or two stars, a good script and a producer).

By 1953, Otto Preminger's *The Moon Is Blue* went out without a Production-code seal of approval and the sky did not fall. In that case, the seal was denied because the word 'pregnant' was on the soundtrack. A great many films were put into production which were adult in theme, and, as the 1950s wound down, there were very few family-fare pictures still coming out of Hollywood.

The big stars – usually male – founded their own production companies, Burt Lancaster being the first with Hecht-Lancaster Productions. Marilyn Monroe founded her own production unit and co-produced *The Prince and the Showgirl* (1957), as well as making three films for Twentieth-Century Fox as a full production partner.

As for the blacklist created by the House Unamerican Activities Committee, which persisted in some cases for nearly twenty years, it insidiously began to change the content of films, while many familiar faces (some of them industry figures whose faces were *not* known to the public), had disappeared from the scene. Gone, of course, was Donald Ogden Stewart, who had written the screenplay for *A Woman's Face* (1941) and who was now an exile in England, a victim of the political purge. Jules Dassin, who had directed Joan in *Reunion in France* (1943), had also fled to Europe after being blacklisted. In Dassin's case, his career later took off magnificently with his international hit film, *Never on Sunday* (1960), starring his uniquely gifted wife, Melina Mercouri. Other victims included Melvyn Douglas, Joan's co-star in *A Woman's Face*, who was blacklisted for ten years, and John Garfield, her leading man in *Humoresque* (1946), who died of a heart attack after being hounded out of films by the House Unamerican Activities Committee.

Joan thought of herself as apolitical, and never did learn that the FBI had opened a large file on her 'subversive' activities before and during the Second World War. Luckily, the HUAC chose to ignore all this because 'after the war, she was known throughout the film community as an anti-communist' (a quote from her FBI file).

★   ★   ★

By the 1950s, sexuality on the screen had altered drastically with the advent of Marilyn Monroe. There had been an uproar about sex in films back in the Jean Harlow era, but, with Marilyn, it suddenly became something so innocent and normal that even children could safely watch her films. Joan did not see this as an immediate threat because her own sexuality was mature and sophisticated, but suddenly it seemed that those two adjectives were potentially deadly.

Ever the careful analyst of industry changes, she invited Marilyn one day to Sunday brunch at her Brentwood house. Marilyn felt honoured by the invitation, and arrived on time for a change. The two women shared an interest in Christian Science, but that topic was quickly exhausted and Joan asked whether Marilyn would like to see her wardrobe. They adjourned to the master suite, where a room-sized closet held a hundred or more of Joan's outfits. Marilyn was wearing something obvious and snug-fitting, and Joan thought she might give her one of her dresses. It turned out, however, that Marilyn was several sizes larger than Joan, and, after she had tried several outfits, it became clear that she could not wear Joan's clothes.

There is some mystery about what happened next. Joan had been drinking all afternoon, whereas Marilyn was sober when she arrived but had then had several drinks with her hostess. Later, Marilyn told her press agent, Rupert Allen, that Joan had made a subtle pass while she, Marilyn, was partially undressed. Perhaps this was true, or perhaps Joan merely made an affectionate gesture – a squeeze of the shoulder or a pat on the cheek – gestures which were immediately misinterpreted by Marilyn, who was at the time deeply involved in an affair she did not want with her drama coach and mentor, Natasha Lytess. Marilyn left almost immediately, and over her vodka Joan nursed her hurt feelings and regretted having invited Marilyn to her home.

Several months later, Marilyn was to appear at the *Photoplay* Magazine Gold Medal Award ceremonies to accept the award as 'Best new star of the year'. Joan arrived a minute or two late, just long enough to make a grand entrance and be photographed and so forth. But the winner of the main award was, as was her custom, *very* late. She arrived on the arm of columnist Sidney Skolsky, wearing a gold-lamé dress into which she had been sewn, and had to take tiny steps because she was hobbled by the gown. Her décolletage was so deep that it ran to her stomach.

All the men in the room seemed charged by Marilyn's presence, and Jerry Lewis leaped on a table and began pawing it with his feet. Joan claimed that she was sickened by the vulgarity of it all, and later told Bob Thomas of the Associated Press: 'There's nothing wrong with my tits, but I don't go around throwing them in people's faces . . . actresses should be ladies.'

Marilyn was distraught upon reading Joan's criticism and truly did not connect it with her own abrupt departure from the

Crawford mansion – that sort of thing happened to her so frequently that she thought it was normal. She told a reporter: 'I've always admired her for being such a wonderful mother – for taking four children and giving them a fine home. Who better than I knows what that means to homeless little ones?'

★   ★   ★

Joan entered the 'new' film world early with *Sudden Fear* (1952). It came as no surprise to anyone that she was the first major female star to take such an independent turn, but she had become thoroughly fed up with the 'trash', as she called it, that Warner Brothers was giving her. Her last film for them, *This Woman is Dangerous*, which was released in early 1952, was so dreadful that she asked to be let out of her contract, and she said of the film: 'That woman wasn't dangerous. She was just a big bore.'

From *Sudden Fear*, onwards Joan only made films as an independent star, although, like Marilyn Monroe, she did enter into one three-picture deal (with Columbia Pictures). Being a free agent was harder on Joan than on some stars, because she had always looked to the studio for guidance as well as for her income. The industry had shifted ground, however, and such paternalism was gone.

Joan was eternally grateful for having been born in a country which allowed someone as bereft of so many elements for success as herself to be given a single chance with her quiver to hit the bullseye. Just one shot, and she had managed it – but, unlike most of her peers, she had never relaxed afterwards. Christina wrote that Joan was extremely edgy as an independent star, and always worried about her next film, but the truth was that she had always been that way about her career. Crowning triumphs in the past had never given her a sense that she had arrived at a particular plateau. She never had taken one success for granted.

The plot of *Sudden Fear* grabs the viewer early in the film and holds tight until the surprising end. Joan is a playwright who marries an actor she once fired. She accidentally overhears a taped conversation between her husband and his old girlfriend, who are plotting her murder. She then plans her revenge, and schemes to outwit her husband and Irene, the girlfriend, by ensuring that Lester, her husband, will die and that Irene will be framed for the murder. Lester discovers her plan at the last minute and, in a car, follows a fleeing woman whom he thinks is his wife, and runs her down. His car goes out of control, however, and it is revealed that the victim is Irene, his girlfriend. Both are killed in the car crash.

Sudden Fear was released by RKO Pictures in late summer, 1952, and the critical acclaim and box-office activity were almost exact repeats of the sensation caused five years earlier by *Possessed.* The film was stylish and suspenseful, and, with it, Joan established herself as mistress of the chic thriller. The film also made its eccentric-looking leading man, Jack Palance, a major star. Not handsome and with a mask-like face, he seemed an unlikely candidate for stardom and Joan had resisted him at first, but she could always listen to reason and in this case it paid off.

At about the same time that she was leaving the security of her Warner contract to become an independent and make *Sudden Fear*, Joan was invited by the New American Library in New York, which published a distinguished list of (mostly original) paperbacks known as Mentor Books, to write a brief account of her rise as a star in the 1920s for a collection of brief memoirs by great Americans. Her section of the book was entitled 'Four Figures in the Amusement Field', the other three being composer W. C. Handy, Babe Ruth, baseball's home run king, and Joe Louis, the legendary world-heavyweight boxing champion. Joan's eight-page account is the most sanitized version of her life to see print. While still not exactly candid, in her ghost-written memoir, *A Portrait of Joan*, published eleven years later, she would be far more forthcoming in talking about her life.

Joan should surely have been content at this point in her life. If we are to believe Christina, however, it was just then, in the wake of *Sudden Fear*'s enormous success around the world, that she turned vicious towards the children. In her book, *Mommie Dearest*, Christina dismisses the unanimous acceptance of her mother's film, and fails to tell us that she had become one of the hottest actresses in town.

One of the chief flaws in Christina's memoir is a distortion of known facts in Joan's life, or, sometimes, a questionable interpretation of those facts. A notable example is near the middle of her book, when she is describing events that took place in the autumn of 1952, after she had entered the ninth grade at the Chadwick School. It should be remembered that *Sudden Fear*, which had opened in August and been a smash hit, had now moved into general world release, and that Joan was on top of her profession again. Scripts were piling up on her desk – some of them very good ones that she would never have the time to do. Joan Crawford was perhaps the most in-demand middle-aged actress in American films. Yet Christina wrote of this same period:

'My mother called me at school one night extremely upset. She said she had very bad news for me. From the tone of her voice and her choice of words, I thought someone died. Then she told me that she'd left Warner Brothers [actually, she had left them the previous year]. She said that she no longer had a contract, she didn't have a job, and she was almost totally broke.'

The month after *Sudden Fear*'s release – the same month that Joan phoned Christina at school, Radie Harris, writing in the *Los Angeles Times*, stated that the film would net Joan over a million dollars as its star, having taken a percentage in lieu of salary. She actually owned fifty per cent of the film. With sums like these flooding into her coffers, it is highly unlikely that she would have given daughter Christina a sob story about having no money and no job. If Joan had accepted all the job offers which flooded her office following the release of *Sudden Fear*, she would have had to work non-stop for two decades.

Christina continued: 'But when the picture finished filming, Mother was right back in the position of having to find another job . . .' Here we move from distortion to borderline falsehood, because Joan had her pick of several film projects. She was still in the forefront for the role of Karen Holmes in *From Here to Eternity*, and, even though that fell through due to her own excessive demands (if she had had a trace of humility in her make-up, she would have withdrawn her demand for the use of her own dress designer, Sheila O'Brien, and got on with the picture). Her fall-back position, of course, was the stack of scripts on her desk, all waiting for her magic approval.

★　　★　　★

Joan spent all of February 1953 working at Paramount on an Irving Asher production, Irving being one of her oldest and dearest friends. *Lisbon* was a tale of international intrigue, and Asher and his writers were changing the gender of the leading role and 'feminizing' it as a vehicle for Joan. The script just did not gel, however, and Joan was often just sitting in her dressing-room, a lavishly furnished suite originally designed for Betty Hutton.

Several years earlier, Warner Brothers tried a similar experiment, buying a novel called *The Fall of Valour* by Charles Jackson about a closet homosexual and his fears of his wife and family learning of his sexual preference. It was Joan's suggestion that they change the protagonist's gender, but everyone then realized that it had simply become another story of a rotten marriage, and the project was abandoned. By the end of February, Asher had also given up on *Lisbon*.

In early March Joan returned to Metro to film a charity-fund appeal to be shown in movie-houses for the United Cerebral Palsy Drive. It was her first visit there since her departure ten years earlier. Her dressing-room was filled with flowers sent by Dore Schary, who had taken over the reins from Louis B. Mayer several years earlier, and Robert Taylor, who vied with Van Johnson for the title of number one fan among her fellow stars. Eddie Mannix, Mayer's longtime aide, led a delegation from the Administration Building to welcome her. Joan's director on *Sudden Fear*, David Miller, was handling the direction of this very short subject as a favour to Joan.

Literally dozens of stage-hands, electricians, grips and gaffers came through the doorway to Stage 16 to see her, a number of them waiting outside while the blinking red light signalled that shooting was underway. Lew Roberts had been number one boy on *Sally, Irene and Mary*, Ralph Pender had been the mixer on *Untamed*, Frank Tanner had been Joan's favourite still photographer.

The entire sound-stage seemed to be overflowing with nostalgia and affection, and Joan did not miss a single first name in greeting them all. She was not the film queen with these old friends, although later they all in one way or another abetted that notion. She honestly felt that she was one of them and that they were her peers, and they clearly felt the same way about her. The entire scene could have been copied from Norma Desmond's return to the old Paramount studio, except that there was no trace of Desmond's egomania and more than a touch of family reunion in the event.

By June, Joan was back at Metro again, this time to do a major feature called *Torch Song*. Everyone was ready for her arrival, and Howard Strickling had hung a banner over the main studio street reading: 'Welcome back, Joan!' The studio had the dressing-rooms of three stars who were not shooting at the time knocked together into one huge dressing-suite, and flowers and candy tributes filled the room on her first day. Clark Gable sent a huge basket of chocolate goodies from Italy, and Ann Blyth (from *Mildred Pierce*), who owed her career as a star to Joan, came on to the set on the first day bearing a huge bouquet of orchids.

Joan's director on the film, Charles Walters, was a specialist in musicals, having directed *Easter Parade* and *Good News*, among others. Joan worked very hard, and she and Walters were together constantly, but he admitted afterwards that she had always remained Joan Crawford, the star, and that he had never seen anything beyond the surface.

In the story, Joan plays Jenny Stewart, an egocentric musical-comedy star whose rehearsal pianist quits, unable to take her stinging criticisms. His replacement is a blind man (Michael

Wilding), of whom Joan turns out to be even more critical than the man he replaced. Joan is desperately lonely inside, however, and slowly she responds to the blind man, who fell in love with her many years ago when he had his sight and was a second-string drama critic. Naturally, they come together by the end because of mutual need and love.

For reasons unknown, India Adams dubbed the songs for Joan, although Joan had been allowed to sing in her previous films. Her voice did have a little quiver in it, but she always sang on-key and in a pleasing contralto (the Brunswick label released two or three of her own renditions of popular tunes which she had introduced on screen). To Joan's fans, of course, the film was a delight, as it was in Technicolor, and she sang, danced and carried the picture.

Screen-writer Michael Hayes made Joan's character, Jenny Stewart, so one-dimensionally tough and hard-edged in the film that it is hard to believe that passive-looking, soft-spoken Michael Wilding will change his mind about her and go off into the Philadelphia or Hartford sunset. Unlike Joan's earlier heroines with a sharp tongue, Jenny Stewart is almost totally unsympathetic.

Helping the film in her own small way was screen veteran Marjorie Rambeau, playing Joan's mother. She is one of the most believable elements in the picture and, when she swigs down her tankard of beer, we know that she is enjoying it and that she is a genuine piece of Jenny's background. On the other hand, Gig Young, the master of sardonic commentary, is wasted as her parasitical lover. The fault is not Young's, however, but Hayes's script and very possibly Charles Walters's surprisingly unexciting direction (he had directed *Lili* only the previous year).

Most of the critics of the day liked the film, however, including Otis Gurnsey, Jr of *The New York Herald Tribune*, who commented:

'Here is Joan Crawford all over the screen, in command, in love and in colour, a real movie star in what amounts to a carefully produced one-woman show. Miss Crawford's acting is sheer and colourful as a painted arrow, aimed straight at the sensibility of her particular fans.'

Michael Wilding, Joan's co-star in *Torch Song*, was born in England in 1912. Unlike many British actors, he spent several years in films before going on to the stage in musical comedy. In 1942, he appeared in Noël Coward's patriotic war film, *In Which We Serve*, and in 1943, ten years before *Torch Song*, he became close to John Gielgud, who was his mentor for several years.

When Elizabeth Taylor first became interested in Wilding, he was one of Marlene Dietrich's several younger lovers. Elizabeth still persuaded him to marry her (it was his second marriage), and the wedding took place in 1952, the year in which he was first mentioned as a lead opposite Joan in *Torch Song*.

Elizabeth had heard of Joan's boast – or admission – that she always slept with her leading men during a production (or her director, or occasionally, both). Elizabeth therefore kept a close eye on her husband's current film, especially as both she and Wilding were shocked to learn that Joan was spending twenty-four hours a day on the set and not going home. 'My god!' Wilding told his young wife. 'She even sleeps there!'

Wilding is one of Joan's few leading men whom she fails to mention in her autobiography. A softly handsome man with a passive look in his very blue eyes, he probably avoided Joan except for the actual work between them. Joan knew, too, that Metro had given him his contract at Elizabeth Taylor's insistence. He never got very far in American films, and readily confessed that he was lazy.

Elizabeth was filming *Rhapsody* (one of her few failures) on an adjoining set, and the couple met at the Metro commissary for lunch. Elizabeth would often come on to the set of *Torch Song* when she was free and at least acknowledged Joan's presence with a nod, but publicity man Dore Freeman recalled that 'One time she came on the set and she snubbed Joan by not saying "hello."' Joan called Freeman over (as with a score of other Metro employees, she had got him the job there) and said: 'You tell that little bitch never to walk in here again without acknowledging me. I want you to teach her some manners.' Freeman commented: 'Of course I didn't say anything to Liz, but I never forgot the incident.'

Despite its shortcomings, *Torch Song* was largely a success and made money for its studio. As far as Joan was concerned, it also established the point within the studio hierarchy (where Dore Schary was now at the production helm) at which Mayer had blundered ten years earlier in letting her slip away to Warner Brothers and then to independence. Schary doubtless had a hand in this film, because it bears the stamp of a liberal mind (overbearing tyrant-boss intimidating the lowly workers around her), but little of the outsized sentiment and 'show-stoppers' which marked Metro's musical films of the 1940s under Mayer. As a general rule, the story had not really mattered with Mayer at the helm. People wanted to be entertained; that was his credo.

As a musical, however, *Torch Song* suffers by comparison with Metro's classic satire, *Singing in the Rain*, which had been released the previous year. Still, great satires and classics are the exception and not the rule, and it seems very clear that this Crawford vehicle was created especially for her return to her old stable. It was not intended to be a parody of anything, although several years later, television comedienne Carol Burnett enacted a take-off of the film (as the whip-cracking, Simon Legree-ish boss-lady of the theatre) which reduced Joan to tears when she viewed it, because she considered Burnett a friend. Joan was much less offended when Burnett did a similar satire of another of Joan's films, which she called *Mildred Fierce*.

★ ★ ★

There has to be an explanation for the resurgence of Joan Crawford's career in the 1950s. In a seminal way, her Warner Brothers films in the 1940s — especially her second film for them, *Possessed*, in 1947 — led almost directly to her popularity and acceptance in 1952 with *Sudden Fear*. The films attracted the same audiences – mostly urban with some college background, and very different from Crawford's fans in the 1930s and '40s.

Joan had known exactly what she was doing when she left Metro and signed with Warner Brothers. There was something artificial about Metro's vision of contemporary life, while Warner Brothers made an effort to capture some realism not only in their stories, but also in their players. In some shrewd way, Joan knew that she belonged there, along with Humphrey Bogart, Bette Davis, Sydney Greenstreet, Ida Lupino, John Garfield and Paul Muni. This is paradoxical when one thinks of her as being formed in thought, manner and appearance by Metro, and ironic when one recalls that nearly everyone around Joan considered her as a film queen, on and off camera, drunk or sober, or in any other human condition.

All those newly won fans lost their patience, however, once Joan had left Warner Brothers and became independent. She was simply too insecure about her abilitities to commit to daring new stories. After the success of *Sudden Fear*, only three Crawford films have survived as worthy of revival in the final years of the twentieth century: the curiosity, *Johnny Guitar* (1954), the bitter-sweet *Autumn Leaves* (1956) and the macabre thriller, *What Ever Happened to Baby Jane?* (1962).

It was a time of profound loneliness for Joan. If Greg Bautzer had not been so involved with himself and his swaggering macho image, he might have saved her many a tearful night. Now he was trying to avoid her. After one of their arguments following a date, she walked unannounced into his office at Hollywood and Vine. He was half expecting her, as, in the past, whenever things between them became impossible, one or the other would sheepishly apologize. This time, however, Bautzer did not want to confront her again, and he had instructed his secretary to tell her that he was out.

Joan refused to believe the young woman, and walked around her desk towards Bautzer's door. When she opened it and peered inside, the office was empty. She searched everywhere – in his private toilet, behind and under the desk, behind the curtains –

but he was not there. She stormed out of the room, and his secretary, knowing that he *was* in, went into the office herself to search for him, to see him edging his way along a narrow ledge towards one of his windows and then crawling back inside. The ledge on which he had stood for five minutes was twelve storeys above Hollywood Boulevard.

★　★　★

Helen Hayes MacArthur went out to Hollywood in 1953 to play a small role in the film *Main Street to Broadway*. She brought with her a protégée, Bethel Leslie, who became a television star in the 1950s in a series of distinguished dramas (including *The Armstrong Theatre* and *Studio One*), although she never managed to win a notable film role. The two women were invited to stay with Joan at the Brentwood mansion. Joan and Helen had been in almost constant touch by telephone and letter over the years, and always had dinner together at least once during Joan's trips to New York. Bethel Leslie recalled that Joan had formal dinners with invited guests almost every night during their stay – perhaps she did not realize that Joan planned these dinners around Helen and her Hollywood friends who wanted to see her.

Bethel Leslie noticed the disciplined children and their 'too correct' manners, and once she caught Joan sobbing for no apparent reason. Her opinion was that Joan Crawford was a very lonely woman.

During their stay, Helen Hayes also stumbled upon young Christopher's long-running joke on his mother. Perhaps the worst of the 'abuse' suffered by Christopher was Joan's use of the 'sleep-safe', whereby the boy was secured in bed each night in a device which kept him tied to his bed until morning so that he could not wander around. Helen's son, Jim MacArthur, spent several nights in Christopher's room and was astonished to see the boy slip out of the 'safe' as easily as Houdini. 'Mother doesn't know I can do this,' Christopher told Jim, and in fact she never discovered that he could slip out and go to the bathroom any time he chose.

ELEVEN

INDEPENDENT OR ADRIFT?

H erbert J. Yates, studio chief at Republic Studios (the home of Gene Autry and Hopalong Cassidy) had made periodic gestures towards cinematic art by producing films such as *Spectre of the Rose*, a ballet film (1946), and Orson Welles's *Macbeth* (1950), and now planned a first-class western in *Johnny Guitar* (1954) to star Joan Crawford. He commissioned Broadway playwright Philip Yordan (*Anna Lucasta*) to write the screenplay, and Nicholas Ray (*Rebel without a Cause*) to direct. Victor Young was brought in to write the score, including the title song, which became a mini-hit recorded by singer Peggy Lee. Joan approved the script and was surrounded by an all-star cast: Mercedes McCambridge, who had won an Oscar for best supporting actress in *All the King's Men* (1949), Sterling Hayden, Scott Brady, Ben Cooper, Ernest Borgnine, Royal Dano and John Carradine.

The film production was marked by a bitter feud between Joan and Mercedes McCambridge, echoing the relationship between them on the screen. McCambridge had come into films from the Broadway stage, and had a commanding presence and a voice to match. Joan was drinking vodka throughout her stay in the Arizona desert, which may have accounted for her violent behaviour (if we deduce that she could be and probably was sometimes violent at home while drinking, this may also explain much of her behaviour at this time towards her two older children). Once, when she could contain herself no longer, she entered McCambridge's motel room, gathered up the latter's costumes and tossed them along the highway next to the location.

There were further problems with the crew as well. Joan insisted that the interior sound-stage back at the Republic Studio should be cooled down to 68°F, which was the temperature she found most comfortable (she may have had an undiagnosed metabolism problem), causing the crew to complain that the frigid air was giving them colds.

The worst upshot of all of this bickering was that it fuelled a five-part series in the *Los Angeles Mirror*, blasting Joan. The reporter, Roby Heard, interviewed Sterling Hayden, who swore that there was not enough money in the world to induce him to work again with Crawford. He also talked to Joan's brother, Hal, who said that he had not seen his sister in five years (disregarding all the phone calls enquiring after him that she had made, or asked Betty Barker to make), and even a servant, who complained that Joan 'made me take my shoes off when I entered the house so I wouldn't get dirt on the rugs'. As all this gossip was based on actual fact, Joan was both livid and helpless to respond. She had no idea what monumental character-maligning would follow her death with Christina's memoir, also based on actual fact.

In general, the critics did not care for *Johnny Guitar*, most of them blaming the script, which was murky and pretentious. The title song outlived the movie by several decades. Like the film based on *Mommie Dearest*, *Johnny Guitar* has become a camp classic.

★ ★ ★

On New Year's Eve 1954, Joan was holed up in her dressing-room suite at the Universal studio, where she was making another of her detested 'dangerous female' films, when Earl Blackwell (a Hollywood commentator and favourite of the tabloids) telephoned from Las Vegas and introduced her to Alfred Steele over the phone. Steele wondered why she was alone on New Year's Eve, and she explained that she was tired after the day's shooting.

Relations had worsened between Joan and her two older children by this time, and it was around then that she had

Christina transferred from the Chadwick School to a Catholic
girls' boarding school (Flintridge Sacred Heart Academy). With
the twins now boarding at Chadwick, too, it is possible that Joan
often did not go home because she was too lonely there with just
the small staff.

Soon after the phone call, Steele turned up in California. Joan
was attracted to him at once. A former football player at college,
Steele now was an executive with the Pepsi-Cola Company and
about to divorce his wife. Joan was fascinated, and, when it
became obvious that he was courting her, she began to see in him
the answer to many of her problems. He was gregarious and she
was lonely; she pictured him as the kind of strong father that she
felt the children needed; and she immediately interested herself
in what he was doing in promoting Pepsi-Cola.

She flew to Las Vegas to marry Al Steele in May 1955. In her
autobiography, Joan implies that she was afraid of flying and that
Steele gave her the courage to put her fears aside, even though
news clippings from the 1940s reveal that she flew regularly
cross-country. They sailed to Europe on a honeymoon. Both Joan
and Steele were strong-willed and used to getting their own way,
and there were some quarrels between them, but they always
made up their differences.

Joan continued making one or two films a year, none of them
very distinguished. She continued her practice of staying
overnight at the studio when she had had a long day in front of
the cameras, and Steele objected so strenuously that on at least
one occasion he blackened her eye and she could not be filmed
the next day. Rumours flew of a possible divorce, but Joan must
have decided that she was going to make a go of this marriage no
matter what, and indeed some years later, she would become
Steele's widow.

Leo Jaffe, Columbia Pictures' president at the time recalled:

'I was very close to her socially when she was married to Al
Steele. In fact, I was at the wedding reception they held at *Les
Ambassadeurs* in London. They had just got there and she was

going to do a picture for us with Jimmy Woolf. I was there at the time, and my wife and I went to the wedding reception. Al Steele was very much her big love.

'I knew Joan for I'd say approximately forty years. I go back a long way with her to when she was still making pictures for Metro and then did some pictures for us (Columbia). Then I was involved in a television series with her called *The Foxes*. A deal had been signed by NBC and was later aborted, but about that time they were cancelling women's shows. They cancelled *The Loretta Young Show, Big Valley – The Barbara Stanwyck Show* and Joan's show, which was supposed to start within a month's time, but they never went ahead with it. For me, it was a personal situation since my son, Howard, was the producer and the originator of the show. NBC explained that the ratings for all women's shows were going way down and so they cancelled.

'When the TV series was aborted, she was let down because she wanted to do it very badly. We had thirteen scripts completed. Then we had a disaster because we had only the thirteen original copies of the scripts and they were misplaced somewhere at William Morris. We were going to start a lawsuit against them, but decided against it after I spoke to their head, Abe Lastfogel.

'As for drinking on her Pepsi appearances, she wouldn't do anything to embarrass Al because she truly loved him. They were wonderful together, and she never went to a point where she could have in any way have created a feeling that she had too much to drink. She was a lady when she was with Al.

'Oh, Joan drank. There was no hiding that. That was public knowledge, and she had a little flask of one hundred per cent proof vodka with her. She often carried that flask with her.'

TWELVE

JOAN AND PEPSI

At first, when Joan began appearing at her husband's side at bottling-plant openings around the country and then the world, it did not seem so terribly unusual that a top executive would be accompanied by his wife. Sometimes, however, Joan would fly to a ground-breaking or an opening on her own, and it became apparent that she had become a good-will ambassador without portfolio for the Pepsi Company. As it was at about this time that Pepsi-Cola drew even with Coca-Cola in sales, there was speculation that Joan Crawford may have made just enough difference to help launch 'the Pepsi generation' in a big way.

Joan was not the first film star to ally herself with corporate America. Polly Bergen had toured for a beauty line, as had Arlene Dahl, and before that, in the 1930s, Irene Rich had become the spokeswoman for Welch's Grape Juice. None of these stars was of the same magnitude as Joan Crawford, however. The only comparable glamour figure to have as great an impact as Joan would be Gloria Vanderbilt, several years after Joan worked with Pepsi.

Joan was wonderfully skilful in handling the press, various bottling executives and their wives, and generally boosting her product wherever she went. The chic woman refined by Metro over the years passed muster as a corporate executive who could draw thousands of people to plant openings and other corporate events. The film factories must have been copying something close to reality when they created Joan to enable her to be so easily absorbed into real life as a businesswoman, with nothing changed except the hours and the people around her. She became so identified with Pepsi that there were thousands of people who thought she ran the company.

Al Steele spoiled Joan, but she had been on her own for so many years that she seemed overdue for a little spoiling. She was now a dozen years away from her days of being pampered by studios. There was a danger in this, however, as Steele allowed her to take over the renovation of a huge Fifth Avenue duplex apartment at 2 East 70th Street on the East Side of Manhattan. Costs soon doubled, and, with expensive new furnishings, they moved into a million-dollar luxury apartment with double-height ceilings and a room-sized closet for Joan's wardrobe and shoes.

In the film, *Mommie Dearest*, there is an argument over the escalating costs involved in renovating the apartment, when Steele tells Joan that he has borrowed against his stock in Pepsi-Cola to help pay for the enormous contractor's bill. The truth was, in fact, that Joan was the one who was worried over the excessive cost because Steele had borrowed heavily against her own life insurance to pay the contractor.

Christina wrote, inaccurately, in her book, that her mother 'had taken a second mortgage on her house, and borrowed against her insurance policies, and she didn't have a job. After the marriage, someone else paid the bills, bought her jewellery, paid the rent, and took her anywhere she wanted to go'. The truth was rather different. Steele not only borrowed on Joan's life insurance *and* his stock in his own company, but, upon his death, Joan discovered that the apartment renovation had all been done on borrowed money. Steele left her in debt – not with an industrialist's fortune, as many believed.

★　　★　　★

In the meantime, it seemed clear that Al Steele wanted Joan to continue making films. He encouraged her so totally in this that, for a long time after her marriage, she no longer needed the prop of alcohol and was sober much of the time. She made three films, almost back to back, between Pepsi junkets in 1955 and 1956, only one of them – *Autumn Leaves* – worth remembering.

The film was released by Columbia Pictures in 1956 as part of a three-film deal with Joan, and had her playing an older spinster who falls in love with a young man (Cliff Robertson in his second film). She was directed by Robert Aldrich, who later would give Joan the best role of her mature years in *What Ever Happened to Baby Jane?* (1962). There are echoes of both *Possessed* (1947) and *Sudden Fear* (1952) in *Autumn Leaves* but it worked well. The *New York Herald Tribune* commented: 'The film is a mature study of loneliness and mental distress . . . The strength of Miss Crawford's performance is that it is natural and controlled . . .'

During the holidays at the end of 1955, Steele took his new family, including all four children, to St Moritz for a skiing holiday. Christina and Christopher were now nearly grown up (sixteen), and were allowed to ski on the beginners' ski slope with an instructor, while Joan, Al and the twins tried to skate near the ski lodge. Cindy recalls: 'It was the only time when we were all together as a family. It was wonderful . . . the one time I can remember him (Al Steele) in that role (as their father).' Al Steele also helped Christopher into his last military school, one of the best in the southwest. It was hoped that the boy's occasional surly behaviour might be curbed. It was a warm and relatively happy time for all of them – a little unreal, in fact, for the older children, who found a 'nice' mother just a little incredible. What is so strange about this is that many of Joan's friends remember only that side of her. Only those who crossed her saw the iron-willed despot.

There is much evidence that Joan was content in her marriage to Steele, perhaps largely because – unlike her previous husbands – he was professionally her equal. He was a 'star' in the business world, and his company gave him much of the credit for its latter-day success. As Joan had made herself a partner in his worldwide promotion of the soft drink, the company was also aware of her contribution. Always straining to move ahead, to be perfect, she now seemed relaxed. She later wrote: 'During the most blissful years of my life, the dead centre of my life was my husband.' It seemed an honest statement, whereas when, many years earlier, she had claimed that her true happiness was with her children, she was once again reinventing her life as she was living it. However, this time she was fairly convincing.

Was this is a new Joan, or had this loving woman always existed, waiting for some man to bring her out? Actually, Joan was the chameleon again. Her career was no longer the focus of her life, and so she became the executive's doting wife. The role had a softer focus than anything she had done on screen: this was no Harriet Craig, endlessly and furtively cleaning her house; no Mildred Pierce being a martyr to her daughter's callous rages; no Crystal Allen gloating over her latest stolen husband. Joan was now past fifty, and no longer needed the public façade of Joan Crawford, film star. Like Greer Garson, Anne Baxter, Susan Hayward and her arch rival of her Metro days, Norma Shearer, she considered retiring from the business of being a leading lady.

For nearly a year, Joan travelled the world with Al Steele, spending weeks in France and Italy, going wherever a new bottling plant was being opened. In Paris, she met her stepdaughter Sally, who urged her without success to try the Metro (Underground). 'You live your life and I'll live mine,' was Joan's response.

The lure of the sound-stage was stronger than pure marital felicity, however, and after all, as Joan must have reasoned, Steele had married her as a film star, and had never asked her to retire. In early 1957, she flew to London to star in *The Golden Virgin* (released as *The Story of Esther Costello*). Her chief regret seemed not to be parting from her children, but having to leave her miniature poodle, Clicquot, in New York. (Like so many other great stars, Joan Crawford was passionately fond of lap-dogs – miniature dachshunds, poodles and shi-tzus. Elizabeth Taylor once spent a week in a boat tied up in the Thames and commuted to her engagement ashore in London by speedboat, rather than have her six lap-dogs quarantined by the British for six months.) On this trip, Joan compromised by carrying a stuffed toy poodle as a substitute along with nearly forty pieces of luggage. In a reversal of her former relationships, Joan's husband came with her for the film. She had become very possessive of Steele, quite unlike her previous marriages. She even resented Christina when she kissed her stepfather on the cheek (Christina later wrote that she had been slapped for this).

Esther Costello would be the last star vehicle to rely for its financing, its drama and its audience on Joan Crawford's considerable artistry. In it she played an American woman, separated from a cad (Rossano Brazzi). She takes on the responsibility for Esther, an Irish deaf-mute (Heather Sears, in her first film role), who has known only poverty in Ireland, and sets up a fund for the girl's future. Joan and her charge begin touring on fund drives for blind charities, but Brazzi returns, takes over the drives and pockets most of the money.

Esther then meets a young reporter, Harry, and they fall in love, but Joan's caddish husband shoves his way into the situation and, in Harry's absence, rapes Esther. This violence shocks her into regaining her hearing and speech. Finally, Joan sacrifices herself by driving her husband to their deaths. The film was tailor-made for Joan, and there are pieces of her old screen character throughout (*A Woman's Face*, *Mildred Pierce*, *Torch Song*). It would be Joan's swan song as the long-suffering heroine.

After the filming, Joan accompanied Steele around Europe and Africa. She said later that she loved touring for Pepsi as much as making films. It should not be forgotten that she had been a sales-girl in Kansas City for several years, and her colleagues from those days recall that she was very good at it. The Pepsi executives back in New York were impressed. The combination of Joan and Al Steele probably did as much to promote the soft drink in its international pitch as the phrase 'The Pepsi Generation'.

★　★　★

Joan's relationship with her children was continuing its difficult course. Although Christina seemed to have come through her troubled adolescence intact, Christopher was in and out of trouble, and, when he was fifteen, Joan had him sent to a correctional institute. The relationship between Joan and her son was a sour one. She did not trust him in any way, and he apparently hated her. The boy rarely articulated his feelings about his mother, however, being handicapped to a degree by the uncertain and off-and-on schooling which he received between escapades.

When Christopher returned from serving in Vietnam, he tried to see Joan at her East Side apartment, but she had instructed the doorman not to admit him. They never met again, and he went to work for a utility company on Long Island, marrying and raising a family. With this inexplicable rejection of her only son returned from the war, suddenly we are in the realm of actress Norma Desmond. Norma was not just a screen character – Billy Wilder, who put her down on paper, had seen a dozen like her: the creation of a film studio, insensitive to those closest to her, kind to the lowly studio workers, who loved her, of course. Was Faye Dunaway, who played the part of Joan as a psychotic throughout the film of *Mommie Dearest*, given clues that Crawford might have been as mad as Norma Desmond? [Joan's archivist, Dore Freeman, spent several hours with Faye Dunaway giving her clues and background to help in her characterization. After seeing the film, he felt betrayed.]

The incident wherein Joan refused to see her son after the war remains a troubling mystery. While it simply cannot be explained away by the troubled relationship over the years, it is significant that Joan had an unforgiving nature. As Betty Barker recalled the specifics of Christopher's catalogue of misdeeds: 'Let's face it. Christopher had been a thief; he had been in jail; he had been expelled from schools. Certainly if Joan had not had in her character this flint-like resolve against certain people she banished from her life, this would have been the moment when mother and son might have had a reconciliation. Joan had supported the war in Vietnam. She considered herself a patriot. But when Metro put Lucille LeSueur onto the studio assembly line and Joan Crawford emerged, the capacity to give people around her a second chance was left out.

If Joan had not been a studio creation, one might assume that she suffered schizophrenic episodes, aggravated by alcohol abuse. But that would be a mistake. Joan could not be judged by normal standards of behaviour. She simply was not a whole person, but being an actress, for the most part, she assumed such a role. As for Christopher, she had closed the door on him a long time ago. Risking his life in a foreign war could not change Joan's resolve.

★ ★ ★

Christina and Joan, on the other hand, were still in touch. Christina had moved into a tenement building on the East Side of Manhattan, with a roommate who had been a fellow-student at the Carnegie Tech Drama School. The roommate, Joan Feldman (Hollander), had, by coincidence, been named after Joan Crawford, and like Christina, was an aspiring actress. Feldman knew that Christina had an uneasy relationship with her mother. She recalled Christina being confined to the dorms during the final summer vacation when the school was closed and there was nothing to do.

Neither of the young women had much money and the flat, which they rented for only $36 a month, had only cold water, but it was on the far East Side with a view of the bridge to Queens on East 59th Street. Feldman said of Christina:

'Living with her in close quarters, I got to know her better than I had at school. Perhaps she wanted to be like her mother. She wanted her own way a lot of the time, but I didn't blame her for this. We were both going through lots of hard places here in New York . . . Her mother wasn't talking to her; she wasn't supporting her . . . She didn't have much money to spend.

'Tina knew that the treatment the so-called twins received was very different from her own, but then she had come along at a very different time in Crawford's life . . . Tina was a very fine home-maker because she had to grow up doing all of that.

She was very good at it. She was a very good cook and knew how to straighten a house. I guess her mother felt that she had to do it when she was young . . .

'Christopher was living out on Long Island and I think he and some other boys got arrested for shooting a beebee gun and breaking street lights and windows. I know he was sent to reform school and he used to visit us from there. I guess he'd get out on pass. He was fairly close to Tina. He was a very quiet person. He would not say a word about his mother. He would not mention her name in front of me . . . He was a real sweet guy, very young, but sweet. And then Christina would go out there to see him at certain times. Now we were living in a $36 a month apartment, but she would hire a car. She would go out à la Crawford . . .

'She had a phone with the longest extension cord I've ever seen and she would be lying on the couch with the dog and the phone would ring and she would reach out for the phone without moving from the couch and indicate she wanted the phone brought to her. And I thought that it was such a movie-star gesture, and I felt it was wilful and very much like her mother, who had a secretary, whereas I was just a roommate there to share expenses. So her will and my will sometimes clashed, but she had a fine sense of humour and sometimes would tell me something that had happened to her and crack up, you know . . .

'She hated to lose arguments. She was very bright, and I always had the feeling that Crawford was very bright. Tina would talk and talk and talk to make a point, just in case you missed it. So I think in all fairness, Tina needed to get her way, but for all intents and purposes her mother had the control . . .

'Several years later, I ran into Christina right after she had begun doing a soap opera, *The Secret Storm*, and she and her mother were close at that time . . . She went on the Merv Griffin Show talking about her mother and publicizing something. So there was that period of time after we had been living together that she did have a reconciliation with her mom . . . She really wanted to understand the good side of her mother. She just didn't want to live under [memories of] the horrendous side of her.

'Incidentally, I didn't like the movie [*Mommie Dearest*]. She pours the drinks into jelly glasses, but when (and if) her mother was ever there, she would never have used anything but the finest of crystal, which she had put away. She had beautiful crystal and china and exquisite things, all put away. So when company came, they were treated royally, and we would spend all our money getting the most expensive foods and whatever was needed. But I fell right into that because when it came down to it, I was just as grand as she was . . .

'So there was a real dichotomy. The book, *Mommie Dearest*, was just one area of their relationship. I don't remember getting from the book just how much she loved her mother, but she truly loved her . . . When I was reading it, I was very sad for Christina. All I could get from it was "Will she ever move on?" . . . [and] all I got from it were those long nights when I used to listen to the horror stories. And the other part where I know there was lightness, where I know there was love, it was left out in favour of complications. The times when they had fun together were missing . . .

'Incidentally, I never remember any mention of wire hangers in her horror stories [she told me] . . . As for physical violence, I think Christopher had the worst of it. Something like the sleep-safe would have scarred him for life. I know that he ran away a lot, but Christina never said she did . . . So he shot out windows. My brother did the same thing and they called it 'mischief' . . . In fact, Christopher was treated like a criminal, and after he went to the reform school, Crawford had nothing further to do with him . . .

'Crawford was an alcoholic, but in those days when I was with Christina, she didn't seem quite sure and she would say, "I wonder if mother is an alcoholic." I learned to drink vodka from Christina, who learned it from her mother. It doesn't smell, you see. In Christina's second book, *Survivor*, she breaks an anonymity on herself and tells us she belongs to AA . . .

'I have this funny fantasy about Christina that I'm going to run into her and let her know that I'm living where I am (on the far East Side near our old cold-water flat), which is now so elegant. I think she'd really get a kick out of that.'

Christina had remained in college long enough to learn the cultural basics. She became a fair actress and a decent writer, and considerable civilized passion went into her diatribes against her mother in *Mommie Dearest* and in her second memoir, *Survivor.* The twins had the equivalent of finishing-school educations and then both married early – one to a farmer and moving to Iowa, and the other to a businessman and moving to Pennsylvania. They made Joan a grandmother, and she loved the babies while deploring the 'ancient' label of 'Grandma'.

Anna LeSueur died in 1958, aged seventy-four, in California, where she still shared the house which Joan had bought for them with son Hal. Joan flew back for the funeral and burial at Forest Lawn. Hal died of appendicitis five years later, and Joan had him buried next to their mother but did not attend the funeral. He had been banished from her life long before.

A detached observer might interpret Joan's coldness towards her own family as a symptom of the old notion that film stars are routinely dysfunctional in domestic situations, and seldom what they seem to be. Joan did, it is true, ensure that she had as little to do with her mother and brother as possible in her later years, largely because of a misplaced shame of their origins as poor folk from the 'wrong side of the tracks'. In her defence, however, she subsidized them financially for many years, gave them a place to live and ensured that they wanted for nothing.

★ ★ ★

In May 1959 Joan and Steele ran into her old friend, Cesar Romero, in Atlanta, where he was promoting a line of men's suits. Nearly always in robust good health himself, Cesar noticed Steele's pallor and lassitude. Steele told him that the present tour had taken a lot out of him. The couple flew back to New York, and the following Sunday morning Joan found him lying face-down on the living-room floor of their apartment. He had died of a heart attack.

If Joan Crawford was fashioned from ordinary human clay by the star-makers at Metro, all hands had succeeded in creating a human being who could weather anything that happened. She did not give way to grief; she planned the funeral, and later went over her financial condition with the men in charge of her assets. She learned from them that her husband had left her in debt. When, shortly afterwards, Joan spoke with Hearst Hollywood columnist Louella Parsons about it, Louella immediately wrote a story for the following day's column, under a headline screaming: 'Joan Crawford Broke!' Joan finally persuaded Louella to modify the story, with an explanation, but some damage had already been done to Joan's reputation as a still successful and wealthy old-time star.

Al Steele had a life insurance policy on himself for four hundred thousand dollars and his first wife had been the original beneficiary. Joan felt that she was not entitled to that money, and allowed the first wife to take it all.

Not all the facts emerged at the time, but Pepsi-Cola then moved to recover almost half-a-million dollars – the amount that Joan and Steele's Fifth Avenue apartment had cost to renovate. Although, she was a great distance from being a charity case, as Louella's column had suggested, Joan did have to make some sacrifices in order to clear the debts.

She confided in producer Jerry Wald, and it was his notion that Joan should go back to work in Hollywood. It was he, of course, who had masterminded her move to Warner Brothers (and an Oscar), and he was now producing a Rona Jaffe novel (*The Best of Everything*, 1959) with a huge cast. The role in which Joan was cast, of Amanda Farrow, a sexually frustrated magazine editor who avenges her assorted miscalculations and disappointments on the girls under her, was a better-written but abbreviated reprise of the character whom she had played in *Torch Song* in

1953. Joan trusted director Jean Negulesco as much as she did
Jerry Wald, but Negulesco and Twentieth-Century Fox sabotaged
her fine work in this film in the final editing. Her best scenes
were excised, and even her last lover, who turned out to be worthy
of her, was cut from the film. Even so, the production gave her six
weeks on the coast, during which she sold the Brentwood
mansion. This was a real wrench for Joan, but her life had
changed far too much for her to continue living there. Betty
Barker, who saw her daily at that time, recalled:

> 'Donald O'Connor bought the house and then sold it to
> Anthony Newley, who could not keep it up. It was an expensive
> house to run. The grounds went all the way back to the street
> at the rear. Then sometimes I would be here and then in New
> York. For her stays in California, she took a large apartment in
> Loretta Young's sprawling apartment building on Fountain
> Avenue. Loretta lived in the building, too, and she and Joan
> became close friends.'

From then on, Joan divided her time between New York and
California. She kept her duplex apartment in Hollywood,
reserving the upstairs for herself, and space for Betty Barker
downstairs. Back east in New York, which she considered her
permanent home, she finally moved into her last apartment in
Imperial House in 1973. The huge duplex on Fifth Avenue, at 2
East 70th Street, had proved to be as much of an unnecessary
expense as the Brentwood mansion had become.

According to the head doorman at Imperial House, Matthew
Curran, Joan even gave up her driver and limousine. From early
on in her residence there, she always hired cars and drivers,
although she had her favourite chauffeurs and would ask for
them in advance. She became friendly with the staff at Imperial
House, and was always very generous at Christmas time. During
one Christmas season, she invited Matthew Curran to come up to
her apartment when he had a moment. When he did so, she took
him into a small ante-room filled with bric-à-brac collected over
the years, and told him: 'Pick out something you would like. I

want you to have it.' Matthew saw a small brandy keg on top of a cabinet and indicated that he would like to have that.

'Oh, but it's empty', she said.

'Ah, yes', Matthew replied in his heavy Irish brogue. 'But it was yours, and I will treasure it, and I will give it to my sons later on, and they will treasure it just as I do, and it will go on down in my family.'

★   ★   ★

The issue of Joan's relationship with her children arose once again in 1960. It was in the October issue of *Redbook* magazine that Christina first publicly stated that she and her mother were on opposite sides of a very 'deep chasm of misunderstanding'. ['The Revolt of Joan Crawford's Daughter', October 1960, *Redbook*.] Of her relationship with Christina, Joan said that 'it has been eighteen years of disappointment'.

'Mummy was with me constantly,' Christina wrote in describing her early childhood. 'No matter where she went, even when she travelled across the country, I went along.' When her adopted brother, Christopher, arrived as an infant, they were 'not shunted off into the nursery', but were there when company came. Christina recalled Louis B. Mayer being a constant visitor, and Judy Garland singing at Joan's parties. 'She had the voice of an angel,' said Christina, 'and was the most beautiful person I had ever seen.' John Garfield came one evening to see his latest film with Joan, *Humoresque* (1946), in her little theatre, and afterwards he carried Christina to her room. 'I decided,' said Christina, 'that if I ever married, it would have to be someone like him.'

Joan was invited by the author Morton J. Golding and the editors at *Redbook* to comment on the article about her relationship with Christina, and to correct it where necessary. In her defence, Joan claimed that she spent more time with her children than most 'normal mothers' do, which could not possibly have been true. She was referring to her 'free time', of course, of which she had very little, even though she gave it to the children.

Joan also gave Christina, intact, the story included in *Mommie Dearest* about Joan winning all the time in the races back and forth across their swimming pool. In *Redbook*, Joan said, 'I'm bigger than you are. I'm faster than you are. I can win all the time ... I picked her up to throw her into the pool and jumped in with her and made her swim.'

By the time Christina was ten years old, she and Joan were quarrelling frequently. This would have been in 1949, when Joan was filming *The Damned Don't Cry* and *Harriet Craig* (both 1950 releases). While she was unhappy with the way which Warner Brothers was beginning to typecast her in tawdry roles with increasing melodrama and loose morality, Joan had a very satisfying time with the making of *Harriet Craig*, with her lover, Vincent Sherman, directing her and looking after her.

Christina asserted in the article that the arguing started in part because Joan was unhappy with the way that her career was going, but, in truth, she was not yet moved to rebellion at Warner Brothers, where Jack Warner had bought her a prize stage property that year (*Goodbye My Fancy*) to keep her happy, and other studios such as Columbia wanted to borrow her. Betty Barker was possibly closer to the mark in her summary of the mother-daughter relationship when she said: 'Joan was wilful, and Christina was wilful and they just clashed.'

★ ★ ★

Joan made herself available to television offers, and from 1953 to 1972 (two full decades) she appeared on *The Twilight Zone*, *The GE Theatre* and *The Zane Grey Theatre*, as well as some variety shows. Pepsi-Cola asked her to continue to lend her glamorous presence to the openings of Pepsi bottling plants, to which she agreed. She had become the company spokeswoman by this time, and was elected to their board of directors. Then, in 1961, Joan became involved in her next film project, *What Ever Happened to Baby Jane?*

Bette Davis was appearing on Broadway in 1961 in Tennessee Williams's *Night of the Iguana*, playing the slatternly hotel owner-manager located in a remote jungle area of Mexico. Joan saw the show one night and came backstage to pay her respects to Davis, but she had an ulterior motive beyond ordinary show-business courtesy. She had read Henry Farrell's book, *What Ever Happened to Baby Jane?*, and wanted Davis to co-star with her in the film version. The book tells a peculiar mystery story with a Hollywood background about two sisters, both formerly in the movies. Baby Jane had been a child star in vaudeville who made the transition to films easily, but not the transition from child star to successful adult actress. The other sister, Blanche Hudson, was formerly a successful movie star, but had been injured in a car accident and was living in seclusion in a decaying Hollywood house.

The roles of Joan and Blanche were obvious, tour-de-force parts for Bette Davis and Joan Crawford respectively, from their inception within the pages of the original story. Joan had brought it to the attention of Robert Aldrich, who had directed her in her last successful film, *Autumn Leaves* (1956). They had had a brief affair during the making of the film, but had not been in close touch for several years.

Aldrich immediately secured the rights and then persuaded Seven Arts to finance the film. It would be made with some of the components still used today to package properties – the director and the two stars would own percentages of the gross. Bette Davis needed some cash on hand, and agreed to five per cent of the gross and $50,000 up front. Joan, still on the Pepsi-Cola payroll as a Director and not so pressed, took ten per cent of the gross and much less cash up front. Her decision would make *Baby Jane* the best investment that she had made in many years.

In 1962 when columnist Hedda Hopper wrote a background story on the making of the film, Joan told her that she had wanted to do a picture with Bette Davis since 1944. 'When I first went to Warners in 1943 I learned they owned *Ethan Frome*; they'd bought it for Bette. But in the meantime Bette had gone off to have a baby. A year later I left Warners [this is typical Crawford confusion about dates: she remained with Warners until the end of the forties] and the property was sold to Jerry Wald. Now

Columbia owns it. But Bette and I never discussed this, she never knew I was after it. Then when I came across *What Ever Happened to Baby Jane?*, I sent it to Bob Aldrich and told him it was for Bette and me.'

Hopper prefaced this by saying: 'I was interested in finding out who first had the story and how they eventually got together. Each of them had been sent the book at different times.'

'A friend of mine, Bill Frye, gave me the story to read two years ago when it was first published,' Bette explained. 'He tried to buy it but nothing came of it. Then a year ago I sent it to Alfred Hitchcock – I thought he should direct it whether or not I was in it, but he had other pictures lined up.' However, a few years before Davis's death, she had published a fragmentary memoir entitled *This 'n That* in which she writes: 'I will always thank her [Joan] for giving me the opportunity to play the part of "Baby Jane" Hudson . . .

'In 1961, I was in a play on Broadway, *The Night of the Iguana* by Tennessee Williams. One night Joan came backstage to see me and told me she had found a novel with parts in it for both of us: *What Ever Happened to Baby Jane?* She said she had sent it to Robert Aldrich with hopes that he would direct it. He had phoned her from Italy, where he was finishing a film, to say he had acquired the rights to the book. He also thought she and I would be ideal for the two leading parts.' (There are three huge egos clashing here in their recollections: Aldrich told writers Charles Higham and Joel Greenberg in an interview published in 1969: 'Right from the beginning, Bette Davis and Joan Crawford were my first choices for the two main parts.' There is no mention here about Joan's or Bette's prior interest. I think that in the case of the phenomenally successful film, it is human nature for each of the participants to take credit for its existence. Since eventually Bette and Joan seemed to agree that Joan brought up the matter of making a movie of the book first, we must accept that story.)

The story begins when Jane, the apparently demented caretaker of Blanche, learns that Blanche is planning to sell the house and put Jane in a sanitarium. Angered, Jane mistreats her helpless sister in every way she can, serving her baked rat and Blanche's beloved parakeet as an entrée, as well as keeping Blanche from outside help by anticipating her every move (when it would appear that Blanche's doctor is somehow convinced that she is in danger and plans to come over, Jane calls the doctor and, in a fine imitation of Blanche's voice, cancels the visit). The sisters' cleaning woman, Elvira, suspects Jane's devilries, and, having pretended to leave the house, returns to find Blanche tied to her bedposts with a gag in her mouth. Jane finds Elvira helping Blanche and, in a panic, hits her over the head with a hammer, killing her.

Meanwhile, Jane is entertaining Edwin, a 'Mama's boy' who responded to her advertisement for an accompanist for Baby Jane's triumphant return to the live stage. Jane has promised him a hundred dollars advance on his salary, but never actually pays it. One day Edwin (beautifully played by a newcomer Victor Buono) overhears Blanche's movements as she knocks down some furniture in her bedroom to attract attention. When he goes upstairs and sees her, he is so terrified that he runs out of the house.

Jane again reacts in panic. She is afraid that Edwin will bring back the police, so she drags her dying sister down to the car and drives her to the beach. Meanwhile, Elvira's family has reported her missing and the police, in searching the old house, find her body. They put out an all-points search for the two sisters. In her dying moments on the beach, Blanche confesses to her sister that she planned the car accident in which she, Blanche, had been injured years ago, but had allowed Jane to believe that it was she who caused her disability. Jane is distraught at this news. 'We could have been friends,' she says, 'all these years'. A beach crowd, including the police, gathers around the two sisters while Jane, reacting to an audience, begins her 'Baby Jane' song and dance.

Of Joan and Bette Davis's relationship on the set, Aldrich said: 'It's proper to say that they really detested each other, but they behaved absolutely perfectly.' Joan sent Davis presents in an effort to make things comfortable between them, but this did not mean that Davis was about to become a friend. Before shooting began, Davis asked Aldrich if he had ever had any 'uh, personal relationship with Miss Crawford'. Aldrich realized that his impartiality would be important to Davis, so he lied and little and said 'no', before adding, 'not that I didn't have the opportunity'.

At first, Aldrich ran into trouble over finding backing for the film, one major company telling him 'We won't give you a dime for those "two old broads".' When Bette Davis was subsequently plugging the film on the *Tonight TV Show* with Johnny Carson, and repeated the quote from the company which turned Aldrich down, she received a letter the following week from Joan telling her never to refer to her as 'an old broad' again. Joan felt that she had to protect her dignity as a lady.

Aldrich discovered the splendid Victor Buono, who played Edwin, in a television show, *The Untouchables.* Davis resisted his Nathanael West Hollywood-gothic mannerisms until halfway through the production, when she smiled at him and said, 'I want you to know that at the beginning of this picture I did everything I could to persuade Bob not to use you, and I'd like to apologize because you're just marvellous.'

Davis created her own make-up for the film, using a clown's white paste and black mascara. Joan, who always knew just how to make herself most presentable, wanted to do *her* own makeup, but, when it was obvious that she even wanted her fingernails painted, Aldrich took charge and saw that she looked properly sick in half her scenes.

Joan was spiking her Pepsis with vodka on the set. As an alcoholic, according to Davis, Joan could not stand the heat at the real beach, so they had to bring in tons of sand to the studio set, where the beach for the final scene was recreated. It was also written into Joan's contract (and in all her contracts going back to the 1940s, when whole studio sound-stages were first air-conditioned) that the studio temperature must be no higher than 68°F. As a result, some of the studio workers went around in lumber jackets, while Davis often wore a scarf or a sweater when she was not in front of the camera.

Davis said that Baby Jane was one of her favourite parts, so that it made Joan's whims 'tolerable'. She was nominated for an Academy Award the following year for her performance as Jane, but did not win because Joan campaigned against her, urging everyone to vote instead for Anne Bancroft in *The Miracle Worker*. Just before her death, Davis was still complaining about 'losing the Oscar because of Joan Crawford'.

What Ever Happened to Baby Jane? became a top-grossing film of 1962. It enabled Joan to recoup her financial situation, wipe out her debts and build the foundation of her future estate.

THIRTEEN

HORROR QUEEN AND A 'LIVING LEGEND'

Joan had established roots in New York during the late 1950s. With her big screen career revived, she might have pulled up stakes in Manhattan and sought another house in Los Angeles in the wake of *Baby Jane*'s great success. Cesar Romero, Willie Haines, Mary Brian and Elsa Martine were all extremely close friends and were still on the west coast.

But Joan now had equally strong ties to friends and places in New York. She was a regular at 21, which became her hangout and chief meeting-place in the city. A banker, Mary Roebling, often came up to have dinner with Joan or take in a film or a play, and Broadway producer Morton Gottlieb often went to dinner and the theatre with her. She also enjoyed entertaining in her apartment, even though it was smaller than her former duplex.

Joan was still touring for Pepsi-Cola whenever they asked her to do so, and earned $40,000 a year for her services. She had earned more as a member of the Board of Directors, but had been dropped from the Board after a clash with Don Kendall, the company's president, over some business point. Behind Kendall's back, she called him 'Fang', picking up this epithet from TV comedienne Phyllis Diller, who used the name for her husband.

Joan followed *What Ever Happened to Baby Jane?* with another study of mental illness, *The Caretakers*, but it was an inferior script, not even as skilful as her similar film, *Possessed*, which she had made fifteen years earlier. Joan went out of her way during this production to help the ageing Herbert Marshall through his scenes.

★   ★   ★

A tradition had begun in the mid-1960s of casting 'over-the-hill' leading ladies in horror films. The success of *Baby Jane* may actually have been the catalyst for this, but thereafter both Joan and Bette Davis each had to suffer through half-a-dozen *grand-guignol* thrillers. Olivia de Havilland and Shelley Winters each made three, Tallulah Bankhead one, Debbie Reynolds two, and so forth. Foremost among the horror-film producers was William Castle, who signed Joan to make two such films: *Strait Jacket* (1964) and *I Saw What You Did* (1965). She played an axe murderess in the first, and a woman trying to keep a killer at bay and save two teenage girls in the second.

Joan's reputation somehow survived the William Castle films. Castle's associate producer, Dona Holloway, an intelligent and warm person who had once been agent Johnny Hyde's girl Friday, became close to Joan during those years and remained so until Joan's death. Then, in midsummer 1964, Robert Aldrich came to Joan with a follow-up to *Baby Jane* entitled *Whatever Happened to Cousin Charlotte?* which later had a title change to *Hush, Hush, Sweet Charlotte* (at Bette Davis's shrewd suggestion). Davis had already agreed to appear, so Joan went to the oppressively hot Louisiana location, near Baton Rouge. Their co-stars were impressive: Joseph Cotten, Bruce Dern, Mary Astor, Agnes Moorhead, Ellen Corby – already a friend of Joan's since *Harriet Craig* (1950) and later to win TV stardom as Grandma Walton – George Kennedy, and the brilliant and sensitive Victor Buono from *Baby Jane*. Fox had given Aldrich unlimited funds for the film.

Davis had not forgotten Joan's profuse 'Bless You's' from their earlier professional relationship, and now she began calling Joan 'Miss Bless You' around the location setting. There were other tensions, too, and no effort on Davis's part to be truly cordial around Joan. Davis could not forgive Joan for trying to scuttle her Academy Award nomination. In truth, both women were very similar in their unforgiving natures. Very soon Joan was flown back to California with what her publicist called 'pneumonia'. A week or so after her departure, when Aldrich had run out of scenes to shoot around her, he was told by the studio and his insurers either to replace Joan or to shut down the production. Davis urged him to call in her old Warners collegue, Olivia de Havilland, who was then living in Europe. This was promptly done, and Joan was out.

Joan should have handled the tensions she knew existed between herself and Davis in a more professional way and continued with production. The film received fair notices, the title song became a hit through a recording by Patti Page, and while never reaching the smash-hit league of *Baby Jane*, it still turned a profit.

★   ★   ★

From the time that Joan had returned to Manhattan in 1960 after selling her Brentwood house, she had often been 'on call' to help in chairing charitable events involving show-business people. By 1964–5, with President Lyndon Johnson's escalation of the Vietnam war, Joan was working increasingly with the revitalized Manhattan chapter of the United Service Organization (USO). She remembered with genuine pleasure her wartime involvement with the Hollywood Canteen, when she was a regular hostess there.

Joan's remarkable business efficiency which had marked her screen career was now transferred to her Pepsi-Cola public-relations work and her USO activities. With a single phone call to the Pepsi Company, she arranged for the Manhattan USO Club to receive free Pepsi on a regular basis. She involved her influential banker friend Mary Roebling in USO work, and USO drew in entertainers Pearl Bailey and Gypsy Rose Lee. She met regularly on a 'man-to-man' basis with industrialists such as Roger Blough (of US Steel) and Harvey Firestone (of Firestone Rubber) to plot strategies for fundraisers. They would meet at Manny Zwaaf's L'Étoile restaurant.

Joan quickly rose to the post of Vice President of the New York USO branch, and, by early 1965, had become such a dependable and inexpendable part of the organization that she was made their first honorary 'Woman of the Year'. The event took place on 2 March 1965 in the Grand Ballroom at the Plaza Hotel. Joan sat on the lower dais with George S. Leisure (her co-Vice President of the USO of New York City), her closest friends (Mary Roebling, Anita Loos, Helen Hayes, Kitty Carlisle Hart, Leo Jaffe, Maureen O'Sullivan and D. Mitchell Cox of the Pepsi-Cola company) and assorted politicos such as Paul Screvane and Herbert Brownell.

Joan then became intimately involved in a special USO event called 'USO A-GO-GO', in this, the decade of the discos and the 'Go-Go' dancers. Partly through Joan's work with Milton Feitelson of the USO, Sammy Davis, Jr (then appearing in the Broadway musical, *Golden Boy*), Eydie Gorme, Johnny Carson, The Beach Boys, Anthony Newley, Henry Fonda and opera diva Eleanor Steber were drawn into the event to perform. It took place at the old Madison Square Garden on 14 November 1965.

★   ★   ★

Joan's drinking had noticeably increased with Al Steele's death in 1959, but New York is a very wet town, and the distinction between an alcoholic and a regular drinker is a fine one. Joan drank at L'Étoile, at Sardi's and at other places where her USO work was often done. No one especially noticed. Everyone knew *what* she drank, of course – one hundred per cent proof Smirnoff vodka. She carried it in a silver flask dropped into her purse.

When, in the late 1960s, she signed to make two Herman Cohen horror films in England, Cohen, who knew how much she drank, made her promise never to drink in the mornings before shooting began. She insisted to Cohen, of course, that she was 'just a sipper'. She even convinced her secretary Betty Barker, who told me that Joan 'only sipped her drinks' of this. Someone who sips vodka all afternoon and into the evening is, however, by anyone's standards a serious alcoholic, and needs help.

Former Columbia Pictures president Leo Jaffe told me in 1993 that Joan had let it be known that she had stopped drinking eighteen months before her death (which makes the date around

Christmas 1975), because she had been frightened by the serious head injury incurred when she fell in her apartment after a long bout of drinking. She never sought outside help to stop drinking.

Just as with the William Castle pictures, the Herman Cohen horror films did Joan's reputation no serious harm, so *Berserk* (1968) and *Trog* (1969) have no special significance as being the last two theatrical films of Joan's career. The latter was shot in England on such a low budget that she had to make her costume changes in a car parked next to the moors location in remote 'mystery' country. These final big-screen productions, although made on the cheap, were not relegated to 'B-movie' status because they carried Joan's name above the title.

★　★　★

At this time, Christina won a leading role in the national company of the play *Barefoot in the Park*, with Joan's old friend Myrna Loy in the cast. During the run, Christina and the director, Harvey Medlinsky, fell in love and decided to get married. Joan was delighted with the news and planned, and paid for, the reception, booking a whole floor at her favourite hang-out, 21. Guests included the author of *Barefoot*, Neil Simon, Mike Nichols, the Sonny Werblins, and even 'Joanie Pants' LeSueur Simon, Uncle Hal's daughter.

During Christina's husband's absence on directorial chores, she and Joan remained in close touch. Whenever Joan over-drank and became hostile, it was Mamacita Brinke, her German maid and companion, who got the brunt of her anger, not Christina.

In 1968, Christina won a role in the long-running daytime-television soap opera, *The Secret Storm*. By October of that year, it was evident that Christina's marriage had fallen apart, and she flew to Mexico for a divorce. Almost immediately upon her return, she fell ill with a gynaecological problem (a tumour in her fallopian tubes) which required surgery. Joan unexpectedly got in touch with the soap opera's producer, and offered to play Christina's part on the show. CBS accepted, and for a week Joan went to their studios to tape the show. Joan was now drinking vodka during the day as well as in the evenings, and took her flask with her to the tapings. On the one day in which the author saw the show it seemed obvious that Joan was drunk, but she still had the professionalism and magnetism to hold her scenes together. In fact, someone who had never seen Joan before might only wonder just how old the character was supposed to be. Christina later wrote that she was very upset with her mother because she was sixty-three years old and drunk on the television screen. Joan, of course, had a ball, and, despite Christina's criticisms, the stint brought the show enormous publicity and shot the ratings skyward all that week.

★   ★   ★

In 1970, Joan signed a contract to write a book about her lifestyle for Simon & Schuster. In it, it becomes obvious that Joan had romanticized her marriage to Al Steele; she insisted in its pages that Steele was the one truly successful marriage of her life. It was the old Joan, recreating her life to conform to some ideal in her mind, forgetting the black eyes that he had given her on occasion and the debts he had piled up, believing that Pepsi-Cola would forgive them.

The book, called *My Way of Life*, was published in 1971 and turned out to be a kind of etiquette guide for corporate wives. It contained some autobiographical passages describing her Hollywood-studio routines, as well as something of her present life as an industrialist's widow. She discussed, in a positive way, her four marriages and her childhood, as well as her children. There were idyllic passages about her going trick-or-treating with the four of them on Hallowe'en, playing football in Brentwood vacant lots, and making transatlantic voyages together. Joan gave details on the three girls and how they turned out, but nothing on Christopher. The falsehood, of course, lies in the fact that, despite the fictional motherhood role, she had one child with whom she was out of touch altogether. Most of her friends loved the book, and Willie Haines said that it was better than her 1962 autobiography (written with Jane Ardmore) called

A Portrait of Joan – a book only slightly less inclined to fuzz over the problems and crises of her life.

Pepsi-Cola officially retired Joan in 1973, when she was officially sixty-five years old (she was in fact sixty-eight). She was furious, but some accommodation must have been made because in March 1976, she wrote to her friend Ken Young, saying, 'Forgive this brief letter but I'm rushing to the airport for several assignments for Pepsi-Cola Company.' Young had recently created a decal to put on his letters showing one large Crawford eye with black eyelashes. He called them 'eye stickers', and when he stuck one on a letter to Joan, she was thrilled and asked him to make up some for her.

Joan's film career, seemingly dead, came briefly to life again in 1972 when publicist and sometime producer John Springer obtained the film rights to Stephen Sondheim's smash Broadway musical *Follies*, which had starred a number of old-time 'legends' such as Yvonne deCarlo, Fifi D'Orsay, Alexis Smith and even Ethel Shutta, band-leader George Olsen's wife, who was famed for shuttling about the stage during the Olsen band appearances. It was John Springer's notion to change the setting of *Follies*, which was about the demise of an old Broadway musical house like the Winter Garden, where the last of the Ziegfeld Follies were performed, to the tearing-down of an old film studio. Springer continues:

'Here's the cast I had lined up: Elizabeth Taylor (in the Alexis Smith part), Richard Burton, Debbie Reynolds, who was on the phone with me around the clock and she was dying to do it, and I had Bette Davis, doing a new role that was being written in, but she would be singing [the show-stopping] "I'm Still Here".'

'I'm still here' is the best song in the show, in which Yvonne de Carlo nostalgically recalled the days when she was up and down – the economic scale – one day wearing a mink and another day putting newspapers in her worn-out shoes, and yet surviving it all. Davis thought that she was just such a survivor, but then so did Joan, who was asked to do the Yvonne deCarlo part. Instead of 'I'm Still Here', however, she would be singing 'Broadway Baby', about an old-time 'hoofer' who never really made it on Broadway, and the song in which Ethel Shutta had stopped the show for the second time.

'Joan was thrilled by all of this', Springer says. 'Peter Bogdanovich was brought in to direct . . . We had Gloria Swanson, Janet Leigh, Anne Jeffreys and Shelley Winters. We also got Fredric March, who was in a wheelchair by that time, to play the producer.'

Then it all collapsed, as many film projects do. Springer cannot recall just who pulled out, but it was doubtless going to cost more than the money-men thought was feasible. The film had become bigger than *Grand Hotel* and *Murder on the Orient Express* combined.

Joan was devastated. She agreed to an interview with writer Patricia Bosworth for the *Sunday New York Times*, which appeared in September under the headline: 'I'm still an actress! I want to act!' The interview came out as rather patronizing, reinforcing old beliefs about Crawford's obsession with plastic-covered furniture, and even including a whole paragraph about her dog's potty training. All this prompted Joan's old friend, Jeanine Basinger, to write a scathing rebuttal, which was almost as long as the interview itself.

Springer responded promptly by adding Joan to his list of 'Legendary ladies of the screen', in which Myrna Loy, Sylvia Sidney and Bette Davis appeared (individually) at Town Hall, along with clips from their hit films. When Jean Arthur backed out, Joan was invited and Springer persuaded her (reluctantly) to appear in a matinée. It was wildly successful – the best in the series. Joan's fans applauded her for ten minutes in a standing ovation the moment she appeared on stage, causing her to exclaim: 'I never knew there was so much love.'

During the 1970s, as Joan became more reclusive, the USO crowd was the first to notice. This embarrassed Joan, and, as poor health had caused her withdrawal in the first place, she changed her will to include the New York USO as a primary beneficiary. Even today, a substantial income from a special trust set up within Joan's estate is funnelled into the USO.

Clicquot, Joan's beloved poodle, had been dead for some years, and Joan had acquired in her place a shi-tzu, which she called Princess Lotus Blossom. The dog went everywhere with Joan, and was on her bed as she lay dying of cancer in 1977. Princess was given an adoptive home two days before Joan's actual death, as Joan had become too weak to look after her little companion properly.

Mrs Markham, a Christian-Science practitioner, came every day to read to Joan from Mary Baker Eddy and to pray with her. She also had a faithful old housekeeper living in until the last week of her life. On her very last day, she insisted on getting out of bed and making breakfast for a dedicated fan who had stayed by her bedside all night. It was a part of Joan's character to insist that a fan should keep this vigil, rather than a member of her family. As the departures of the housekeeper and then Princess were so strange, someone might have guessed that her death was imminent. One Imperial House neighbour, Doris Lily (author of *How to Marry a Millionaire*), believed that it was a suicide. Doug Fairbanks, Jr was of two minds on the subject, admitting that it was in Joan's character to do such a thing, meaning that Joan always had to be in control of the events in her life. With the knowledge that she was dying, she would control that, too, if she had the means to do so; with her painkiller pills, she had. However, her family accepted the opinion of the doctor on call that she had died of a heart attack. There was no autopsy to confirm this, and Cesar Romero expressed great shock and surprise upon hearing of her death 'because she had not been ill' to the best of his knowledge. Joan's death occurred on 10 May 1977. She was seventy-two years old, although she had admitted to sixty-nine.

Joan Crawford's fame had not dimmed much in the latter years; it was only in the wings waiting for the final act. Word of her death was flashed around the world on radio and television, and on every front page in America and abroad.

★ ★ ★

Christina claims that she began her memoir that summer (although this has been called into question, as Joan apparently knew about the book months before her death), which she called *Mother of the Year*, picking up her title from Joan's proudest moment when honoured by the USO as 'Woman of the Year'. Christina's book could equally have been called *Monster of the Year*. The film of *Mommie Dearest* followed in 1981, and was very popular despite uniformly bad reviews. The notoriety and wide coverage did have the effect of giving Christina an individual identity as well as a cause, both previously denied her because she was living in her mother's shadow. She had become one of the best-known enemies of child abuse in America.

Joan would have been outraged by it all, but, had she lived long enough, she would have seen her last major rival consumed by the same bitter gall when Bette Davis's daughter published *My Mother's Keeper*. It is even possible that Joan would have noted that the Davis brouhaha was minor compared to the one stirred up by her own Christina.

And wherever she is, she probably knows that now – in part in these pages, and to a larger degree in her indelible image on the screen – she has regained her own lustre, diminished very little by the passing notoriety. God knows, she was used to that in her lifetime.

EPILOGUE

When Joan Crawford died, she surrendered herself to history, which she had never altogether trusted. Her tight control over the facts of her life did not loosen immediately. Most obituaries, for instance, stated that she was only sixty-nine. Even *Variety* magazine pointed out that in the late 1940s she had 'concentrated on raising her four adopted children . . . her only survivors'.

Joan's obituary along with a (fairly) recent photograph, made the front page of the *New York Times*. It said: 'Miss Crawford was a quintessential superstar — an epitome of timeless glamour who personified for decades the dreams and disappointments of millions of American women.' She even made the editorial pages of countless daily papers, such as the *Lancaster* (Pennsylvania) *Intelligencer-Journal*, which headlined its piece: 'Quite a lady!'

Some of Joan's control began to unravel with the weeklies. In the issue published a week after her death, *Time Magazine* pointed out that:

> 'The customs of stardom clung to her even after death. In the obituaries of Joan Crawford, who died of a heart attack last week, some newspapers felt compelled to note a certain confusion about her age . . . Small, image-enhancing fibs like that are a habit of the profession whose code she helped to shape . . .'

Ten days after Joan's death, word of her exclusion of Christina and Christopher from any inheritance broke in the press.

Christina knew perfectly well that being cut out of her mother's will was a confirmation of the fact that Joan knew – probably many months earlier – about the book she was writing. Joan had in fact held a conversation with Betty Barker expressing concern about Christina's book at least a year before she died. Christopher, too, who had been refused admittance to Joan's apartment several years earlier, could not have been surprised by the wording of the exclusion 'for reasons which are well known to them'.

A controversy raged following the publication of *Mommie Dearest* in the autumn of 1978. The book's publication date may have been delayed by the William Morrow company to lessen the impact of Joan's disinheritance of her oldest children and ensure that the book was not viewed as having been written for recrimination and revenge. Joan's two younger children, Cathy and Cindy, called the book a collection of 'malicious lies'. Their protests were, however, overwhelmed by the willingness of the public to accept Christina's word as gospel, almost no one making the connection between mother and daughter as interested parties to the conscious manipulation of the truth that is as old as Hollywood itself. Since its publication, the book has never been out of print, and doubtless Christina would attribute that longevity to its being such a strong condemnation of child abuse. Certainly, the issue is an important one, and *Mommie Dearest* is an indictment of one of the twentieth century's major celebrities. The reader of this book will, however, have become aware of the distortions and the critical omissions made by Christina, and also now has some background facts – badly needed before – giving Joan at least the motivation behind some of her abusive behaviour.

The question will remain as to why *Mommie Dearest* continues to be read so widely. Is it because of its theme, or, because, in a world in which tabloid sensation is all too often accepted as fact, the book purports to give us the truth at last about a legend which never tried to pass as anything but what Joan Crawford wanted the public to know?

★ ★ ★

Of all of the leading ladies who had been as prominent as Joan during her peak years in the thirties, none of their deaths has been especially noted by the movie industry – not Constance Bennett's, not even Lillian Gish's nor Garbo's, both of whom died a dozen years after Joan. But Joan Crawford was special. She was not just a superstar; she was what Hollywood was all about – glamour and style, ability and self-confidence, and most of all, the adaptability to move forward with the times. There was nothing superannuated about Joan Crawford.

The memorial service at All Souls Unitarian Church in New York was crowded with her friends: Pearl Bailey sang, and a friend read Joan's credo, *Desiderata*: 'Go placidly amid the noise and haste, and remember what Peace there may be in Silence. As far as possible without surrender be on good terms with all people . . .' (found in Old Saint Paul's Church, Baltimore, dated 1692, according to Joan).

In Hollywood, there was a consensus that Motion Picture Authority head Jack Valenti's request for a minute of silence on all Hollywood lots on the Friday following her death was not enough. All of the industry's various guilds and organizations, from the American Film Institute to the Screen Directors' Guild, felt something more meaningful was called for. And so, more than two months after her death, an industry-wide tribute to her memory was held at the Samuel Goldwyn Theatre in the Academy of Motion Picture Arts and Sciences. For almost two hours, a packed throng of Hollywood's leading citizens, including director George Cukor (who read his perceptive eulogy from the *New York Times*), Myrna Loy, John Wayne, Steven Spielberg and hostess Kathleen Nolan, reminisced about Joan and the pleasures of working with her. There was frequent laughter; there was nothing sombre about it. Singer Jack Jones sang 'Everything I Have Is Yours' from Joan's *Dancing Lady*, and spoke about his being Joan's godson. Clips from her most famous films were shown, although the ones from *Rain* were aborted when the old reel snapped halfway through (an omen, Joan would have said, since she had come to hate the movie).

The ceremony was unique. Not even the death of Gloria Swanson was marked in such a way. No one there had not heard the gossip about Joan's children and the way they had been raised: like Sarah Bernhardt, Joan was not a lovable person; she was wilful and unforgiving, but she had become more important than the details of her life and its big and little scandals.

★　★　★

Would such a tribute have been held if *Mommie Dearest* had been published in the spring of 1977? Probably not. Christina's book effectively destroyed her mother's reputation. More to the point, can the passage of time ameliorate this dark and offensive image? As Joan herself once said of another matter, 'Time will tell.'

★　★　★　★　★　★　★　★　★　★　★

BIBLIOGRAPHY

Bacon, James *Hollywood is a Four-Letter Word*, Avon Books, New York (1977)

Bacon, James *Made in Hollywood*, Contemporary Books, Inc, Chicago (1977)

Baxter, John *Hollywood in the Thirties*, A. S. Barnes, New York (1968)

Behlmer, Rudy *Memo from David O. Selznick*, Viking Press, New York (1972)

Brownlow, Kevin *The Parade's Gone By*, Alfred Knopf, New York (1969)

Clurman, Harold *All People are Famous*, Harcourt, Brace, Jovanovich, New York (1974)

Cooper, Jackie *Please Don't Shoot My Dog*, William Morrow, New York (1988)

Crawford, Christina *Mommie Dearest*, William Morrow, New York (1978)

Crawford, Christina *Survivor: A Long Night's Journey from Anger and Chaos to the Peace of an Inner Awakening*, Donald I. Fine, Publisher, New York (1988)

Crawford, Joan 'I Couldn't Ask for More', article in the *Ladies' Home Journal*, Philadelphia (December 1942)

Crawford, Joan *My Way of Life*, Simon and Schuster, New York (1971)

Crawford, Joan *A Portrait of Joan* (with Jane Kesner Ardmore), Doubleday, Garden City (1962)

Crowther, Bosley *Hollywood Rajah: The Life and Times of Louis B. Mayer*, Dell Publishing Co, New York (1961)

Davis, Bette *The Lonely Life*, Lancer Books, New York (1963)

Davis, Bette *This 'N That* (with Michael Herskowitz, Putnam, New York (1987)

Fairbanks, Douglas, Jr *Salad Days*, Doubleday, New York (1988)

Fairbanks, Douglas, Jr *The Fairbanks Album* (with Richard Schickel), New York Graphic Society, Boston (1975)

Finch, Christopher and Rosenkrantz, Linda *Gone Hollywood: The Movie Colony in the Golden Age*, Doubleday, Garden City (1979)

Fonda, Henry *My Life* (with Howard Teichmann), New American Library, New York (1981)

Golding, Morton J. 'The Revolt of Joan Crawford's Daughter', article in *Redbook* magazine, New York (October 1960)

Goodman, Ezra *The Fifty-Year Decline and Fall of Hollywood*, Simon and Schuster, New York (1961)

Guiles, Fred Lawrence *Hanging On in Paradise*, McGraw-Hill, New York (1975)

Guiles, Fred Lawrence *Marion Davies*, McGraw-Hill, New York (1972)

Haver, Ronald *David O. Selznick's Hollywood*, Bonanza Books, New York (1985)

Higham, Charles and Greenberg, Joel *The Celluloid Muse: Hollywood Directors Speak*, Signet/New American Library, New York (1972)

Higham, Charles and Greenberg, Joel *Hollywood in the Forties*, Paperback Library, New York (1970)

Houston, David *Jazz Baby: A Biography of Joan Crawford*, St Martin's Press, New York (1983)

Kobal, John *Legends: Joan Crawford*, Little, Brown, Boston (1986)

Lambert, Gavin *GWTW: The Making of Gone With the Wind*, Atlantic, Little, Brown, Boston (1986)

Lambert, Gavin *Norma Shearer: A Life*, Knopf, New York (1990)

Lambert, Gavin *On Cukor*, Putman Publishing Group, New York (1972)

Loos, Anita *Cast of Thousands*, Grosset & Dunlap, New York (1977)

Loos, Anita *Kiss Hollywood Goodbye*, Viking Press, New York (1974)

Marx, Samuel *Mayer and Thalberg: The Make-Believe Saints*, Random House, New York (1975)

Mott, Frank Luther *A Gallery of Americans*, Mentor/New American Library, New York (1951)

Mowrey, George E. (ed.) *The Twenties: Fords, Flappers & Fanatics*, Prentice-Hall, Englewood Cliffs, NJ (1965)

Newquist, Roy *Conversations with Joan Crawford*, Citadel Press, Secaucus, NJ (1986)

Niven, David *Bring On the Empty Horses*, Putnam, New York (1975)

Parsons, Louella *Tell It to Louella*, Putnam, New York (1961)

Quirk, Lawrence J. *The Films of Joan Crawford*, Citadel Press, Secaucus (1968)

Quirk, Lawrence J. *Norma: The Life of Norma Shearer*, St Martin's Press, New York (1988)

Richman, Harry *A Hell of a Life* (with Richard Gehman), Duell, Sloan & Pearce, New York (1966)

Schulberg, Budd *Moving Pictures: Memoirs of a Hollywood Prince*, Stein and Day, Briarcliff Manor, New York (1981)

Selznick, Irene Mayer *A Private View*, Knopf, New York (1982)

Springer, John 'The Classic Crawford: A Montage of Memories', article in *After Dark* magazine (March 1978)

Swindell, Larry *Spencer Tracy*, World Publishing Co, New York and Cleveland (1969)

Temple, Shirley (Black), *Child Star*, McGraw-Hill, New York (1988)

Thomas, Bob *Joan Crawford: A Biography*, Simon and Schuster, New York (1978)

Thomas, Bob *Thalberg: Life and Legend*, Doubleday, Garden City (1969)

Tornabene, Lyn *Long Live the King: A Biography of Clark Gable*, Putnam, New York (1976)

Walker, Alexander *Joan Crawford: The Ultimate Star*, Weidenfeld & Nicolson, London (1983)

Wayne, Jane Ellen *Crawford's Men*, Prentice-Hall, New York (1988)

FILMOGRAPHY

Note: all release dated listed are for New York City. All films are Metro-Goldwyn-Mayer Productions unless otherwise indicated.

1925

PRETTY LADIES
Story by Adela Rogers St Johns
Adaptation by Alice D. G. Miller
Direction by Monta Bell
Cinematography by Ira Morgan
Cast
Ann Pennington, Lilyan Tashman,
Tom Moore, Conrad Nagel,
Bernard Randall, Helen D'Algy,
George K. Arthur, Norma Shearer,
Lucille LeSueur, Paul Ellis, Roy
D'Arcy, Gwendolyn Lee, Dorothy
Seastrom, Lew Harvey, Chad
Huber, Walter Shumway, Dan
Crimmins and Jimmy Quinn
Released 14 July 1925

OLD CLOTHES
Produced by Jack Coogan, Sr
Story by Willard Mack
Direction by Eddie Cline
Cinematography by Frank B. Good
Cast
Jackie Coogan, Max Davidson,

Lillian Elliott, Joan Crawford, Alan
Forrest, James Mason and Stanton
Heck.
Released 9 November 1925

THE ONLY THING
Story by Elinor Glyn
Supervised by Elinor Glyn
Direction by Jack Conway
Cinematography by Chester Lyons
Cast
Eleanor Boardman, Conrad Nagel,
Edward Connelly, Louis Payne,
Arthur Edmond Carew, Vera Lewis,
Carrie Clark Ward, Constance
Wylie, Dale Fuller, Ned Sparks,
Mario Carillo, David Mir, Michael
Pleschkoff, Buddy Smith, Joan
Crawford, Frank Braidwood, Derke
Glynne and Mary Hawes
Released 23 November 1925

SALLY, IRENE AND MARY
From the musical play by Eddie
Dowling and Cyrus Woods
Adaptation by Edmund Goulding
Directed by Edmund Goulding
Cinematography by John Arnold
Cast
Constance Bennett, Joan Crawford,
Sally O'Neil, William Haines,

Douglas Gilmore, Ray Howard,
Aggie Herrin, Kate Price, Lillian
Elliott, Henry Kolker, Sam
DeGrasse and Mae Cooper
Released 7 December 1925

1926

THE BOOB
Adaptation by Kenneth Clarke
Story by George Scarborough and
Annette Westbay
Direction by William A. Wellman
Titles by Katherine Hiliker and
H. H. Caldwell
Cinematography by William
Daniels
Cast
Gertrude Olmstead, George K.
Arthur, Joan Crawford, Charles
Murray, Antonio D'Algy, Hank
Mann and Babe London
(Release date unknown)

TRAMP, TRAMP, TRAMP (*A First
National Production*)
Produced by Harry Langdon
Corporation
Story by Frank Capra, Tim
Whelan, Hal Conklin, J. Frank
Holliday, George Duffy and
Murray Roth
Direction by Harry Edwards
Cinematography by Elgin Lesley
and George Spear
Cast
Harry Langdon, Joan Crawford,
Edwards Davis, Carlton Griffith,
Alec B. Francis, Brooks Benedict
and Tom Murray
Released 24 May 1926

PARIS
Story by Edmund Goulding
Direction by Edmund Goulding
Cinematography by John Arnold
Cast
Charles Ray, Joan Crawford,
Douglas Gilmore, Michael Visaroff,
Rose Dione and Jean Galeron
Released 1 June 1926

1927

THE TAXI DRIVER
Story by Robert Terry Shannon
Adaptation by A. P. Younger
Direction by Harry Millarde
Cinematography by Ira H. Morgan
Cast
Joan Crawford, Owen Moore,
Douglas Gilmore, Marc
McDermott, Willam Orlamond,
Gertrude Astor, Rockcliffe
Fellowes, Claire McDowell and
Bert Roach
Released 8 March 1927

WINNERS OF THE WILDERNESS ('THE
GLORIOUS ADVENTURE')
Story by John Thomas Neville
Direction by W. S. 'Woody' Van
Dyke
Cinematography by Clyde De
Vinna
Cast
Tim McCoy, Joan Crawford,
Edward Connelly, Frank Currier,
Roy D'Arcy, Louise Lorraine,
Edward Hearn, Will R. Walling
and Tom O'Brien
Released 1 April 1972

THE UNDERSTANDING HEART
Story by Peter B. Kyne

Adaptation by Edward T. Lowe, Jr
Direction by Jack Conway
Cinematography by John Arnold
Cast
Francis X. Bushman, Jr, Joan
Crawford, Rockcliffe Fellowes,
Carmel Myers, Richard Carle and
Harvey Clark
Released 10 May 1927

THE UNKNOWN
Story by Tod Browning
Scenario by Waldemar Young
Direction by Tod Browning
Cinematography by Merritt
Gerstad
Cast
Lon Chaney, Norman Kerry, Joan
Crawford, Nick de Ruiz, John
George and Frank Lanning
Released 13 June 1927

TWELVE MILES OUT
From the play by William Anthony
McGuire
Adaptation by Sada Cowan
Direction by Jack Conway
Cinematography by Ira H. Morgan
Cast
John Gilbert, Ernest Torrence, Joan
Crawford, Betty Compson, Bert
Roach, Eileen Percy (Ruby),
Edward Earle, Tom O'Brien and
Harvey Clark
Released 26 July 1927

SPRING FEVER
From the play by Vincent Lawrence
Scenario by Albert Lewin and
Frank Davies
Direction by Edward Sedgwick
Titles by Ralph Spence
Cinematography by Ira H. Morgan

Cast
William Haines, Joan Crawford,
George K. Arthur, George Fawcett,
Eileen Percy (Ruby), Edward Earle,
Bert Woodruff and Lee Moran
Released 18 October 1927

1928

WEST POINT
Story by Raymond L. Schrock
Direction by Edward Sedgwick
Titles by Joe Farnham
Editing by Frank Sullivan
Cinematography by Ira H. Morgan
Cast
William Haines, Joan Crawford,
Neil Neely, William Bakewell,
Ralph Emerson, Edward
Richardson, Baury Bradford
Richardson, Leon Kellar, Major
Raymond G. Moses and Major
Philip B. Fleming
Released 2 January 1928

ROSE MARIE
From the operetta by Otto Harbach
and Oscar Hammerstein, II
Scenario and direction by Lucien
Hubbard
Editing by Carl F. Pierson
Cinematography by John Arnold
Cast
Joan Crawford, James Murray,
House Peters, Creighton Hale,
Gibson Gowland, Polly Moran,
Lionel Belmore, William
Orlamond, Gertrude Astor, Ralph
Yearsley, Sven Hugo Borg and
Harry Gribbon
Released 13 February 1928

ACROSS TO SINGAPORE
Story by Ben Ames Williams
Continuity by E. Richard Schayer
Direction by William Nigh
Editing by Ben Lewis
Cinematography by John Seitz
Cast
Ramon Novarro, Joan Crawford,
Ernest Torrence, Frank Currier,
Dan Wolheim, Duke Martin,
Edward Connelly and James Mason
Released 30 April 1928

THE LAW OF THE RANGE
Story by Norman Houston
Scenario by E. Richard Schayer
Titles by Robert Hopkins
Direction by William Nigh
Editing by Dan Sharits
Cinematography by Clyde DeVinna
Cast
Tim McCoy, Joan Crawford, Rex
Lease, Bodil Rosing and Tenen
Holtz
(Release date unknown)

FOUR WALLS
Story by Dana Burnet and George
Abbott
Continuity by Alice D. G. Miller
Titles by Joe Farnham
Direction by William Nigh
Editing by Harry Reynolds
Cinematography by James Wong
Howe
Cast
John Gilbert, Joan Crawford, Vera
Gordon, Carmel Myers, Robert
Emmet O'Connor, Louis Natheaux
and Jack Byron
Released 20 August 1928

OUR DANCING DAUGHTERS (*A
Cosmopolitan Production* [*MGM*])
Story and Scenario by Josephine
Lovett
Titles by Marion Ainslee and Ruth
Cummings
Direction by Harry Beaumont
Editing by William Hamilton
Cinematography by George Barnes
Cast
Joan Crawford, Johnny Mack
Brown, Dorothy Sebastian, Anita
Page, Nils Asther, Dorothy
Cummings, Huntley Gordon,
Evelyn Hall, Sam De Grasse and
Edward Nugent
Released 8 October 1928

DREAM OF LOVE
From the play *Adrienne Lecouvreur*
by Eugene Scribe and Ernest
Légouve
Continuity by Dorothy Farnham
Titles by Marion Ainslee and Ruth
Cummings
Direction by Fred Niblo
Editing by James MacKay
Cinematography by Oliver Marsh
and William Daniels
Cast
Joan Crawford, Nils Asther, Aileen
Pringle, Warner Oland, Carmel
Myers, Harry Reinhardt, Harry
Myers, Alphonse Martell and
Fletcher Norton
Released 24 December 1928

1929
───────────────────────────
THE DUKE STEPS OUT
Story by Lucien Cary
Adaptation by Raymond Schrock
and Dale Van Every

Titles by Joe Farnham
Direction by James Cruze
Editing by George Hively
Cinematography by Ira H. Morgan
Cast
William Haines, Joan Crawford,
Karl Dane, Tenen Holtz, Eddie
Nugent, Jack Roper, Delmer Daves,
Luke Cosgrave and Herbert Prior
Released 15 April 1929

OUR MODERN MAIDENS
Produced by Hunt Stromberg
Story and screenplay by Josephine
Lovett
Titles by Ruth Cummings and
Marion Ainslee
Direction by Jack Conway
Editing by Sam Zimbalist
Cinematography by Oliver Marsh
Cast
Joan Crawford, Rod LaRocque,
Douglas Fairbanks, Jr, Eddie
Nugent, Anita Page, Josephine
Dunne and Albert Gran
Released 7 September 1929

HOLLYWOOD REVUE OF 1929 (*A
Cosmopolitan Production [MGM]*)
Produced by Harry Rapf
Dialogue by Al Boasberg and
Robert Hopkins
Directed by Charles F. Reisner
Art direction by Cedric Gibbons
and Richard Day
Costumes by David Cox
Dances and Ensembles by Sammy
Lee
Orchestra and Musical Score by
Arthur Lange
Music and Lyrics by Gus Edwards,
Joe Goodwin, Nacio Herb Brown,
Arthur Freed, Dave Snell, Louis

Alter, Jessie Greer, Ray Klages,
Martin Broones, Fred Fisher, Jo
Trent, Avy Rice and Ballard
MacDonald
Editing by William Gray
Cinematography by John Arnold,
Irving G. Reis and Maximilian Fabian
Cast
Conrad Nagel, Bessie Love, Joan
Crawford, William Haines, Buster
Keaton, Anita Page, Karl Dane,
George K. Arthur, Gwen Lee,
Ernest Belcher's Dancing Tots,
Marie Dressler, Marion Davies,
Cliff Edwards, Charles King, Polly
Moran, Gus Edwards, Lionel
Barrymore, Jack Benny, the Brox
Sisters, Albertina Rasch Ballet,
Natacha Natova and Company, the
Rounders, Norma Shearer, John
Gilbert, and Laurel and Hardy
Released 15 August 1929

UNTAMED
Story by Charles E. Scoggins
Adaptation by Sylvia Thalberg and
Frank Butler
Dialogue by Willard Mack
Titles by Lucile Newmark
Direction by Jack Conway
Editing by William Gray and
Charles Hockberg
Cinematography by Oliver Marsh
Cast
Joan Crawford, Robert
Montgomery, Ernest Torrence,
Holmes Herbert, Joan Miljan,
Gwen Lee, Edward Nugent, Don
Terry, Gertrude Astor, Milton
Farney, Lloyd Ingram, Grace
Cunard, Tom O'Brien and Wilson
Benge
Released 30 November 1929

1930

1931

MONTANA MOON
Story and screen play by Sylvia
Thalberg and Frank Butler
Dialogue by Joe Farnham
Direction by Malcolm St Clair
Music and lyrics by Nacio Herb
Brown and Arthur Freed
Editing by Carl L. Pierson and
Leslie P. Wildier
Cinematography by William
Daniels
Cast
Joan Crawford, Johnny Mack
Brown, Dorothy Sebastian, Ricardo
Cortez, Benny Rubin, Cliff
Edwards, Karl Dane and Lloyd
Ingraham
Released 14 April 1930

OUR BLUSHING BRIDES
Story by Bess Meredyth
Screenplay by Bess Meredyth and
John Howard Lawson
Additional dialogue by Edwin
Justus Mayer
Direction by Harry Beaumont
Editing by George Hively and
Harold Palmer
Cinematography by Merritt B.
Gerstad
Cast
Joan Crawford, Anita Page,
Dorothy Sebastian, Robert
Montgomery, Raymond Hackett,
John Miljan, Hedda Hopper, Albert
Conti, Edward Brophy, Robert
Emmett O'Connor, Martha Sleeper,
Gwen Lee, Mary Doran, Catherine
Moylan, Norma Drew, Claire Dodd
and Wilda Mansfield
Released 2 August 1930

PAID
From the play *Within the Law* by
Bayard Veiller
Adaptation by Lucien Hubbard and
Charles MacArthur
Dialogue by Charles MacArthur
Direction by Sam Wood
Editing by Hugh Wynn
Cinematography by Charles Rosher
Cast
Joan Crawford, Robert Armstrong,
Marie Prevost, Kent Douglass, John
Miljan, Hale Hamilton, Purnell B.
Pratt, Polly Moran, Robert Emmett
O'Connor, Tyrell Davis, William
Bakewell, George Cooper, Gwen
Lee and Isabel Withers
Released 3 January 1931

DANCE, FOOLS, DANCE
Story by Aurania Rouverol
Continuity by Richard Schayer
Dialogue by Aurania Rouverol
Direction by Harry Beaumont
Editing by George Hively
Cinematography by Charles Rosher
Cast
Joan Crawford, Lester Vail, Cliff
Edwards, William Bakewell,
William Holden, Clark Gable,
Earle Fox, Purnell B. Pratt, Hale
Hamilton, Natalie Moorhead, Joan
Marsh and Russell Hopton
Released 21 March 1931

LAUGHING SINNERS
From the play *Torch Song* by
Kenyon Nicholson
Continuity by Bess Meredyth
Dialogue by Martin Flavin
Direction by Harry Beaumont

Editing by George Hively
Cinematography by Charles Rosher
Cast
Joan Crawford, Neil Hamilton,
Clark Gable, Marjorie Rambeau,
Guy Kibbee, Cliff Edwards, Roscoe
Karns, Gertrude Short, George
Cooper, George F. Marion and Bert
Woodruff
Released 4 July 1931

THIS MODERN AGE
From the story 'Girls Together' by
Mildred Cram
Continuity and Dialogue by Sylvia
Thalberg and Frank Butler
Direction by Nicholas Grinde
Editing by William LeVanway
Cinematography by Charles Rosher
Cast
Joan Crawford, Pauline Frederick,
Neil Hamilton, Monroe Owsley,
Hobart Bosworth, Emma Dunn,
Albert Conti, Adrienne
d'Ambricourt and Marcelle Corday
Released 7 September 1931

POSSESSED
From the play *The Mirage* by
Edgar Selwyn
Adaptation by Lenore Coffee
Direction by Clarence Brown
Cinematography by Oliver T.
Marsh
Cast
Joan Crawford, Clark Gable,
Wallace Ford, Skeets Gallagher,
Frank Conroy, Marjorie White,
John Miljan and Clara Blandick
Released 28 November 1931

1932

GRAND HOTEL
Adapted from the play by Vicki
Baum
Scenario by William A. Drake
Directed by Edmund Golding
Editing by Blanche Newell
Cinematography by William
Daniels
Cast
Greta Garbo, John Barrymore, Joan
Crawford, Wallace Beery, Lionel
Barrymore, Jean Hersholt, Robert
McWade and Purnell B. Pratt
Released 12 April 1932

LETTY LYNTON
From the novel by Marie Belloc
Lowndes
Adaptation by John Meehan and
Wanda Tuchock
Direction by Clarence Brown
Costumes by Adrian
Editing by Conrad A. Nervig
Cinematography by Oliver T.
Marsh
Cast
Joan Crawford, Robert
Montgomery, Nils Asther, Lewis
Stone, May Robson, Louise Closser
Hale, Emma Dunn, Walter Walker
and William Pawley
Released 30 April 1932

RAIN (*Produced by United Artists*)
From the play by John Colton and
Clemence Randolph
From the story, 'Miss Thompson',
by W. Somerset Maugham
Screenplay by Maxwell Anderson
Direction by Lewis Milestone
Editing by W. Duncan Mansfield

Cinematography by Oliver T. Marsh

Cast

Joan Crawford, Walter Huston, William Gargan, Beulah Bondi, Matt Moore, Kendall Lee, Guy Kibbee, Walter Catlett, Ben Hendricks, Jr and Fred Howard

Released 13 October 1932

1933

TODAY WE LIVE

From the story by William Faulkner

Screen play by Edith Fitzgerald and Dwight Taylor

Direction by Howard Hawks

Editing by Edward Curtiss

Cinematography by Oliver T. Marsh

Cast

Joan Crawford, Gary Cooper, Robert Young, Franchot Tone, Roscoe Karns, Louise Closser Hale, Rollo Lloyd and Hilda Vaughn

Released 15 April 1933

DANCING LADY

Produced by David O. Selznick

From the novel by James Warner Bellah

Screenplay by Allen Rivkin and P. J. Wolfson

Direction by Robert Z. Leonard

Music and lyrics by Burton Lane, Harold Adamson, Richard Rodgers, Lorenz Hart, Jimmy McHugh, and Dorothy Fields

Conducted by Lou Silvers

Costumes by Adrian

Editing by Margaret Booth

Cinematography by Oliver T.

Marsh

Cast

Joan Crawford, Clark Gable, Franchot Tone, May Robson, Winnie Lightner, Fred Astaire, Robert Benchley, Ted Healy, Gloria Foy, Art Jarrett, Grant Mitchell, Maynard Holmes, Nelson Eddy, The Three Stooges and Sterling Holloway

Released 1 December 1933

1934

SADIE MCKEE

Produced by Lawrence Weingarten

From the story 'Pretty Sadie McKee' by Vina Delmar

Screenplay by John Meehan

Direction by Clarence Brown

Costumes by Adrian

Editing by Hugh Wynn

Cinematography by Oliver T. Marsh

Cast

Joan Crawford, Gene Raymond, Franchot Tone, Edward Arnold, Esther Ralston, Earl Oxford, Jean Dixon, Leo Carrillo, Akim Tamiroff, Zelda Sears, Helen Ware, Helen Freeman, Gene Austin and Candy and Coco

Released 19 May 1934

CHAINED

Produced by Hunt Stromberg

From the story by Edgar Selwyn

Screenplay by John Lee Mahin

Direction by Clarence Brown

Costumes by Adrian

Editing by Robert J. Kern

Cinematography by George Folsey

Cast
Joan Crawford, Clark Gable, Otto
Kruger, Stuart Erwin, Una
O'Connor, Marjorie Gateson and
Akim Tamiroff
Released 1 September 1934

FORSAKING ALL OTHERS
Produced by Bernard H. Hyman
From the story by Edward Barry
Roberts and Frank Morgan Cavett
Screenplay by Joseph L.
Mankiewicz
Direction by W. S. 'Woody' Van
Dyke
Costumes by Adrian
Editing by Tom Held
Cinematography by Gregg Toland
and George Folsey
Cast
Joan Crawford, Clark Gable, Robert
Montgomery, Charles Butterworth,
Billie Burke, Frances Drake,
Rosalind Russell, Tom Rickets,
Arthur Treacher and Greta Moyer
Released 21 December 1934

1935
_____

NO MORE LADIES
Produced by Irving Thalberg
From the play by A. E. Thomas
Screenplay by Donald Ogden
Stewart and Horace Jackson
Direction by Edward H. Griffith
and George Cukor
Costumes by Adrian
Editing by Frank E. Hull
Cinematography by Oliver T.
Marsh
Cast
Joan Crawford, Robert
Montgomery, Charlie Ruggles,

Franchot Tone, Edna May Oliver,
Gail Patrick, Reginald Denny,
Vivienne Osborne, Joan Burfield,
Arthur Treacher, David Horsley
and Jean Chatburn
Released 22 June 1935

I LIVE MY LIFE
Produced by Bernard H. Hyman
From the short story
'Claustrophobia' by A. Carter
Goodloe
Development by Gottfried
Reinhardt and Ethel Borden
Screenplay by Joseph L.
Mankiewicz
Direction by W. S. 'Woody' Van
Dyke
Costumes by Adrian
Editing by Tom Held
Cinematography by George Folsey
Cast
Joan Crawford, Brian Aherne,
Frank Morgan, Aline MacMahon,
Eric Blore, Fred Keating, Jessie
Ralph, Arthur Treacher, Hedda
Hopper, Frank Conroy, Etienne
Girardot, Edward Brophy, Sterling
Holloway, Hilda Vaughn, Vince
Barnett, Lionel Stander and Hale
Hamilton
Released 12 October 1935

1936
_____

THE GORGEOUS HUSSY
Produced by Joseph L. Mankiewicz
Based on the novel by Samuel
Hopkins Adams
Screenplay by Ainsworth Morgan
and Stephen Morehouse Avery
Direction by Clarence Brown
Art direction by Cedric Gibbons

Musical score by Herbert Stothart
Costumes by Adrian
Editing by Blanche Sewell
Cinematography by George Folsey
Cast
Joan Crawford, Robert Taylor,
Lionel Barrymore, Franchot Tone,
Melvyn Douglas, James Stewart,
Alison Skipworth, Louis Calhern,
Beulah Bondi, Melville Cooper,
Sidney Toler, Gene Lockhart, Clara
Bandick, Frank Conroy, Nydia
Westman, Charles Trowbridge,
Willard Robertson, Ruby DeRemer,
Betty Blythe and Zeffie Tilbury
Released 5 September 1936

LOVE ON THE RUN
Produced by Joseph L. Mankiewcz
From the story by Alan Green and
Julian Brodie
Screenplay by John Lee Mahin,
Manuel Seff and Gladys Hurlburt
Direction by W. S. 'Woody' Van
Dyke
Costumes by Adrian
Editing by Frank Sullivan
Cinematography by Oliver T. Marsh
Cast
Joan Crawford, Clark Gable,
Franchot Tone, Reginald Owen,
Mona Barrie, Ivan Lebedeff,
Charles Judels and William
Demarest
Released 28 November 1936

1937

THE LAST OF MRS CHEYNEY
Produced by Lawrence Weingarten
Adapted from the play by Frederick
Lonsdale
Screenplay by Leon Gordon,

Samson Raphaelson, and Monckton
Hoffe
Direction by Richard Boleslawski
Art direction by Cedric Gibbons
Music by Dr William Axt
Editing by Frank Sullivan
Cinematography by George Folsey
Cast
Joan Crawford, William Powell,
Robert Montgomery, Frank
Morgan, Jessie Ralph, Nigel Bruce,
Colleen Clare, Benita Hume, Ralph
Forbes, Aileen Pringle, Melville
Cooper, Leonard Carey, Sara
Haden, Lemsden Hare, Wallis
Clark and Barnett Parker
Released 19 February 1937

THE BRIDE WORE RED
Produced by Joseph L. Mankiewicz
Based on the unpublished play *The
Girl from Trieste* by Ferenc Molnar
Screenplay by Tess Slesinger and
Bradbury Foote
Direction by Dorothy Arzner
Art direction by Cedric Gibbons
Costumes by Adrian
Music by Franz Waxman
Editing by Adrienne Fazan
Cinematography by George Folsey
Cast
Joan Crawford, Franchot Tone,
Robert Young, Billie Burke,
Reginald Owen, Lynne Carver,
George Zucco, Mary Phillips, Paul
Porcasi, Dickie Moore and Frank
Puglia
Released 15 October 1937

1938

MANNEQUIN
Produced by Joseph L. Mankiewicz

Developed from an unpublished
story by Katharine Brush
Direction by Frank Borzage
Costumes by Adrian
Editing by Frederic Y. Smith
Cinematography by George Folsey
Cast
Joan Crawford, Spencer Tracy, Alan
Curtis, Ralph Morgan, Mary
Phillips, Oscar O'Shea, Elizabeth
Risdon and Leo Gorcey
Released 21 January 1938

1939

THE SHINING HOUR
Produced by Joseph L. Mankiewicz
Based on the play by Keith Winter
Screenplay by Jane Murfin and
Ogden Nash
Direction by Frank Borzage
Costumes by Adrian
Dance arranged by De Marco
Music by Franz Waxman
Editing by Frank E. Hull
Cinematography by George Folsey
Cast
Joan Crawford, Margaret Sullavan,
Robert Young, Melvyn Douglas,
Fay Bainter, Allyn Joslyn, Hattie
McDaniel, Oscar O'Shea, Frank
Albertson and Harry Barris
Released 20 January 1939

THE ICE FOLLIES OF 1939
Produced by Harry Rapf
From the story by Leonard
Praskins
Screenplay by Leonard Praskins,
Florence Ryerson and Edgar Allan
Woolf
Direction by Reinhold Schunzel
Costumes by Adrian

Music by Rodger Edens
Editing by W. Donn Hayes
Cinematography by Joseph
Ruttenberg and Oliver T. Marsh
Cast
Joan Crawford, James Stewart, Lew
Ayres, Lewis Stone, Bess Ehrhardt,
Lionel Stander, and Charles D.
Brown
'The International Ice Follies' with
Bess Ehrhardt, Roy Shipstad, Eddie
Shipstad and Oscar Johnson
Released 17 March 1939

THE WOMEN
Produced by Hunt Stromberg
Based on the play by Clare Boothe
Screenplay by Anita Loos and Jane
Murfin
Direction by George Cukor
Art direction by Cedric Gibbons
Costumes by Adrian
Music by Edward Ward and David
Snell
Editing by Robert J. Kerns
Cinematography by Oliver T.
Marsh and Joseph Ruttenberg
Cast
Norma Shearer, Joan Crawford,
Rosalind Russell, Mary Boland,
Paulette Goddard, Phyllis Povah,
Joan Fontaine, Virginia Weidler,
Lucile Watson, Florence Nash,
Muriel Hutchinson, Esther Dale,
Ann Moriss, Ruth Hussey, Dennie
Moore, Mary Cecil, Mary Beth
Hughes, Virginia Grey, Marjorie
Main, Cora Witherspoon and
Hedda Hopper
Released 22 September 1939

1940

STRANGE CARGO
Produced by Joseph L. Mankiewicz
Based on the book *Not Too Narrow, Not Too Deep* by Richard Sale
Screenplay by Lawrence Hazard
Direction by Frank Borzage
Art direction by Cedric Gibbons
Music by Franz Waxman
Editing by Robert J. Kern
Cinematography by Robert Planck
Cast
Joan Crawford, Clark Gable, Ian Hunter, Peter Lorre, Paul Lukas, Albert Dekker, J. Edward Bromberg, Eduardo Ciannelli, John Arledge, Frederick Worlock, Bernard Nedell and Victor Varconi
Released 26 April 1940

SUSAN AND GOD
Produced by Hunt Stromberg
Based on the play by Rachel Crothers
Screenplay by Anita Loos
Direction by George Cukor
Art direction by Cedric Gibbons
Costumes by Adrian
Music by Herbert Stothart
Editing by William H. Terhune
Cinematography by Robert Planck
Cast
Joan Crawford, Fredric March, Ruth Hussey, John Carroll, Rita Hayworth, Nigel Bruce, Bruce Cabot, Rita Quigley, Rose Hobart, Constance Collier, Gloria DeHaven, Richard O. Crane, Norman Mitchell and Marjorie Main
Released 12 July 1940

1941

A WOMAN'S FACE
Produced by Victor Saville
From the play *Il Etais Une Fois* by Francis de Croisset
Screenplay by Donald Ogden Stewart
Direction by George Cukor
Art direction by Cedric Gibbons
Costumes by Adrian
Music by Bronislau Kaper
Editing by Frank Sullivan
Cinematography by Robert Planck
Cast
Joan Crawford, Melvyn Douglas, Conrad Veidt, Osa Massen, Reginald Owen, Albert Bassermann, Marjorie Main, Donald Meek, Connie Gilchrist, Richard Nichols, Charles Quigley, Gwili Andre, Clifford Brooke, George Zucco, Henry Kolker, Robert Warwick, Gilbert Emery, Henry Daniell, Sarah Padden and William Farnum
Released 16 May 1941

WHEN LADIES MEET
Produced by Robert Z. Leonard and Orville O. Dull
Based on the play by Rachel Crothers
Screenplay by S. K. Lauren and Anita Loos
Direction by Robert Z. Leonard
Art direction by Cedric Gibbons
Costumes by Adrian
Music by Bronislau Kaper
Editing by Robert Kern
Cinematography by Robert Planck
Cast
Joan Crawford, Robert Taylor,

Greer Garson, Herbert Marshall,
Spring Byington, Rafael Storm,
Florence Shirley, Leslie Francis,
Olaf Hytten and Mona Barrie
Released 5 September 1941

1942

THEY ALL KISSED THE BRIDE
(*Produced by Columbia Pictures*)
Produced by Edward Kaufman
From the story by Gina Kaus and
Andrew P. Solt
Screenplay by P. J. Wolfson
Direction by Alexander Hall
Art direction by Lionel Banks and
Cary Odell
Costumes by Irene
Music by Morris Stoloff
Editing by Viola Lawrence
Cinematography by Joseph Walker
Cast
Joan Crawford, Melvyn Douglas,
Roland Young, Billie Burke, Allan
Jenkins, Andrew Tombes, Helen
Parrish, Emory Parnell, Mary
Treen, Nydia Westman, Ivan
Simpson, Roger Clark, Gordon
Jones and Edward Gargan
Released 31 July 1942

1943

REUNION IN FRANCE
Produced by Joseph L. Mankiewicz
Based on original screen-story by
Ladislaus Bus-Fekete
Screenplay by Jan Lustig, Marvin
Borowsky and Marc Connelly
Direction by Jules Dassin
Art direction by Cedric Gibbons
Costumes by Irene
Music by Franz Waxman

Editing by Elmo Veron
Cinematography by Robert Planck
Cast
Joan Crawford, John Wayne, Philip
Dorn, Reginald Owen, Albert
Basserman, John Carradine, Ann
Ayars, J. Edward Bromberg, Moroni
Olsen, Howard Da Silva and Henry
Daniell
Released 5 March 1943

ABOVE SUSPICION
Produced by Victor Saville
Based on the novel by Helen
MacInnes
Screenplay by Keith Winter,
Melville Baker and Patricia
Coleman
Direction by Richard Thorpe
Art direction by Randall Duell
Music by Bronislau Kaper
Costumes by Irene and Gile Steele
Editing by George Hively
Cinematography by Robert Planck
Cast
Joan Crawford, Fred MacMurray,
Conrad Veidt, Basil Rathbone,
Reginald Owen, Cecil
Cunningham, Richard Ainley, Ann
Shoemaker, Sara Haden, Felix
Bressart, Bruce Lestor, Johanna
Hoper, Lotta Palfi and Alex Papana
Released 6 August 1943

1944

(*Warner Brothers productions unless
otherwise indicated*)
HOLLYWOOD CANTEEN
Produced by Alex Gottlieb
Original screenplay by Delmar
Daves
Direction by Delmar Daves

Art direction by Leo Kuter
Musical direction by Leo F.
Forbstein
Musical numbers created by LeRoy
Prinz
Music adapted by Ray Heindorf
Editing by Christian Nyby
Cinematography by Bert Glennon
Cast
Joan Leslie, Robert Hutton, Dane
Clark and Janis Paige.
Guest stars: Andrews Sisters, Jack
Benny, Joe E. Brown, Eddie Cantor,
Kitty Carlisle, Jack Carson, Joan
Crawford, Bette Davis, John
Garfield, Sydney Greenstreet, Paul
Henreid, Peter Lorre, Ida Lupino,
Irene Manning, Joan McCracken,
Dennis Morgan, Eleanor Parker,
Roy Rogers and Trigger, Barbara
Stanwyck and Jane Wyman
Released 16 December 1944

1945

MILDRED PIERCE
Produced by Jerry Wald
From the novel by James M. Cain
Screenplay by Ranald MacDougall
Direction by Michael Curtiz
Art direction by Anton Grot
Costumes by Milo Anderson
Music by Max Steiner
Editing by David Weisbart
Cinematography by Ernest Haller
Cast
Joan Crawford, Jack Carson,
Zachary Scott, Eve Arden, Ann
Blythe, Bruce Bennett, George
Tobias, Lee Patrick, Moroni Olsen,
Jo Anne Marlow and Barbara
Brown
Released 29 September 1945

1946

HUMORESQUE
Produced by Jerry Wald
Based on the story by Fannie Hurst
Screenplay by Clifford Odets and
Zachary Gold
Direction by Jean Negulesco
Art direction by Hugh Reticker
Joan Crawford's costumes by
Adrian
Music conducted by Franz Waxman
Musical direction by Leo F.
Forbstein
Music consultancy by Isaac Stern
Editing by Rudi Fehr
Cinematography by Ernest Haller
Cast
Joan Crawford, John Garfield,
Oscar Levant, J. Carroll Naish, Joan
Chandler, Tom D'Andrea, Peggy
Knudsen, Ruth Nelson, Craig
Stevens, Paul Cavanagh, Richard
Gaines, John Abbott, Bobby Blake,
Tommy Cook, Don McGuire, Fritz
Leiber, Peg La Centra, Nestor Paiva
and Richard Walsh
Released 26 December 1946

1947

POSSESSED
Produced by Jerry Wald
Based on story 'One Man's Secret'
by Rita Weiman
Screenplay by Silvia Richards and
Ranald MacDougall
Direction by Curtis Bernhardt
Art direction by Anton Grot
Joan Crawford's costumes by Adrian
Music by Franz Waxman
Cinematography by Joseph
Valentine

Cast
Joan Crawford, Van Heflin,
Raymond Massey, Geraldine
Brooks, Stanley Ridges, John
Ridgley, Moroni Olsen, Erskine
Sanford, Gerald Perreau, Isabel
Withers, Lisa Golm, Douglas
Kennedy, Monte Blue, Don
McGuire, Rory Mallinson, Clifton
Young and Griff Barnett
Released 30 May 1947

DAISY KENYON (*Produced by
Twentieth-Century Fox*)
Produced by Otto Preminger
From the novel by Elizabeth
Janeway
Screenplay by David Hertz
Direction by Otto Preminger
Art direction by Lyle Wheeler and
George Davis
Costumes by Charles LeMaire
Musical score by David Raskin
Musical direction by Alfred
Newman
Editing by Louis Loeffler
Cinematography by Leon Shamroy
Cast
Joan Crawford, Dana Andrews,
Henry Fonda, Ruth Warrick,
Martha Stewart, Peggy Ann
Garner, Connie Marshall, Nicholas
Joy, Art Baker, Robert Karnes, John
Davidson, Victoria Horne, Charles
Meredith, Roy Roberts and Griff
Barnett
Released 25 December 1947

1949

FLAMINGO ROAD
Produced by Jerry Wald
From the play by Robert and Sally
Wilder

Screenplay by Robert Wilder
Direction by Michael Curtiz
Art direction by Leo K. Kuter
Joan Crawford's costumes by
Travilla, executed by Sheila
O'Brien
Musical score by Max Steiner
Musical direction by Ray Heindorf
Editing by Folmar Blangsted
Cinematography by Ted McCord
Cast
Joan Crawford, Zachary Scott,
Sydney Greenstreet, Gladys
George, Virginia Huston, Fred
Clark, Gertrude Michael, Alice
White, Sam McDaniel and Tito
Vuolo
Introducing David Brian as 'Dan
Reynolds'
Released 7 May 1949

IT'S A GREAT FEELING
Produced by Alex Gottlieb
From a story by I.A.L. Diamond
Screenplay by Jack Rose and Mel
Shavelson
Direction by David Butler
Art direction by Stanley Fleischer
Music by Ray Heindorf
Editing by Irene Morra
Cinematography by Wilfrid M.
Cline
Cast
Dennis Morgan, Doris Day, Jack
Carson, Bill Goodwin, Irving
Bacon, Claire Carlton, Harlan
Warde and Jacqueline deWit
Guest stars: Gary Cooper, Edward
G. Robinson, Joan Crawford, Danny
Kaye, Errol Flynn, Ronald Reagan,
Jane Wyman, Eleanor Parker and
Patricia Neal
Released 1 August 1949

1950

THE DAMNED DON'T CRY
Produced by Jerry Wald
Story by Gertrude Walker
Screenplay by Harold Medford and
Jerome Weidman
Direction by Vincent Sherman
Art direction by Robert Haas
Wardrobe by Sheila O'Brien
Music by Daniele Amfitheatrof
Editing by Rudi Fehr
Cinematography by Ted McCord
Cast
Joan Crawford, David Brian, Steve
Cochran, Kent Smith, Hugh
Sanders, Selena Royle, Jacqueline
deWit, Morris Ankrum, Edith
Evanson, Richard Egan, Jimmy
Moss, Sara Perry and Eddie Marr.
Released 8 April 1950

HARRIET CRAIG (*Produced by
Columbia Pictures*)
Produced by William Dozier
Based on the play *Craig's Wife* by
George Kelly
Screenplay by Anne Froelick and
James Gunn
Direction by Vincent Sherman
Art direction by Walter Holscher
Wardrobe by Sheila O'Brien
Music by Morris Stoloff
Editing by Viola Lawrence
Cast
Joan Crawford, Wendell Corey,
Lucile Watson, Allyn Joslyn,
William Bishop, K. T. Stevens,
Viola Roache, Raymond Greenleaf,
Ellen Corby, Fiona O'Shiel, Patric
Mitchell, Virginia Brissac,
Katharine Warren, Douglas Wood,
Kathryn Card, Charles Evans and

Mira McKinney
Released 3 November 1950

1951

GOODBYE MY FANCY
Produced by Henry Blanke
Based on the play by Fay Kanin
Screenplay by Ivan Goff and Ben
Roberts
Directed by Vincent Sherman
Art direction by Stanley Fleischer
Wardrobe by Sheila O'Brien
Music by Ray Heindorf
Editing by Rudi Fehr
Cinematography by Ted McCord
Cast
Joan Crawford, Robert Young,
Frank Lovejoy, Eve Arden, Janice
Rule, Lurene Tuttle, Howard St
John, Viola Roache, Ellen Corby,
Morgan Farley, Virginia Gibson,
John Qualen, Anne Robin and
Mary Carver
Released 30 May 1951

1952

THIS WOMAN IS DANGEROUS
Produced by Robert Sisk
Original story by Bernard Firard
Screenplay by Geoffrey Homes and
George Worthing Yates
Direction by Felix Feist
Art direction by Leo K. Kuter
Wardrobe by Sheila O'Brien
Music by David Buttolph
Editing by James C. Moore
Cinematography by Ted McCord
Cast
Joan Crawford, Dennis Morgan,
David Brian, Richard Webb, Mari
Aldon, Philip Carey, Ian

MacDonald, Katherine Warren,
George Chandler, William Challee,
Sherry Jackson, Stuart Randall and
Douglas Fowley
Released 28 February 1952

SUDDEN FEAR (*Produced by RKO
Pictures*)
Produced by Joseph Kaufman
Based on the novel by Edna Sherry
Screenplay by Leonore Coffee and
Robert Smith
Direction by David Miller
Art direction by Boris Leven
Wardrobe by Sheila O'Brien
Music composed and directed by
Elmer Bernstein
Editing by Leon Barsha
Cinematography by Charles Lang, Jr
Cast
Joan Crawford, Jack Palance, Gloria
Grahame, Bruce Bennett, Virginia
Huston and Touch Connors
Released 8 August 1952

1953
_____

TORCH SONG (*Produced by Metro-
Goldwyn-Mayer*)
Produced by Henry Berman and
Sidney Franklin, Jr.
From the story 'Why Should I Cry?'
by I.A.R. Wylie
Screenplay by John Michael Hayes
and Jan Lustig
Direction by Charles Walters
Art direction by Cedric Gibbons
Costumes by Helen Rose
Music by Adolph Deutsch
Editing by Albert Akst
Cinematography by Robert Planck
Cast
Joan Crawford, Michael Wilding,

Gig Young, Marjorie Rambeau,
Henry Morgan, Dorothy Patrick,
James Todd, Eugene Loring, Paul
Guilfoyle, Benny Rubin, Peter
Chong, Maidie Norman, Nancy
Gates, Chris Warfield and Rudy
Render
Released 13 October 1953

1954
_____

JOHNNY GUITAR (*Produced by
Republic Pictures*)
Produced by Herbert J. Yates
Based on the novel by Roy Chanslor
Screenplay by Philip Yordan
Direction by Nicholas Ray
Art direction by James Sullivan
Wardrobe by Sheila O'Brien
Music by Victor Young
Theme song by Peggy Lee and
Victor Young
Editing by Richard L. Van Enger
Cinematography by Harry
Stradling
Cast
Joan Crawford, Sterling Hayden,
Mercedes McCambridge, Scott
Brady, Ward Bond, Ben Cooper,
Ernest Borgnine, John Carradine,
Royal Dano, Frank Ferguson, Paul
Fix, Rhys Williams and Ian
MacDonald
Released 28 May 1954

1955
_____

FEMALE ON THE BEACH (*Produced
by Universal-International*)
Produced by Albert Zugsmith
Based on the play *The Besieged
Heart* by Robert Hill
Screenplay by Robert Hill and

Richard Alan Simmons
Direction by Joseph Pevney
Art direction by Alexander
Golitzen
Wardrobe by Sheila O'Brien
Music by Joseph Gershenson
Editing by Joseph Shoengarth
Cinematography by Charles Lang
Cast
Joan Crawford, Jeff Chandler, Jan
Sterling, Cecil Kellaway, Natalie
Schafer, Charles Drake, Judith
Evelyn, Stuart Randall, Marjorie
Bennett and Romo Vincent
Released 20 August 1955

QUEEN BEE (*Produced by Columbia
Pictures*)
Produced by Jerry Wald
Based on the novel by Edna Lee
Screenplay and direction by Ranald
MacDougall
Art direction by Ross Bellah
Gowns by Jean Louis
Music by Morris Stoloff
Editing by Viola Lawrence
Cinematography by Charles Lang
Cast
Joan Crawford, Barry Sullivan,
Betsy Palmer, John Ireland, Lucy
Marlow, William Leslie, Fay Wray,
Katherine Anderson, Tim Hovey,
Linda Bennett, Willa Pearl Curtis,
Bill Walker and Olan Soule
Released 23 November 1955

1956

AUTUMN LEAVES (*Produced by
Columbia Pictures*)
Produced by William Goetz
Story and screenplay by Jack Jevne,
Lewis Meltzer and Robert Blees

Direction by Robert Aldrich
Art direction by Bill Glasgow
Gowns by Jean Louis
Music composed by Hans Salter,
Conducted by Morris Stoloff
Editing by Michael Luciano
Cinematography by Charles Lang
Cast
Joan Crawford, Cliff Robertson,
Vera Miles, Lorne Greene, Ruth
Donnelly, Sheppard Strudwick,
Selmer Jackson, Maxine Cooper,
Marjorie Bennett, Frank Gerstle,
Leonard Mudie, Maurice Manson
and Bob Hopkins
Released 2 August 1956

1957

THE STORY OF ESTHER COSTELLO (*A
Romulus production for Valiant
Films, released by Columbia
Pictures*)
From the novel by Nicholas
Monsarrat
Screenplay by Charles Kaufman
Produced and directed by David
Miller
Art direction by George Provis and
Tony Masters
Gowns by Jean Louis
Music by Lambert Williamson
Editing by Ralph Kemplen
Cinematography by Robert Krasker
Cast
Joan Crawford, Rossano Brazzi,
Heather Sears, Lee Patterson, Ron
Randell, Fay Compton, John Loder,
Denis O'Dea, Sidney James, Bessie
Love, Robert Ayres, Maureen
Delaney, Harry Hutchinson, Tony
Quinn, Janina Faye, Estelle Brody,
June Clyde, Sally Smith, Diana

Day, Megs Jenkins, Andrew
Cruikshank, Victor Rietti and
Sheila Manahan
Released 6 November 1957

1959

THE BEST OF EVERYTHING
(*Produced by Twentieth-Century
Fox*)
Produced by Jerry Wald
From the novel by Rona Jaffe
Screen play by Edith Summer and
Mann Rubin
Direction by Jean Negulesco
Art direction by Lyle R. Wheeler,
Jack Martin Smith and Mark-Lee
Kirk
Costumes by Adele Palmer
Music by Alfred Newman
Editing by Robert Simpson
Cinematography by William C.
Mellor
Cast
Hope Lange, Stephen Boyd, Suzy
Parker, Martha Hyer, Diane Baker,
Brian Aherne, Robert Evans, Brett
Halsey, Donald Harron, Sue
Carson, Linda Hutchings, Lionel
Kane, Ted Otis, Jane Blair, Myrna
Hansen, Alena Murray, Rachel
Stephens, Julie Payne, and Nora
O'Mahoney; and starring Louis
Jourdan as 'David Savage' and Joan
Crawford as 'Amanda Farrow'
Released 9 October 1959

1962

WHAT EVER HAPPENED TO BABY
JANE? (*Produced by Seven Arts,
Released by Warner Brothers*)

Executive Producer: Kenneth
Hyman
Associate Producer: Robert Aldrich
Based on the novel by Henry
Farrell
Screenplay by Lukas Heller
Direction by Robert Aldrich
Art direction by William Glasgow
Costumes by Norma Koch
Musical score by Frank DeVol
Editing by Michael Luciano
Cinematography by Ernest Haller
Cast
Bette Davis, Joan Crawford, Victor
Buono, Marjorie Bennett, Maidie
Norman, Anna Lee, Julie Allred,
Barbara Merrill, Dave Willock,
Gina Gillespie and Ann Barton
Released 7 November 1962

1963

THE CARETAKERS (*Produced by
United Artists*)
Produced and directed by Hall
Bartlett
Screen-story by Hall Bartlett and
Jerry Paris
Based on a book by Daniel Telfer
Screenplay by Henry F. Greenberg
Music by Elmer Bernstein
Editing by William B. Murphy
Cinematography by Lucien Ballard
Cast
Robert Stack, Polly Bergen, Joan
Crawford, Janis Paige, Diane
McBain, Van Williams, Constance
Ford, Sharon Hugueny, Herbert
Marshall, Robert Vaughn, Ana St
Clair, Barbara Barrie, Susan Oliver
and Ellen Corby
Released 22 August 1963

1964

STRAIT JACKET (*Produced by William Castle, Released by Columbia Pictures*)
Produced and directed by William Castle
Screenplay by Robert Bloch
Music by Van Alexander
Editing by Edwin Bryant
Cinematography by Arthur Arling
Cast
Joan Crawford, Diane Baker, Leif Erickson, Howard St John, John Anthony Hayes, Rochelle Hudson, George Kennedy, Edith Atwater, Mitchell Cox, Lee Yeary, Patricia Krest, Vachel Cos, Patty Lee, Laura Hess, Robert Ward and Lyn Lundgren
Released 23 January 1964

1965

I SAW WHAT YOU DID (*Produced by Universal-International*)
Produced and directed by William Castle
Based on the novel by Ursula Curtiss
Screenplay by William McGivern
Music by Van Alexander
Editing by Edwin H. Bryant
Cinematography by Joseph Biroc
Cast
Joan Crawford, John Ireland, Leif Erickson, Sara Lane, Andi Garrett, Sharyl Locke, Patricia Breslin, John Archer, John Crawford and Joyce Meadows
Released 22 July 1965

1968

BERSERK ('*Circus of Blood*')
(*Produced by Columbia Pictures*)
Produced by Herman Cohen
Associate producer: Robert Sterne
Original story and screenplay by Aben Kandel and Herman Cohen
Direction by Jim O'Connolly
Art direction by Maurice Pelling
Costumes by Jay Hutchinson Scott
Wardrobe by Joyce Stoneman
Music composed and conducted by John Scott
Editing by Raymond Poulton
Cinematography by Desmond Dickinson, BSC
Cast
Joan Crawford, Ty Hardin, Diana Dors, Michael Gough, Judy Geeson, Robert Hardy, Geoffrey Keen, Sydney Tafler, George Claydon, Philip Madoc, Thomas Cimarro, Ambrostine Phillpotts, Peter Burton, Golda Casimir, Ted Lune, Milton Reid, Marianne Stone, Miki Iveria, Howard Goorney, Reginald Marsh and Bryan Pringle
Released 11 January 1968

1970

TROG (*Produced by Warner Brothers*)
Produced by Herman Cohen
Screen play by Peter Bryan, John Gilling and Aben Kandel
Direction by Freddie Francis
Cast
Joan Crawford, Michael Gough, Joe Cornelious, Kim Braden and Bernard Kay
(Release date unknown)

Wilkerson, Billy 144
Williams, Tennessee 183, 185
Wilson, Teddy 36
Wilson, President Woodrow
  25, 32
Winchell, Walter 101
Winters, Shelley 190, 196
Wiser Sex, The 90
Within the Law (play) 66
Woman of Affairs, A 64
'Woman of the Year' (USO)
  192, 198

Woman's Face, A 68, 115,
  126–7, 131, 138, 154, 174
Women, The (play) 70
Wood, President, James
  Madison (of Stephens
  College) 35–6
Woolf, Jimmy 169
Wyman, Jane 152

Yates, Herbert J 166
Yordan, Philip 166
Young, Ernie 38–9

Young, Mrs Ernie 38–9
Young, Gig 161
Young, Ken 195
Young, Lester 28
Young, Loretta 138, 180
Young, Victor 166
Young Woodley (play) 64

Ziegfield Follies 51, 194
Zwaaf, Manny 191